FORGOTTEN WIVES
How Women Get Written Out of History

Ann Oakley

First published in Great Britain in 2021 by

Policy Press, an imprint of
Bristol University Press
University of Bristol
1-9 Old Park Hill
Bristol
BS2 8BB
UK
+44 (0)117 954 5940
bup-info@bristol.ac.uk

Details of international sales and distribution partners are available at
policy.bristoluniversitypress.co.uk

British Library Cataloguing in Publication Data
A catalogue record for this book is available from the British Library

ISBN 978-1-4473-5583-0 hardcover
ISBN 978-1-4473-5584-7 paperback
ISBN 978-1-4473-5586-1 ePub
ISBN 978-1-4473-5585-4 ePdf

Cover design: Liam Roberts
Front cover image: Olga Seredenko 1222859600

Bristol University Press and Policy Press use environmentally responsible
print partners.

Printed in Great Britain by CMP, Poole

For Robin

All women by marriage acquire a new economic and social status, with risks and rights different from those of the unmarried.

Social Insurance and Allied Services, Report
by William Beveridge, 1942, p 49

Contents

List of illustrations and sources

[1] BPLES = The British Library of Political and Economic Science; LSE = London School of Economics and Political Science

About the author

Ann Oakley is Professor of Sociology and Social Policy at the Social Research Institute, University College London. She has been a social researcher for more than fifty years, and is the author of many academic publications as well as biography, autobiography and fiction. Her books include *Sex, Gender and Society*, *The Sociology of Housework*, *From Here to Maternity* and *The Men's Room*, which was serialised by the BBC in 1991. Her most recent book, published by Policy Press in 2019, is *Women, Peace and Welfare: A Suppressed History of Social Reform, 1880–1920*.

Preface and acknowledgements

The subtitle of this book, 'how women get written out of history', overstates its argument. *Forgotten Wives* isn't a comprehensive guide to all the strategies that have ever been used to achieve this ignoble aim. But I've been researching and writing about gender for more than half a century, and I'm tired of careful phrasing and modest claims. It is obvious to anyone who has followed the trajectory of gender through and beyond the 20th century that the social processes shaping a second-class citizenship for women remain firmly in place. We are drowning in evidence about what these processes are and how they work, but evidence – of which there is plenty in this book – remains hugely important. At the same time, there's nothing to be gained by understating the impact on all our lives of systematic discrimination against women.

Marriage is a central plank in this system. Women in many societies are formally wives much less than they were, as other kinds of intimate relationships have joined heterosexual marriage in popularity and social acceptance (although these rarely match the legal and economic status of the normative wedded union). This book argues that the status of women as wives continues to manipulate the status of women in general. Women are seen as proto-wives, wives in the making, wives when they aren't; they are persistently judged by standards of behaviour, personality and presentation which are tied to the character of the female half of a married couple. Wifehood is the default prism through which women's individual agency is blurred and often effectively dissolved. Culture shapes the form this process takes, so that in some places in the world the discriminations of wifehood continue to have personally disastrous consequences: deprivation of human rights, forced seclusion, physical and mental violence, deliberate injury and murder.

There are many ways to illustrate how the default prism of wifehood works. The method I adopt in *Forgotten Wives* is to take some historical examples of British women married to well-known men and consider how the biographers of these men, and historians who have written about their various projects, have failed to entertain the possibility of the wives also being people who made contributions to history in their own right.

In order to do this it has been necessary to go back to the beginning as far as possible: that is, to read the original documents left by the women (and their husbands and others) rather than depend on the biographical and historical stories produced by those who have made assumptions about women's lives and labours based on the gendered stereotypes of wifehood. During the early part of research for this book I spent much time in libraries and archives. Then in March 2020 the UK government's response to the threat of the COVID-19 virus closed many public spaces, including these. At the time of writing (November 2020) most archives remain out-of-bounds, and there's no timetable for their reopening. Rather than waiting for this to be resolved, I decided to finish the book with the material I'd already gathered. By the time it's published I shall be well into my 78th year and patience doesn't grow with age. So I need to apologise for the gaps, some of which I know about but many of which I probably don't, that are a consequence of not having the time or the patience to wait. Although I assume that the general drift of my case in *Forgotten Wives* wouldn't be altered substantially by more time in the archives, this is only an assumption. The photographs might have been better, however, as in some places I've had to depend on the early imperfect images collected on my mobile phone. Thanks to archival staff in Senate House and the London School of Economics (especially Indy Bhullar), and to Aaron Brown for indispensable technical help.

Among those I want to thank for the emergence of this book are all the staff in the archives and libraries where I've worked. Foremost among these are the staff in The Women's Library at the British Library of Political and Economic Science, the London School of Economics (LSE), an institution whose history forms a kind of sub-plot in this book. Sue Donnelly, the LSE archivist, was especially helpful with the lives of Charlotte Shaw and Janet Beveridge. At Senate House Library, the University of London, Richard Temple and the other archive staff patiently guided me through the labyrinth of the Booth archives. For access to William Beveridge papers held at University College, Oxford, I am grateful to Robin Darwall-Smith. Helen Burton at the Foundations of British Sociology Archive, Keele University, Ceri Sugg at Eton College Archives, and staff at the Scott Polar Research Institute, University of Cambridge, and at the John J. Burns Library at Boston College in the US have also provided valued help. The Titmuss-Meinhardt Fund at LSE has been generously contributing to my work on various forgotten women for some years, and I am extremely grateful for their continued support. And as always, it has been a pleasure to work with the dedicated and thoughtful team at Policy Press.

It has been a great privilege to have met or otherwise communicated with members of Janet Beveridge and Mary Booth's families in the course of researching the book. These are the two out of the four women in *Forgotten Wives* who were also mothers. The interest shown by their descendants in their legacies is a sharp acknowledgement of the role families can play in preserving and directing the historical record. David Burn, George Gwilt, Richard Gwilt and Jennifer Ward have been a source of information about Janet Beveridge; and Theresa Booth, Charles Macnaghten, Charles Martineau, Christopher Stephens and Mark Stephens have drawn my attention to many aspects of Mary Booth's life and work. Our encounters have included highly enjoyable and informative (and safe) meetings during the COVID-19 lockdown. I am especially grateful to Mary Booth's sole surviving grand-daughter, Fanny Hugill, for sharing her memories of an engagingly memorable grandmother. At the Charles Booth Centre in Thringstone, Leicestershire, the Friends of Thringstone community group and Nita Pearson and Ann Petty did an excellent job in enabling me to understand Mary Booth's work in the community. Thanks to my daughter Laura Oakley for reducing Mary Booth's complex genealogical background to the neat table in Chapter 2.

While I was writing this book historian John Stewart was engaged on the biography of my father, Richard Titmuss. The conjunction of these two enterprises prompted many spirited interchanges about the challenges of making sense of other people's lives. John read the manuscript of *Forgotten Wives* for me, and gave me many useful comments. So also did Graham Crow, Karen Dunnell, Robin Oakley, Joy Schaverien and Mark Stephens. I am grateful to all of them for the care they took to identify typos, tell me when they thought I was wrong, suggest improved orderings and phrasings, and generally provide moral encouragement. Since most of the book was written under the restricted social conditions of the COVID-19 lockdown, my engagement with these interested others has been absolutely indispensable. They're not, of course, responsible for the interpretative decisions that shaped the ultimate form of the text.

My youngest grandchild, Sylvie Oakley-Brown, told me to get on and publish this book so we can have another launch party (she much enjoyed the last one). So here you are, Sylvie. And thanks, as always, for the love and support of all my family. *Forgotten Wives* is dedicated to Robin, who is not a forgotten husband, and who did not do the typing.

Ann Oakley
Rutland
November 2020

1

The condition of wifehood

'Why be a wife?' was the byline of a vigorous 1975 women's liberation campaign in Britain against the institution of marriage. Pamphlets were produced, and we wore YBAW badges. Some of us took the message to heart and undid our own marriages. The argument was that neither the Equal Pay Act of 1970 nor the Sex Discrimination Act of 1975 improved the situation of women that much, because they failed to tackle the root of the problem: women's 'wedlocked' position in marriage. Tax and social security systems still treated wives as dependants. Public services, as well as husbands, counted on women's unpaid labour at home. Therefore, 'The question "why be a wife?" needs to be asked by us all.'[1]

This focus on the condition of wifehood is a dimension that is mostly missing from accounts of the first 20th-century feminist movement, which have concentrated overwhelmingly on media-worthy images of angry women in picture hats throwing bricks in their pursuit of the vote. Yet the legal, economic, social and political treatment of wives has historically occupied far more of feminist activists' attention than the missing right to vote. Wives were traditionally the property of men and allowed no property of their own, and property ownership was for a long time a necessary criterion for voting. The oppressions of married women have generally been worse and more extensive than those of single women (which is not to say that single women, especially unmarried mothers, haven't been subject to awful oppressions of their own).

Forgotten Wives is about marriage as a primary political experience and an institution that defines the work and identity of women. It's about both what actually happens to women in marriage and what is assumed to happen, and the dissonance between these two. It uses four case studies of wives who lived and worked in the late 19th and the first part of the 20th centuries to illustrate the argument that history and biography can be distorted by prior assumptions about who wives are and what they do. This first chapter outlines the themes of the book and introduces the women who feature in it. It considers the history and sociology of marriage as the background against which a focus on wifehood is an intelligent and necessary way of understanding the social representation of women, even today. The four wives in the book were all comfortably off, middle- or upper-middle class, and they were all married to men with reputations that placed them at the centre of developments in social welfare and public policy in Britain. Although their social milieu is specific, *Forgotten Wives* argues that the situations and treatment in historical narratives of these wives illustrate general aspects of wifehood as a condition – in some ways *the* condition – of women. The four case studies date from a time when people, and certainly women, were still expected to marry as a mark of adult status. Today we have civil partnerships, and we have marriages in which two wives or two husbands figure out how to make sense of gender in intimate relationships, and in many cohabitations, too, the idea of 'heteronormativity' still governs the landscape of intimate relations. Remnants of the Victorian ideology to which the four women in this book were exposed continue to dog modern expectations of women as both formal and informal wives.

There is, of course, an enormous literature on marriage – its history, its anthropology, its sociology, its psychology, its legal, economic and social status. People have been impressed, puzzled, angered and generally fascinated and obsessed with what marriage is and what it does to individuals and society. Much of this literature fastens on the gender disparities that lie at the heart of marriage. Her marriage is not the same thing as his marriage: their domestic and emotional labour is different; marriage has a different impact on their public lives; intimacy is a gendered experience; and marriage divides the economic position, psychology, and physical and mental health of men and women. In the 21st century we still struggle with the conflict between these systemic inequalities and the goal of equal citizenship. Academics tangle with the question of whether it is marriage per se that's the problem, or whether the real culprit is something intrinsic to heterosexual relationships, or whether it's the monolithic structures of capitalism and patriarchy that condemn us to a lockdown in gender divisions. Interestingly, there's been relatively little social science research on one of the main themes of *Forgotten Wives* – wives' relationships to husbands' work.

The relationship between marriage and gender means that we've inherited an enormous skewed collection of narratives shaping the ways in which the lives and achievements of married people are remembered. *Forgotten Wives* takes a little bit of this history and asks how being married might have altered the ways in which wives and husbands are differently remembered. Its focus is on wifehood as a political filter through which women's lives are passed so as to yield a product which only partially records what they actually did.

Husbandhood calls for comments of various kinds, but it doesn't have at all the same effects as wifehood. Marriage offers a particular case of forgetting with respect to women: 'forgetting' here is an umbrella term that covers assorted forms of ignoring, devaluing, marginalising and distorting. Marriage functions as a paradigm, a cipher, an exemplar of the status of women in societies that are still dominated, despite many moves towards sex equality made over the last hundred years, by the rule of male superiority. Wives are especially likely to be forgotten, more likely than other women, who cannot so easily be concealed behind men (though fathers and even brothers may sometimes do instead of husbands here).

The habit of forgetting

Forgotten Wives follows on from the research I did for *Women, Peace and Welfare: A Suppressed History of Social Reform, 1880–1920*, published by Policy Press in 2018. That earlier book remembers 328 women around the world who were active either in peace movements or developing the tools of social research or in the field of social welfare, and often in all three areas, which many of them saw as fundamentally interconnected. The research for *Women, Peace and Welfare* exposed me to a breathtaking expanse of forgotten-ness – the omission of women's individual and collective agency from most standard accounts of peace movements and the history of both social welfare and social science. The peace movement belonged to men, social science was the invention of male theorists, and 'the welfare state' had a father, but no mother. The writer Joanna Russ listed some standard strategies for demoting women's writing in her *How to Suppress Women's Writing* (1983): she didn't write it at all; she didn't write it, he did; she did write it, but she ought not to have done; she wrote it, but look what she wrote about; she wrote only one of it; she had help; yes, she did write it but she's an anomaly. There's a whole methodology here of ways in which what women do gets omitted from history, so that history remains predominantly a story of what men have done in those spheres of action – party politics, warfare, industry, technology, sport – that have traditionally occupied masculine attention and concern.

The accounts that appeared in *Women, Peace and Welfare* of what women contributed to the theory and practice of pacifism, social welfare and social science required detailed archival digging. While many had suffered from dismissive comments or silences in histories/ biographies of the period, a consistent theme was the sidelining of the contributions made by women who were also wives, especially those married to men with public reputations. This phenomenon of wife-forgetting seemed to demand some attention. We are fairly used now to the inroads of scholarship on women's general invisibility as subjects of study: both academic books and articles and books for the general reader give us no excuse for the 'where are the women?' question that has traditionally preoccupied opponents of women's rights. A veritable tsunami of books about forgotten women has hit the bookshops in recent years: broadcaster Jenni Murray's *A History of Britain in 21 Women* (2016), and *A History of the World in 21 Women* (2018); Kerstin Lücker and Ute Daenschel's *A History of the World with the Women Put Back in* (2019); Kate Pankhurst's *Fantastically Great Women Who Made History* (2018); and *Bloody Brilliant Women: The Pioneers, Revolutionaries and Geniuses Your History Teacher Forgot to Mention* (2018) by Cathy Newman are just some of them.

But wives? How does being a wife *specifically* affect the likelihood of an individual female human being's life and work being given the same consideration as a husband's? This is a question about wives' work both outside the home and inside it. The cumulative amount of domestic labour performed by the four women whose lives are recounted in *Forgotten Wives* to care for husbands, homes and children was truly enormous, but there are few glimpses of it anywhere in any existing accounts of the women's or their husbands' lives. Most importantly, almost no attention is given by biographers and historians to what the famous husbands might have been able to achieve without this subterranean industry of wifely labour. The gendered assumption that this is what wives do has clouded the vision, so that wives' domestic labour, being unremarkable, is simply not there at all. This cultural neglect of domestic labour is one issue. The second issue is what *she* does to help *his* work. Husbands thank their wives, often fulsomely in discourse and in publications, but perhaps she was also an author of it, and might have liked the world to know that? Then there is what she herself did as an individual, with some degree of independence from her husband and their joint marital life, and – as two of the case studies in this book show – sometimes it's an accomplishment he didn't actually know much about, which can get in the way of other people knowing anything about it at all.

The four women

The four women whose lives are discussed in the next four chapters were born between 1847 and 1881 in England, Scotland, Ireland and India respectively. None of them is famous in the sense of being a household name, or being known for some outstanding contribution to the history of feminist struggles. They married between 1871 and 1909, and what they have in common is that all their husbands are well known for the key contributions they made to the formation of Britain's modern welfare state. The life stories of these wives and husbands intersect at many points, offering an entry point into the landscape of powerful social networks that helped to develop the foundations of modern Britain. The wives would have known each other: they shared 59 years of mutual existence, although there's no outstanding record of any especially intimate relationship. The husbands all have multiple biographical entries, including in the *Oxford Dictionary of National Biography* (ODNB) and Wikipedia and at least one full-length biography each. Only one of the wives appears in the ODNB, and only one (a different one) in Wikipedia, and only one has merited a full-length biography: Charlotte Shaw's life is recorded under the telling title *Mrs G.B.S.* The two of the wives who were also mothers had children who wrote accounts of their mothers' lives, which consciously set out to correct this anti-wife record. All four wives left considerable amounts of archival records – letters, diaries, unpublished manuscripts – which have to be searched for under the headings of their husbands' archive collections. It is sadly true that the best place to look for wives' stories is in material catalogued under the names of husbands and other male relatives. The histories of the wives in this book are those of white European privileged middle classes because its focus is on the political and social networks that shaped modern Britain. This isn't a book about working-class wifehood, which is a condition of multiple deprivation and disadvantage, something of which all four of the middle-class wives in this book were in their different ways aware.

Mary Catherine Booth, née Macaulay, was born in 1847 and at the age of 24 in 1871 she married the business man and social investigator Charles Booth whose multi-volume work *Life and Labour of the People in London*, published between 1889 and 1903, alerted the governing classes to the problem of poverty and the need for state action to alleviate it. For 17 years Mary devoted much of her time to Charles's poverty research. She steered the work, contributed to its analysis and writing, oversaw its publication and coordinated and hosted endless research meetings. She was a partner 'in all but name' in the lucrative Booth shipbuilding and leather industry, which funded the poverty research. While giving birth to seven children, caring for her family, and ministering to the idiosyncrasies of an often-absent husband, Mary was independently involved in social reform. She set up community aid and healthcare associations in the Leicestershire coalmining district where the Booths lived.

Charlotte Frances Shaw, née Payne-Townshend, was born a decade after Mary Booth in 1857. She married the radical playwright George Bernard Shaw in 1898 when she was 41. Before this she played an important role as one of the founders of the London School of Economics and Political Science (LSE), which is today a leading international centre for social science research, teaching and policy work. At LSE Charlotte Shaw also founded a programme of research into women's history, which aimed to correct the masculine bias in much history at a time before this was a common activity. In her marriage to Shaw, Charlotte proposed ideas for his plays, did much of the research for some of them, chose suitable actors, and was closely involved in performance arrangements. She actively promoted and translated the work of a radical French playwright, Eugène Brieux, regarded by some as the greatest French dramatist of the early 20th century. Another significant plank in Charlotte Shaw's work was her role in the life and writings of T.E. Lawrence ('Lawrence of Arabia'). Charlotte contributed much to Lawrence's famous *Seven Pillars of Wisdom*, his insider account of the Arab revolt against the Ottoman Turks in 1916–18, although this role is frequently assigned to her husband instead.

Jeannette Tawney, née Beveridge, born in 1881, was the sister of William Beveridge, the 'father' of Britain's welfare state. At the age of 28, in 1909, Jeannette married William Beveridge's close friend, the socialist economic historian Richard Henry ('Harry') Tawney, who is known for his work in adult education, at LSE, for providing the Labour Party with a useful case for moral socialism, and as the author of such classic historical texts as *The Acquisitive Society* (1921), *Religion and the Rise of Capitalism* (1926), and *Equality* (1931). Jeannette Tawney was a historian in her own right, publishing work on women and unemployment, the history of occupational statistics and the development of economic ideas. She contributed to her husband's research, was one of the first women factory inspectors, and a writer of autobiography and fiction. As an obituary by the Labour politician Lena Jeger observed, Jeannette 'suffered the disability of being thought of too often as either Professor Tawney's wife or Lord Beveridge's sister'.[2]

Janet Beveridge, née Jessy Thomson Philip, and previously Jessy Mair, was born in 1876. She worked with her second husband William Beveridge in a variety of roles for at least twenty-five years before marrying him at the age of 66. The marriage took place two weeks after the publication in 1942 of William's famous Beveridge Report, which outlined the blueprint for Britain's post-war welfare state. William Beveridge was a cousin of Janet's first husband, David Beveridge Mair, who died in 1942; the Mairs had four children together. During the First World War, Janet worked as a senior civil servant in the Ministry of Food with responsibility for food rationing. The Beveridges' most-celebrated (pre-marriage) partnership was the running of LSE as Director (him) and Secretary (her) for 18 years during a period which saw its 'second foundation' as the pre-eminent institution it is today. Janet made a major contribution both to the development of LSE and to the shaping of the Beveridge Report as a document, which inspired both public and (eventually) policy support.

Table 1 on page 24 summarises the key demographic information for the four women, who are referred to throughout the book by their married names, because wifehood is its subject matter. In the case of Janet Beveridge, who was married twice, I use her second married name since it's this one that connects her to her famous husband, and the forename 'Janet' which she chose to use instead of 'Jessy' after this second marriage.

Choosing examples

Many wives could have been chosen as illustrations for this book. The reasons for settling on these particular four are that the work they and their husbands did was important to three wider stories. The first is about the development of something that much later came to be called evidence-based social policy: the discipline of basing policy initiatives on what is reliably known about public welfare. The second story is the rather better-known one about how the British welfare state came to emerge in the years before, during and after the Second World War. Social science as a feeder discipline for these two initiatives is the third story; this was a subject in its infancy during the lifetimes of Mary Booth, Charlotte Shaw, Jeannette Tawney and Janet Beveridge, but it was one which they all saw as necessary to the goal of better government and improved civic welfare.

'Forgetting' hides different forms of misremembering. History is littered with examples of forgotten or misremembered wives. In the 19th century, when the wives in *Forgotten Wives* were born, there was, for example, Clara Schumann, an epoch-making concert pianist and composer, wife to the more famous Robert, who regarded their artistic lives as one (his). Clara was the family's main breadwinner, the mother of eight children, champion of Robert's compositions and those of Brahms, Chopin and Mendelssohn, and neglectful of her own, as was Robert, and most music lovers since, who simply forgot them. Another case is the Polish scientist Marie Skłodowska, who discovered (and named) radioactivity, and who married in 1895 the French scientist Pierre Curie, of whom it was said that she was his greatest discovery. Marie was at pains to point out that radioactivity was entirely her discovery, not her husband's – she knew people would have difficulty crediting a woman with such world-changing work. And so it was that, when the Curies were invited to speak at the Royal Society in London in 1903 about 'their' discovery, Marie, as a woman, wasn't allowed to speak. Pierre talked about what she'd done as though he'd done it. Marie Curie was the first woman to get the Nobel Prize for physics, yet this happened only because another female scientist alerted Pierre to the fact that the Nobel Committee intended to honour him only. Access to the full records of Marie Curie's life is impeded because many of the documents are radioactive and considered too dangerous to handle.

In the fields of interest and action to which the four wives in this book belong, other contenders jostle for a role in exemplifying the pitfalls of wifehood. Consider, for instance, the case of Alice Stopford Green. Alice Green was one of a considerable band of women who collaborated with Charles Booth on his great poverty enquiry. She was a historian and influential Irish nationalist, but she's mainly remembered as Mrs J.R. Green, the wife of another historian who broke new ground by organising the historical narrative according to what people in general did rather than by the more usual kings and conquests. Mrs Green's widowhood outlasted her marriage by 35 years, which makes it even more extraordinary that her place in history tends to be limited to being her husband's helpmeet. The standard story of Alice Green's development as a historian is that she learnt its methodology by serving as her husband's assistant and secretary. Yet most of his work was done after the marriage, when she was 'a major force' spurring him on and actually carrying out the research.[3] With her help, J.R. Green turned his one-volume *A Short History of the English People* into a four-volume longer one. The two Greens wrote a book about the geography of the British Isles together. After her husband died, Alice was exceptionally busy. The longevity of J.R. Green's *A Short History* owes much to Alice, who looked after all subsequent editions following her husband's early death at the age of 45.

Aside from promoting her husband's work, Alice Green published *Town Life in the Fifteenth Century* (1894), one of the texts demonstrating the practical freedom many married women had to trade and own property before the era of restrictive 19th-century legislation. She wrote several significant texts on Irish history, including one, *The Making of Ireland and Its Undoing*, that revealed a far richer culture in medieval Ireland than was usually supposed – a flourishing civilisation smashed by English imperialism. Among Alice Green's other achievements, she published a startling essay on 'Woman's place in the world of letters' in the journal *Nineteenth Century* in 1913. This essay is a formidable argument about women as a class existing outside a masculine social system. 'Woman is herself no better than a stranger in the visible established order of this world,' wrote Alice, 'a strayed wanderer from some different sphere – a witness, a herald it may be, of another system … She does not speak the tongue of this world, nor does she in her heart think its thoughts … Of all pilgrims and sojourners in the world, woman remains in fact the most perplexed and the most alien.'[4] Some aspects of Alice Green's pilgrimage in this world were picked up in a short but sensitive biography by the Irish historian Robert McDowell, who quoted from the French literary critic Sainte-Beuve on its first page the unpleasantly dismissive view that: 'A woman should never have a biography … woman can only lose charm in the text of a continuous narrative. Can a woman's life be told? It is felt, it passes, it appears.'[5]

The first edition of Green's *Short History*, published in 1874 and covering 14 centuries, fell into the hands of Mary Booth, who looked up King Alfred in it to see if Green's opinion tallied with her own (it did), and then put the book aside in favour of Arnold's sermons and the works of the Brontë sisters. Alice Green was a close friend of Mary's and she makes multiple appearances in the latter's diaries. Another of Alice Green's closest friends for 30 years was the marvellously erudite social scientist and Fabian reformer, Beatrice Webb, who thought Alice's historical work of real social value. Beatrice is an enormously important figure in the background stories of *Forgotten Wives* about the evolution of state welfare, evidence-based policy and social science. She weaves her authoritative presence through all four case studies. Beatrice Webb knew Charlotte Shaw well; when Charlotte was still (the wealthy) Miss Payne-Townshend, Beatrice had her eye on her, it turned out most aptly, as a potential source of funds for the infant LSE. It was in one of the Webbs' holiday houses that Charlotte first met her future husband George Bernard Shaw. Beatrice was never quite sure whether she liked Charlotte or not, but the two Webbs and the two Shaws settled down to a comfortable ménage à quatre together in which they shared cycling trips, stayed in one another's houses, took holidays with one another, and discussed both bodily ailments and the ailments of the body politic with mutual commitment and energy. For fifty years, wrote Beatrice in her diary in 1942, the year before both she and Charlotte were to die, the Webbs and the Shaws 'lived together in constant intercourse, sharing the same opinions and cooperating in spreading the same gospel'.[6]

Beatrice Webb features in Mary Booth's life as Charles Booth's cousin, who worked with him on the great poverty enquiry, learning the craft of social investigation by taking jobs as a 'plain trouser-hand' in the sweatshops of East London. (Her cover was blown by her inability to produce a sufficiently working-class accent and what George Bernard Shaw described as her 'hopeless inferiority as a needlewoman'.[7]) Beatrice turned to Mary Booth, 11 years her senior, for advice and solace in affairs of the heart, and also for Mary's valued intellectual input to her first attempts at writing up her research. When we come to Jeannette Tawney, Beatrice is there too, as a friend of Harry Tawney, and commentator on Jeannette's own role as a wife. The acerbic nature of Beatrice's views, as expressed in her diary and in letters, comes into its own in the fourth story, of how Janet Beveridge, who dominated LSE for 18 years, managed to annoy almost everyone so much that they forgot what she actually did for that institution, and in her life of public service more generally.

Beatrice Webb was a wife too, but clearly not a forgotten one. Unlike the case studies in this book, Beatrice was an inveterate compiler and promoter of her own autobiographical observations. She wrote *My Apprenticeship* (first published in 1926) and *Our Partnership* (published in 1948), and bequeathed to Webb scholars and the rest of us four volumes of diaries covering the years 1873 to 1943, together with a great deal of correspondence. Much of this material is available on the LSE website, some of it in typescript form, which is a relief since Beatrice's handwriting was notoriously undecipherable. Ensuring the production and accessible survival of sufficient documentary evidence may be an important prerequisite for wives wishing to escape being forgotten, whereas famous men seem to achieve fame without this. It is important, too, not to be over-modest about one's own achievements. Charlotte Shaw and Mary Booth were both too good at modesty, thus encouraging their disappearance in relevant narratives, or at least their assignment to a subsidiary role. Janet Beveridge and Jeannette Tawney erred in the opposite direction, speaking with their own voices too much and incurring the disapproval of biographers. Wives can't win.

However, the record of Beatrice Webb's life and work isn't entirely free from the biases of wifehood. The books she co-authored with Sidney all appeared with Sidney's name first, even when she did most of the work. Their signal text *Methods of Social Study*, published in 1932, a really impressive and ahead-of-its-time stab at outlining the combined qualitative and quantitative methodology of social science, was based mainly on Beatrice's sole-authored *My Apprenticeship*. 'I' morphed into 'we'. In his preface to Beatrice's *My Apprenticeship*, Charlotte Shaw's husband referred to the 'firm of Sidney and Beatrice Webb whom a Labour Government tried vainly to disguise as Baron and Lady Passfield'.[8] Shaw went on to note that most of Beatrice's work was inseparable from this corporate entity, although he acknowledged that 'a separate Beatrice' did exist, especially in the important work she did before she 'collided' with Sidney Webb. Others have noted the unfortunate influence of Sidney on the trajectory of Beatrice's work of social investigation; he thought, and persuaded her, that studying documents was a better strategy than studying actual social relations, something at which she, but not he, was exceptionally skilled.

Beatrice Webb also studied her own marriage, observing the differences between her and Sidney's approach to the world. He liked statistical abstracts and committee agendas, and he related to the actual social world primarily through her. She believed in studying social facts at first hand. Most critically, she experienced a certain disjunction between herself and herself-as-wife: 'When Sidney is with me,' she confessed to her diary 12 years into her marriage in 1904, 'I cannot talk to the other self with whom I commune when I am alone – "it" ceases to be present and only reappears when he becomes absent. Then the old self who knew me and whom I have known for that long period before Sidney entered into my life – who seems to be that which is *permanent* in me – sits again in the judgement seat and listens to the talk of the hours and days, acts, thoughts and feelings.'[9]

Marriage and the subjection of women

A once highly popular anthropological text on marriage was written by Janet Beveridge's daughter Lucy Mair, an LSE professor. In it she argues that all human societies have some system for the formal licensing of childbearing. In most, children inherit their social status from their fathers. In many, it's men who wish to become husbands and women who have no choice but to be wives. Much to do with marriage isn't about love but about property, lineage and reputation. Beyond these basic precepts, everything is very variable, depending on economic conditions, political systems and so forth. The history and sociology of marriage in Britain tracks the importance of religious doctrines about men being the 'natural' heads of families to whom women defer as subservient wives. This system left the heart of marriage a most unequal place. Men were citizens but women, denied citizenship, had no chance of establishing any claim to equal treatment in the home. Another way to put this is to say that contesting the subordinate status of wives, the *confirmation* in the marriage contract of women's political subjection, was absolutely essential to the movement for women's enfranchisement and then their liberation. This importance to women's movements of changing *specifically* the position of women as wives isn't sufficiently acknowledged in most of the relevant histories.

There's a long history of texts, mainly by women, which fix on wifehood as the paramount problem. The philosopher Mary Astell caused a storm with her *A Serious Proposal to the Ladies*, published in two parts in 1694 and 1697, which excoriated in an arrestingly modern way the oppressive gender roles constructing women as passive, silly and sentimental: Astell said women should instead exercise their minds and reject this false femininity. In her later *Some Reflections Upon Marriage* (1700) she incited women to avoid the tyranny of marriage as imposing on them a further layer of inferiority. Writing in the aftermath of the 1688–89 revolution that transformed most of Britain into a constitutional monarchy, Astell's elegant rhetoric deconstructed the new doctrine of individual liberty as completely omitting women. Government for the people, she declared, was simply government for and by men. Women, hidden under the rule of men in the family, were property: slaves without citizenship rights. Astell showed how the principle of male domination in personal life imprinted itself effortlessly onto the pattern of social relations in public life, so that wifehood effectively defined the status of *all* women. Her impertinent connection of private and public spheres didn't endear her at all to the philosophers of liberty at the time. But her insight was enthusiastically taken up by 20th-century feminists, who demonstrated how the original conflation of political with patriarchal rights means that civil society as we know it today is thoroughly contaminated with the ideology of wifehood.

The best known of these early feminist texts about marriage and the position of women was published a century after Astell's, in 1792. Mary Wollstonecraft's *A Vindication of the Rights of Woman* turned its author into the most famous woman in Europe for a while. But *A Vindication* is passionate, full of pyrotechnics and hyperbole, and it lacks the logical analytic air of Astell's text or of another one called *Enfranchisement of Women* published half a century later in 1851. The author of this latter primer, Harriet Taylor Mill, was herself the wife of a famous man, the philosopher and political economist John Stuart Mill. 'The real question,' wrote Harriet in *Enfranchisement of Women*, 'is whether it is right and expedient that one-half of the human race should pass through life in a state of forced subordination to the other half.' While the first half has 'a will and a substantive existence', the second half are just 'humble companions to these persons, attached, each of them to one, for the purpose of bringing up *his* children, and making *his* home pleasant to him.' Why should a woman be 'a mere appendage to a man', allowed to have no interests of her own'? Because men like it, concludes Harriet. 'It is agreeable to them that men should live for their own sake, women for the sake of men: and the qualities and conduct in subjects which are agreeable to rulers, they succeed for a long time in making the subjects themselves consider as their appropriate virtues.'[10] This argument, that women are seduced by patriarchal ideology into believing themselves especially suited to the subjections of wifehood, is a common theme in feminist protest. It was to re-emerge in the 1970s women's movement as 'false consciousness'.

There was nothing false about Harriet Taylor Mill's own consciousness. Her understanding of how marriage interfered with the necessary goal of completely equal rights for men and women was what fired her husband John Stuart Mill's much more famous *The Subjection of Women*, originally published in 1869. 'All that is most striking and profound' in that text, wrote Mill, 'belongs to my wife'.[11] Both Mill's famous book and Harriet's almost-unremembered polemic gave very little space to the suffrage cause, treating as their main subject the general subordination of women as continually reproduced and reinforced through the institution of marriage. The Mills enjoyed 21 years of a very close collaboration and companionship, the last seven as a married couple. Before that, Harriet was married to her first husband, with whom she had three children. She travelled and worked closely together with John Stuart Mill during this first marriage; the two Taylors set up separate households and remained on affectionate terms and involved in their children's lives. Harriet married John Stuart Mill two years after nursing John Taylor through terminal cancer. The married state was one of which both Mills 'entirely and conscientiously' disapproved, and John Stuart Mill wrote a disclaimer before the marriage in which he declared his 'will and intention' to be that Harriet 'retains in all respects whatever the same absolute freedom of action, & freedom of disposal of herself and of all that does or may at any time belong to her, as if no such marriage had taken place'.[12] The general pattern of the Mills' relationship is very like the one between Janet and William Beveridge described in Chapter 5 of

Forgotten Wives. Like Janet, Harriet incurred negative assessments for being an unconventional wife. Like William, John Stuart Mill largely escaped such moralising. (For more on how these moral judgements impeded any sensible understanding of Harriet's own life and work see Chapter 6.)

Disputes about authorship and the ownership of ideas thread their way through many commentaries on wifehood. Another renowned statement of women's right to be liberated from wifehood, *Appeal of One Half the Human Race, Women, Against the Pretensions of the Other Half, Men* (1825) has a male author, William Thompson, but it had a co-author, a radical woman philosopher called Anna Wheeler. Thompson credited her in a 'letter to Mrs. Wheeler' at the beginning of the book as sharing its authorship with him: it was their 'joint property'. Appropriately, the focus of the *Appeal* is the unpicking of the common political argument that women's interests are naturally included in men's interests. No, they are not, argue Thompson and Wheeler.

William Thompson, John Stuart Mill and William Beveridge all recognised and praised their wives' roles in sharing their work, but they were all castigated in their lifetimes and afterwards for being over-extravagant and unrealistic in such acknowledgements. For example, Harriet Taylor Mill's connection with John Stuart Mill has 'proved a stumbling block' to generations of Mill scholars, who found it troubling to witness the incursion of a woman into masculine intellectual territory.[13] As the American sociologist Alice Rossi said, 'the hypothesis that a mere woman was the collaborator of so logical and intellectual a thinker as Mill, much less that she influenced the development of his thought, can be expected to meet resistance in the minds of men'.[14] The 20th-century economist Friedrich Hayek became obsessed with unravelling this puzzle through a meticulous examination of all the available textual evidence – the writings of both Mills, their correspondence and other commentaries of the period. Hayek concluded that Harriet Taylor Mill was actually one of the major figures shaping opinion during the later Victorian era. Hayek, who was a professor of economics at LSE, resurfaces in *Forgotten Wives* as one of the toughest critics of Janet Beveridge's relationship to William.

One of the witnesses of the original apocalyptic meeting round the dinner table between Harriet Taylor and John Stuart Mill in 1830 was Harriet Martineau, the first British sociologist, and a relative of the Booth family. Martineau considered the treatment of women – 'the condition of that half of society over which the other half has power' – the strongest test of any civilisation.[15] Her writings on marriage in her extraordinary sociological travelogue, *Society in America* (1837), and what is probably the world's first sociological methods treatise, *How to Observe Morals and Manners* (1838), written on board ship on the way to the US, connect the gendering of society irretrievably with the inequalities of wifehood and husbandhood. Like Astell, Wollstonecraft and Wheeler, Martineau described women as brought up to be subservient, ill-educated, unoccupied, undemanding, passive and sentimental, while men were dominant, rational, educated, assertive, aggressive, and connected always to the public life of society: and so it is that these roles exactly fit the expectations for both sexes in marriage. Along with other protesters, Martineau considered the case against wifehood to be especially compelling in the field of education. If women were educated for anything, it was for marriage, which meant that essentially they were educated for nothing at all.

Man and wife

Of the four wives in this book, only one (Janet Beveridge) received an education parallel to that of men her same age and class. The upbringing of the others was permeated by traditionally gendered customs prescribing the domestic arts and the private life of the home for women. When the Mill texts were published, and the four wives in the present book were born, the legal position of wives in England remained governed by the insulting doctrine of '*femme covert*' or 'covered woman'. The 18th-century jurist William Blackstone defined this in his *Commentaries on the Laws of England*: 'By marriage, the husband and wife are one person in law: that is, the very being or legal existence of the woman is suspended during the marriage, or at least is incorporated and consolidated into that of the husband: under whose wing, protection, and cover, she performs every thing.'[16] By contrast, unmarried women, or '*femmes soles*', had legal personhood and the same property rights as men, as did widows. The doctrine of *femme covert* emerged from medieval practices, particularly those of the Catholic Church, which regarded the sacrament of marriage as necessarily entailing the dominion of man over wife. Paradoxically, however, the wholesale adoption of the *femme covert* ideology by the Victorians has misled us as to the variable extent to which it did actually govern married women's behaviour before the 18th century. This is an illustration of the way in which prejudiced assumptions about the practices of wifehood get in the way of a reliable history. Some of the historical work carried out as a result of the labours of two of the forgotten wives in the present book, Charlotte Shaw and

Jeannette Tawney, alert us to a revised view of history in which wives did have some practical freedom to make contracts, run businesses and own property separately from their husbands. It was industrialisation that brought this freedom to an end. 'Protective' legislation against the employment of wives and mothers in factories and workshops interrupted their freedom to take paid work; this legislation was more about cutting women's labour market participation in favour of men's than it was about maximising women's own welfare. The so-called 'marriage bar' prevented wives from being employed in professional jobs, requiring that women give up employment on marriage. This particular injustice wasn't finally abolished until the mid-1970s. Charting all these negative consequences of wifehood was a preoccupation of the Fabian Women's Group set up by Charlotte Shaw and others in the early 1900s. Both Jeannette Tawney and Janet Beveridge had personal encounters with the middle-class prohibition on wives' employment.

Before the Married Women's Property Act of 1870 in Britain the property and earnings of all wives belonged to their husbands. Because their identities were subsumed in those of their husbands', wives were prevented from entering into contracts and trusts and from carrying on any business or trade, and they weren't considered legally liable for their actions. The 1870 Act began to unravel the legal custom of coverture, allowing women who were wives to keep their own earnings and inherit some property. This and the other Married Women's Property Acts that followed were responsible for one of the greatest (and quietest) wholesale reallocations of property in English history. Many millions of pounds were undramatically transferred from men to women. Married women's bodies and their children also belonged to their husbands (single women retained ownership of theirs). Wives had to live where their husbands said, and physical coercion by husbands was a male right. Fathers had an absolute legal right to custody of children and could do with them what they wanted; married mothers had no rights at all. It took much agitation over many decades to overturn these unsavoury practices. The 1839 Infant Custody Act gave married mothers very limited rights over young children, though only via the intercession of the courts. The extension of the Act in the legislation of 1873, 1886 and 1925 increased these rights, but it wasn't until the Guardianship of Minors Act of 1973 that British mothers acquired the same rights as fathers.

Wives have also historically had trouble with nationality: here the law in the late 19th century was definitely retrogressive rather than progressive. Women kept their own nationality when they became wives until 1870 when a Naturalization Act abolished this right (leaving men's unchanged). Thereafter British-born women marrying men born elsewhere became aliens. Classed with 'infants, lunatics, and idiots', they were also deprived of the right to apply for naturalisation. Alien wives were automatically debarred from any form of suffrage or representation on local government bodies, and (in the early years of state welfare provision) from old age pensions and national health insurance. Only in 1948 were British-born women granted the right to their own nationality, regardless of marital status, and this is despite the fact that the 1919 Sex Discrimination (Removal) Act singled out both sex *and* marriage as grounds on which people shouldn't be disqualified from any public function.

It's easy to forget how long these injustices lasted – and how much effort it took to get them removed. This is the background against which the four forgotten wives in this book entered, grappled with and lived out the institution of marriage. Marrying in 1871, 1897, 1898 and 1909 respectively – with Janet Beveridge contracting her second more famous marriage in 1942 – they were variously aware of the constraints of wifehood. Jeannette Tawney found it difficult to come to terms with her limited freedom to engage in public work and she railed against her wifely duty to care for (a particularly untidy) husband and home. Janet Beveridge disliked the role of suburban housewife and mother (in her first marriage), and found the civil service a misogynistic environment, while much enjoying the reflected glory (in her second marriage) of being 'the wife of the Beveridge Report'.[17] Charlotte Shaw and Mary Booth both interpreted wifehood as an executive and administrative position, a strategy that helped to bury their own intellectual work.

Marriage as a trade in a man-made world

Even if they didn't read the early feminist texts, the four wives would certainly have been familiar with others that appeared in their own lifetimes. Marriage was a popular subject for Victorian and Edwardian feminist texts. The year, 1897, when the young Janet Beveridge married her university mathematics tutor and put her own academic ambitions on hold, the feminist writer and progressive thinker Mona Caird published *The Morality of Marriage and Other Essays on the Status and Destiny of Women*. Caird's book reprinted a radical article about marriage she had earlier published in the *Westminster Review* in which she called marriage the primary institution keeping women in bondage and treating them like slaves. 'In entering the marriage relation …

she takes upon herself a tie infinitely more stringent, infinitely more imperious and extensive in its action than the bond into which the man enters'.[18] Caird argued for the total rejection of marriage or, at the very least, its rebirth as a completely equal relationship in law and practice. Her outspoken views caused a media storm that reflected the level of contemporary public interest in marriage and women. *The Daily Telegraph*, inviting readers to comment, received 27,000 letters in reply.[19]

The quotation at the front of Caird's book was from another spirited anti-marriage campaigner, Charlotte Perkins Gilman, who puts in a brief appearance in *Forgotten Wives* as a guest of the Webbs at a Fabian house party in Suffolk in 1896. Gilman published a notorious text, *Woman and Economics*, two years later in 1898, the year Charlotte Payne-Townshend, whom Gilman had met at the Webb's house party, became Mrs G.B.S. *Woman and Economics* was translated into seven languages, and all the four wives in this book would certainly have been familiar with it. Gilman rehashed some of the old arguments with an endearing turn of phrase: 'The labor of women in the house, certainly, enables men to produce more wealth than they otherwise could; and in this way women are economic factors in society. But so are horses ... But the horse is not economically independent, nor is the woman.'[20] Gilman's analysis of marriage as a service industry exposed the ideological fancies that sustain it. She was known for her railings against the insanity of a system that mistook the onerous scientific labours of nutrition and sanitation for family life, and that assigned the socially important work of motherhood and child-rearing to an enfeebled subject sex. Like other feminist theorists before and after her, Gilman identified a sinister process of socialisation, which manufactured what she called 'excessive sex-distinction', with damaging effects for women, men and children. Today we would call this gender. *Woman and Economics* isn't actually about women and economics, it's about wives and economics. What Gilman argues is that marriage requires a degrading specialisation of the sexes, which is accordingly built into the entire social system.

Gilman published a wider-ranging analysis of patriarchy in 1911, *The Man-Made World, or Our Androcentric Culture*. In the same year the South African writer Olive Schreiner let her *Woman and Labour* loose on the world, or at least that part of it which was engaged in trying to disentangle the rights from the wrongs of women. Jeannette Tawney sent a copy of *Woman and Labour* to her husband, hoping its arguments about the unbearable dependence of wives would make him listen more carefully to her own on this same topic. Schreiner's florid, exclamation-marked prose isn't easy to read, and may well have prevented the precise economic historian Harry Tawney from being persuaded by it to alter his own marital habits. The first 117 pages of *Woman and Labour* are about parasitism, which Schreiner dubbed the main characteristic of women in industrial society, where three-quarters of women's traditional labours had been discarded by processes of technological and social change. Instead of parasitic wifehood, women, said Schreiner, needed to have 'honourable and socially useful human toil' restored to them.[21] An unpublished essay by Mary Booth covers very much the same ground of women's lost productive domestic labour.

One Edwardian tract on wifehood which would definitely have been well known to another wife in this book, Charlotte Shaw, was Cicely Hamilton's *Marriage as a Trade*, published in 1909. Hamilton was a writer, an actress, a pacifist, an energetic campaigner for women's rights and an unswerving anti-maritalist. She and Charlotte Shaw met through their mutual work in the theatre; Charlotte's friend, the actress-manager Lena Ashwell, produced Cicely Hamilton's first stage-play, *Diana of Dobson's*, in 1911, and Charlotte and Cicely shared membership of the advisory committee for a feminist outfit called the Pioneer Players, which staged non-commercial plays on issues of contemporary social interest. Hamilton's *Marriage as a Trade* is indignant, funny, perceptive and quite unforgiving about what marriage does to women. 'The only excuse for this book', announces Hamilton at the outset, 'is the lack of books on the subject with which it deals – the trade aspect of marriage. That is to say, wifehood and motherhood considered as a means of livelihood for women.' The trade of wifehood, which Hamilton analyses in her book in the same manner as one would approach any trade, is women's staple industry. 'Language bears the stamp of the idea that woman is wife, actually, or in embryo. To most men – perhaps to all – the girl is some man's wife that is to be; the married woman some man's wife that is; the widow some man's wife that was; the spinster some man's wife that should have been – a damaged article, unfit for use, unsuitable. Therefore a negligible quantity.'[22] This narrowing down of women's ambitions to 'the sole pursuit and sphere of marriage' is, in Hamilton's eyes, one of the main causes for all the disabilities that attach to the position of women.

Transformations

The lives of the four women in *Forgotten Wives* were lived in stirring years. These saw the replacement of Victorian values and institutions by a social, economic and moral system more in tune with the democratic needs of modern industrialised and urbanised societies, although desperately lagging behind in terms of gender equality. Mary Booth married just in time to benefit from the Act, which allowed wives to keep their own property and earnings, but her husband, not she, remained the legal arbiter of her children's upbringing and education, despite the fact that he actually had very little to do with such decisions in their household. When women gained the vote on the same terms as men in 1928, Mary was 81 and Jeannette Tawney had notched up 19 years of marriage to her untidy husband, and was typing documents for him while writing her own frustrations into fiction. In that same year, the Prince of Wales opened the Founders' Room on the sixth floor of LSE as a library and a place of leisure for students. The library was endowed by Charlotte Shaw, one of the founders; she, with her strong aversion to publicity, declined to have her portrait painted for the occasion, but later consented to the room being known as 'the Shaw Library'. In 1928, Janet Beveridge, then Jessy Mair, spent a fair amount of time dealing with an epidemic of rodents in the Shaw Library, arranging for the installation of fires and telephones, and trying to prevent students misusing it to sleep in. Otherwise Janet was busy administering a multi-million-pound grant from an American charitable foundation that put both LSE and British social science on a much sounder foundation than would otherwise have been possible. Under the influence of the social reformer Eleanor Rathbone and her campaign for family allowances, Janet and William Beveridge had just made LSE the first educational establishment in Britain to pay child allowances to staff. The sustained case Rathbone laid out in her *The Disinherited Family* (1924) against the mythology of 'the family wage' for ignoring the labour and true needs of women and children was as unwavering in its commitment to piercing the sentimental veil of wifehood as those earlier feminist texts. The core of Rathbone's argument was that the economic dependence of wives could only be alleviated by state intervention, which would bypass husbands entirely. Rathbone shared with Charles Booth an upbringing in Liverpool, and she had Booth's statistics in front of her when she wrote up her own (rather ignored) enquiry into Liverpool dock labour.

All four of the wives lived through the First World War, the roaring twenties, and the 1930s depression. They saw many changes of government and enormous changes in Britain's political life. Two of them endured the Second World War, one (Charlotte Shaw) died during it, and Mary Booth died the day before war was declared. She didn't live to see the flowering of the welfare state that brought into force many of the reforms for which she and her husband had worked, but Janet Beveridge and Jeannette Tawney, dying in the late 1950s, did. Jeannette's brother and Janet's husband William Beveridge launched his famous Beveridge Report on *Social Insurance and Allied Services* in 1942, which laid down the structure of social security and public health that was eventually introduced by the post-war Labour government. It was Janet's influence that was responsible for the Report's accessibility to a public eager for change. Although the Report did not in itself establish the welfare state, and William Beveridge's reputation as the welfare state's main architect has been over-inflated, his Report was an important international testament 'for what it said could be done by governments throughout the developed world'.[23] Janet was not, however, able to shift William Beveridge's muddled thinking about wives, which she shared with him. In his scheme, wives retained their traditional economic dependence on men, and married women who worked for pay lost their full entitlements to unemployment and sickness benefits, receiving only 60 per cent of the pensions available to men and single women. Provision for separated, divorced or abused wives defeated Beveridge entirely. This 'incredibly crude chauvinism' excluded wives from the life-changing social security benefits of the welfare state.[24]

Problems of method

Forgotten Wives aims to show some of the ways in which the work and experiences of wives have been subject to an entrenched process of historical neglect and burial. Methodologically, this is complicated, as two things have to happen at the same time. First, there has to be an attempt to uncover and recount what these wives actually did; and second, there needs to be a focus on how the wives were treated in the relevant histories and biographies. I try to do both together in the four chapters that follow. My attempts aren't biographically comprehensive; I couldn't possibly fit in everything that happened in four long lives (77, 82, 86 and 91 years respectively), nor could I read (in the timespan of my own advancing 77 years) all the archival material and commentaries that exist. Instead I've tried to 'bring to life' the buried stories of their lives and point out some of the places where these stories conflict with what's been perceived and written about them.

This process is useful in identifying the kinds of stratagems that underlie the historical neglect of wives: the assumptions, the stereotypes, the one-sided interest, the laudatory attitude to some types of work and the derogatory silence about others. The writing of 'great man' biographies by historians often starts with the (usually unarticulated) premise that marriage is a relationship which consigns women to the margins of public interest. In fact, 'great man' biographies are the rule, as the education historian Jane Martin noted when she analysed entries in the *Oxford Dictionary of National Biography*: most are of alpha males. This gendering of history writing is unlikely to give any prominence to wives' achievements or perspectives. What *she* did as an individual is mentioned, perhaps, but there's rarely any attempt to quantify *her* input of intellectual, political, domestic or emotional labour to the partnership – without which her husband might not have been great at all. The other side of this coin is what the effort may have cost her in terms of reduced health and lost opportunities. Importantly too – something that is very clear in the four case-studies that follow – these standard assumptions about marriage don't permit much appreciation of diversity and nonconformity in individual marriages.

Biographers' default assumption tends to be that of traditional marital roles. This makes them query any seeming divergences and fail to comment on conformity. Thus untidy households are the fault of miscreant wives (Jeannette Tawney), whereas superb domestic administration (Mary Booth) hardly gets a mention. Wives who contribute to their husbands' intellectual or artistic work (Charlotte Shaw, Mary Booth, Janet Beveridge and Jeannette Tawney) are demoted to performing merely secretarial tasks. The absence of motherhood calls for attention (Charlotte Shaw, Jeannette Tawney), whereas its presence (Mary Booth, Janet Beveridge) is barely recognised as incurring huge burdens of domestic labour which support husbands' public achievements. The sexual relationship between husband and wife is a most mysterious thing, causing much puzzlement. Did they or didn't they? Mary and Charles Booth obviously did, with at least eight pregnancies to show for it, but what about the Shaws, the Tawneys and the Beveridges? Were the men incapable and/or the wives unwilling? Biographers' 'obsession with genital heterosexuality'[25] is another default prejudice, which has distracted them from appreciating the unique quality of individual marriages.

None of the women in *Forgotten Wives* conformed to prevailing sentimental stereotypes of the dutiful wife at home, but each deviated in her own particular way. In this they were undoubtedly typical of many other married women at the time. Mona Caird in 1897 put it like this: 'when a man or woman marries a great curtain seems to fall. As human beings they have both lost their position; they are more or less shut away in their little circle, and all the rest of the world is emphatically outside.'[26] This is what makes marriage such a tantalising and challenging subject for biographers. We are prying into secret places, guessing, interpreting and feeling faintly guilty all the time. But marriage as a political institution connects wives and husbands to wider social and economic structures: it inflicts a seamless welding of public with private patriarchy. The 'male breadwinner' model of the family with subservient and undervalued wives at home isn't just a historical story: it underlies the philosophy of all modern welfare regimes. The themes of *Forgotten Wives* are thus relevant to current debates about gender inequalities and the ways in which these are sustained by deeply patriarchal ways of thinking and seeing – and their counterparts: ways of not thinking, not seeing and therefore not remembering.

Table 1: The four wives, in birth order

	Mary Catherine Booth, née Macaulay	Charlotte Frances Shaw, née Payne-Townshend	Janet Beveridge, previously Jessy Mair, née Jessy Thomson Philip	Annette Jeanie [Jeannette] Tawney, née Beveridge
Birth	04/11/1847, Bristol, England	20/01/1857, Derry, Cork, Ireland	26/11/1876, Dundee, Scotland	11/09/1880*, Bankipur, India
Marriage	29/04/1871 to **Charles James Booth** [1840–1916]	01/06/1898 to **George Bernard Shaw** [1856–1950]	14/10/1897 to David Beveridge Mair [1868–1942]; 15/12/1942 to **William Henry Beveridge** [1879–1963]	28/06/1909 to **Richard Henry Tawney** [1880–1962]
Death	25/09/1939, aged 91	12/09/1943, aged 86	25/04/1959, aged 82	20/01/1958, aged 77
ODNB entry	Yes	No	No	No
Wikipedia entry	No	Yes [as Charlotte Payne-Townshend]	No	No
Full length biography	No	Yes	No	No

* This is a probable date taken from the Tawney Papers in LSE. The actual date is not given in any of the relevant biographies, and I have not been able to find it on any British India database. The grave in Highgate Cemetery, London, just gives 'September, 1880' as Jeannette Tawney's birth date.

2

Mary Booth

1847–1939

On 26 June 1878, 30-year-old Mary Booth composed one of her regular letters to her husband, Charles, who was on one of his frequent forays to look after the family shipping and leather business in New York. She was at home in their London house, 6 Grenville Place, South Kensington, a generous stuccoed mansion, though sunless and prone to draughts. Mary's cousin Beatrice Potter, the future Beatrice Webb, dubbed it 'dark, dull and stuffy and somewhat smelly' – the Victorians had a lot of problems with drains. In the summer of 1878 Mary Booth was in Grenville Place, with her five-year-old daughter Antonia, and two sons, Thomas, aged four, and baby George, who was nine months old. Her husband Charles had been worried about her. She had been having palpitations and complaining of stress, some clearly caused by the death two years earlier of their little girl, Polly, whose birth and death from croup had occurred between the births of the two boys. So there was Mary, in her comfortable house, with a considerable number of servants,[1] in constant communication with her liberal intellectual parents and a wide circle of relatives, friends and acquaintances who together made up 'the intellectual aristocracy of London',[2] a husband much occupied with business affairs, and a great deal of house- and child- and servant-management work to do. There were gnawing subterranean questions about the singular purpose of her own life, but in her letter to Charles she reflected on what the two of them had already achieved together, and what might await them in the future: 'At present there are only beginnings,' she wrote, 'a fair and promising opening of such a serious life of effort as we may hope to carry on to some perhaps not wholly satisfying; but still worthy and intelligent conclusion.' They needed, she estimated, another ten or twelve years in which adequately to impress themselves on their children and their surroundings. This was an effort in which, 'We need each other absolutely. We can't stir a step without each other.'[3]

It was during the ensuing twelve years that Charles Booth's most publicly lauded achievement, the 17-volume *Life and Labour of the People in London*, was conceived, gestated and born. This was an endeavour that changed political thinking in Britain about poverty and the role of the state. It was the first systematic and detailed attempt to catalogue the extent and nature of British urban poverty, and in the course of the 17 years the project occupied many steps were taken to develop the methodological tools of social science. The Booth inquiry into poverty, and Charles Booth's work on allied subjects, particularly the condition of the aged poor, would prove to be key to the 20th-century extension of state provision. The poverty inquiry suggested what would become a cornerstone of the welfare state: the concept of a 'minimum accepted standard' below which society should not allow anyone to sink. Charles Booth also had a special interest in the fate of older people. The central argument of his work on old age pensions, that pensions must be counted as a right of citizenship, entered public life as a new and lasting welfare concept. When William Beveridge launched his celebrated report on *Social Insurance and Allied Services* in 1942, the findings of Booth's poverty survey were among those he drew on as demonstrating that Britain held enough wealth to eradicate poverty: the problem was one of unequal distribution. A major impact of Booth's work was thus to nudge into being a new tradition of basing social policy on scientific study.

Life and Labour has been intensively studied by academics, who have been both aided and impeded by the vast quantities of (not always well-organised) archival material available in London and Liverpool. One line of enquiry has been the *collective* nature of the research and writing that went into the finished volumes. Charles Booth was the leader, 'the Chief', but, altogether, no fewer than 34 different researchers contributed. Some names are well known: the economist Clara Collet, for example, who lived in the East End for the Booth study and became an expert on women's work; and Beatrice Potter (later Webb), who learnt about life as a seamstress in the East End, and about dock labour and the Jewish community for 'cousin Charlie's' investigation – she and Mary Booth had grandparents in common. Others are more shadowy figures. Mary Booth, one of the team of 34, is in many ways the most intriguingly shadowy of them all. She is there in accounts of

Charles Booth's life and work, as his 'hidden collaborator', his 'critic and editor', a 'helpmeet' who made 'an active intellectual and practical contribution';[4] she is noted to have read books for him, explaining socialism, theories of trade unionism, the principles of the cooperative movement and the new science of positivism to a man who didn't have the time to read; she wrote passages of his books and rewrote others; she managed his team of researchers when he was away; she acted as his business secretary; she went to meetings for him or with him; and, above all, she was very thoroughly enmeshed in the endless entertaining his social investigation work entailed.

Mary is there, but she is at the same time also not there. Mary was a wife, and the historians and social scientists who have probed Charles Booth's work have incuriously located Mary in the background, at the margins, and often in footnotes. Although they've been troubled occasionally by Mary's haunting presence, they've not really wondered whether *Life and Labour* would have happened without her, or how different it might have been. Accepting unquestioningly the nature of wifehood, they have also not taken account of the enormous inputs of domestic labour Mary Booth supplied, nor have they, for the most part, considered how she shaped what is known as exclusively Charles Booth's contribution to modern social policy. There are other questions. What did Mary feel about the role history has conferred on her of being Mrs Booth? Did she have any kind of independent life, apart from Charles and the survey and his other work, and the rearing of children – there were to be seven in all (one of Mary's pregnancies ended in miscarriage) – and the overseeing of the houses and the servants and the orchestration of manifold social duties and relations?

Coming down to dinner

She described herself as 'a puzzling child. I loved solitude & brooding by myself. I used to go down from the nursery to the library where I could be quite by myself, and could browse among the books, reading & skimming all sorts, some not at all suitable to a child.'[5] Precocious might be another word for her. She was said to have been reading Plutarch's *Lives* at the age of three. It was a thoroughly intellectual and upper-middle-class household: Mary's father, Charles Zachary Macaulay, was a senior civil servant in the Board of Trade, a highly educated and well-networked man who came from a family with strong Liberal reforming ties. His father, Zachary Macaulay, had been a prominent member of the Clapham Sect, a community of evangelical Christian families devoted to the abolition of slavery and generally raising the moral tone of late Georgian society. Mary's uncle, Thomas Babington Macaulay, was the famous historian, whose *History of England* disturbed Victorian Britain with a new view of history as containing ordinary lives, and, even more unusually, of drawing on novels as sources of historical data. Mary's mother's family, which connected her to the famous Beatrice Webb, was no less radical. Her and Beatrice's common grandfather, Richard Potter, known as 'Radical Dick', was MP for Wigan, a textile merchant, a member of a group of wealthy Unitarians committed to improving the welfare of the poor. He campaigned for the reform of parliament, and was one of the founders of *The Manchester Guardian*. (In order to help the reader, these dense genealogical connections are laid out in Table 2 on page 64.) Mary Booth lived in Richard Potter's house in Manchester as a young child with her elder brother and mother when her father was Colonial Secretary in Mauritius.

Mary Catherine Macaulay was born in Bristol in 1847 but her brother Thomas had been born in Mauritius in 1843.[6] Richard Potter's son, also called Richard, and his wife Lawrencina had nine daughters, and as a child Mary often joined some of the nine female cousins for holidays at the Potters' Gloucestershire house, Standish, overlooking the Severn valley full of meadows and orchards. Later, Mary Booth and her own family would visit another Potter house in Monmouthshire, Wales, a dilapidated Jacobean fantasy called the Argoed, where they encountered such notables as the social philosopher Herbert Spencer, the housing reformer Octavia Hill, Toynbee Hall Settlement founders Samuel and Henrietta Barnett, the economist and first Director of LSE, W.A.S. Hewins, Beatrice and Sidney Webb, and Charlotte and George Bernard Shaw.

Mary Booth was connected through her Macaulay and Potter heritages to many of the moulders of Victorian and Edwardian society. When she married Charles Booth, 'the family tree became a forest'.[7] As one of her obituarists put it: 'By her birth and her marriage she was related to something like a score of families who for three or four generations ... played a leading part in shaping British events, commercial, political, and sociological ... At the height of her activity she went everywhere [and] met almost everybody of consequence.'[8] Describing her childhood, Mary noted how she had regularly been given the opportunity to hear much about the views and interests of her elders. In the Macaulay household, 'a great many people turned up often to dinner'. The children were brought down to the dining room in time for dessert. Mary would go the round of any visitors, answer a few kind questions, and then take her seat by her father's side, 'with a little dessert on a plate before me & a glass of wine & water'. After that, she wasn't expected to speak; 'in fact should hardly have been allowed to do so'. So she listened, 'and often with deep interest'. Thus, 'at the time of the Crimean war, I knew of Lord Raglan's leadership & of his death, & Codrington succeeding him, & of Miss Nightingale in her efforts'.[9]

These encounters with public and literary life, along with her mother's reading to her of Walter Scott's novels, constituted Mary Booth's informal education. Her formal education was a matter of sharing a governess with her elder brother and then, when he was dispatched to school, being entered as a pupil at an elite girls' school in Kensington, Hyde Park College, and later moved to a small boarding school intended for delicate or backward girls (a doctor had, probably incorrectly, diagnosed a problem with Mary's heart). There she was 'infinitely bored' for two years with an 'education' consisting of writing out French, German and Italian verbs, practising the piano, and drawing and sketching. Every day before tea the girls had to lie flat on the floor and recite either the catechism, or the list of the British imperial possessions, and Queen Victoria's claim to the throne, going all the way back to Egbert, the 9th-century King of Wessex.[10]

Both Mary Booth's mother and her maternal grandmother, who were also called Mary — there are many Marys and Charles and Richards in this story — are described by biographers as being 'mentally unstable'. It's not easy to decipher what this means. The Mary Potter who was married to grandfather Richard Potter appears to have developed some form of 'puerperal insanity' after the birth of her fourth child in 1823; she's said to have rejected her husband, had hallucinations, been suicidal and become obsessively interested in Zionism, at one point buying a donkey and heading off to Jerusalem. This Mary is fortunate in having had a grand-daughter, Georgina Meinertzhagen, who wrote a memoir of the Potter family which gives an alternative impression of her as 'cultivated, witty, full of fun ... a sensitive and restless creature, impatient of restraint'.[11] Her impatience extended to the restrictions imposed by the conventional roles of wife and mother. Women who depart from received norms of wifehood have often been called crazy (but of course acute postnatal illness also does happen).

Mary Booth's own mother had married at 21, and gave birth to three children, and not much is known about her, her interests or psychological health. 'Mama' and 'Father' are frequent references in Mary Booth's diaries and letters. Mary was evidently closer to her father, a closeness that commentators — but not Mary herself — attribute to maternal instability and the consequent emotional dependence of Mary's father on his only daughter. The letters exchanged between

Mary and her father bear witness to a prodigious and all-encompassing affection. 'I am sure that I shall think of you to-morrow morning before I think of any other woman, you & you only can be my real valentine,' writes the 66-year-old Charles Zachary Macaulay to his 31-year-old daughter on 13 February 1879.[12] Mary poured out her worries in letters to her father in a way she did not do when writing to Charles. Her admission elicited this sort of reply from her father: 'Oh! My darling – How I wish I could see you, and put my arms quite round you, and soothe you as I used to do.'[13] Mary does confess in a letter to her husband that nothing helps her with her worries as much as 'being with Papa'. She spends so much time with Papa and the children at the seaside while Charles is away in the early years of their marriage that he gets almost jealous and she has to reassure him that she loves both men.[14] There are few clues in Mary Booth's papers as to her mother's mental health – the letters from her mother that survive are much less frequent, more practical, and less effusive. But there is this tantalising acknowledgement in one of Mary's letters to Charles written in 1888: 'One can't expect to have no trouble,' she philosophises, 'and my life has been and is singularly free from it considering the strange tragedy in the middle of which I have grown up. Thank heaven my own married relation is a straightforward one.'[15]

'This interesting new relative'

It wasn't perhaps quite as straightforward in the living as it became in the retrospect. Mary Booth left her little boarding school at 14,[16] and continued her informal education at home until she married Charles in 1871, when she was 23. They met in 1868, in Liverpool, when Mary went to stay with one of her Potter cousins who had recently married the shipowner Robert Holt. It was this shipping connection that first brought Charles Booth into Mary's life. In the complex kinship network without which stories such as Mary Booth's can't be grasped, Charles was a cousin of William Lamport, the co-founder of Robert Holt's shipping line, and Charles had worked in Lamport and Holt's business until leaving to start his own with his brother Alfred in 1863. Most of the Booth family's money was made, not in running steamships, but in leading the world in the business of turning animal skins into products people wanted to buy. The Booth companies – there were eventually a total of 33 – played a pivotal role in the commercial network that transformed the production, distribution and use of leather in the late 19th century. The original Booth partnership exported sheepskins from Bermondsey to a tannery in the US in a place aptly named Gloversville in upstate New York. The Booth brothers bought their own ships; by 1900 the company owned 14 and, by 1914, more than thirty. Profitable contracts were signed to transport mail, gunpowder and other cargoes to northern Brazil, returning with cotton, sugar, coffee and nuts. The invention of the pneumatic tyre by John Boyd Dunlop in 1888 expanded their trade substantially to include natural Brazilian rubber. The leather trade involved the opening of Booth offices in Australia to source kangaroos; in the early 1900s the Booths dominated the world trade in kangaroo skins, processing up to 2,400 a day. It is a side-story, but the sinking of the Lusitania in 1915, which killed 1,195 people, quite possibly happened because it was carrying armaments for the Booth business, disguised on the ship's manifest as sheepskins.[17]

Charles Booth was tremendously occupied with this commercial business when he met Mary Macaulay. He was much engaged with its technical aspects, but also with the challenge of administering staff and offices in far-flung places, and with the capitalist need to seek constantly expanding opportunities for profit making. Mary presented an opposite set of interests. This 'brilliant, brown-eyed, vehement London-Scottish girl', 'sophisticated and intelligent', 'marvellously well-read and well-informed, and an astonishingly vital person',[18] took, it is said, a startlingly dim view of the preoccupations of Charles Booth's Liverpool: Mary considered them stilted, provincial and trivial. Her urbane, cultured, literary, intellectual attitude to life was a magnet to Charles.

Charles Booth's only talent at school had been arithmetic, so he had been sent into business rather than to university. Although interested in current social and political debates, he was said to lack any intellectual resources with which to appraise these, and to suffer from 'a curious inability to absorb ideas from books'.[19] His family remembers his study as being completely bookless, and it is abundantly clear from Mary's letters and diaries that she was the reader in the family. Charles's youth had been marred by several deaths – those of both parents, and then the young woman with whom he had fallen in love, Antonia Prange, the daughter of a German merchant in Liverpool and the sister of a school friend. 'To the end of his life, his feelings towards her memory remained unchanged,' wrote Mary's daughter Meg.[20] Mary and Charles named their first daughter Antonia in the young woman's memory, and Mary was assiduous, right up until her late eighties, well after Charles's death, in keeping up contact with the Prange family, who continued to receive financial aid from the Booth estate.

At the beginning of Mary and Charles's marriage, it had not been at all obvious that this mixture of different temperaments, attitudes and styles of life would yield a successful couple. On meeting her 'interesting new relative', Beatrice Webb said of him: 'No longer young' (Charles was seven years older than Mary) 'he had neither failed nor succeeded in life'; to a stranger he might have passed for 'a self-educated idealistic compositor or engineering draughtsman; or as the wayward member of an aristocratic family or … as an ascetic priest'. He was abnormally thin, with his clothes hanging off him as though on pegs, 'a distinctly queer figure of a man';[21] and he had the most peculiar eating habits, picking at a potato or nibbling at a dry biscuit while those around him ate full-scale meals. This behaviour signalled some kind of nervous disorder that was associated with recurrent breakdowns in health throughout Charles's life. Mary Booth called it in her *Memoir* of Charles 'a distressing form of indigestion' which sometimes led to him avoiding food altogether.[22]

Whatever was wrong with Charles was the cause of 18 months' rigorous isolation in a remote Swiss valley early in the marriage. In 1873, Charles, Mary and the infant Antonia, their first child, departed to 'a quiet secluded house at a little distance from Bex in the Canton de Vaud' in Switzerland in the hope of a cure.[23] Charles brooded, thought and walked among the wildflowers. According to their grand-daughter Belinda Norman-Butler, Mary showed exceptional sympathy and courage at what must have been a very difficult time for her. In mid-April 1874, with snow still thick on the ground, Mary gave birth, alone – Charles was out looking for the doctor – to her second child. Focusing on the impact of the Swiss episode on him, rather than on her, Mary concluded that it had been a failure, and Charles was still an invalid when they returned to England.

Charles Booth's health had a considerable impact on Mary Booth's life, and it remains a biographical puzzle. What kind of physical or mental condition was this? To us in the 21st century the symptoms read like anorexia.[24] It isn't so much a scarcity of archival evidence that leaves the question unanswered, but a surfeit of it: a sea of evidence spattered with myriad conflicting clues. The only full-length biography of Charles – there is none of Mary – written by the Liverpool social scientists Tom and Margaret Simey in 1959 offers little clarity, deciding that Charles suffered both mental anguish and physical ailments of an unspecified kind. The Simeys relied in their biography on documents supplied to them by the Booth family. In return they had to take on board the family's opinions about the story they put together. The Booths' son George, their daughters Imogen and Meg, and Meg's husband W.T.D. (Billy) Ritchie, were the main correspondents in this attempt to arrive at a collective diagnosis. Billy Ritchie was particularly angry at the implied insult that Charles had been prey to mental anguish. This was simply not so. He was a man with a mission, quite without self-doubt, and simply so driven that he periodically wore himself out.[25] However, the evidence of Charles's letters to Mary, which recurrently admit to self-doubt, low-spiritedness, depression and anxiety about the 'ease with which I break down', weigh against this interpretation.[26]

The shipping and leather business made possible the poverty inquiry. By the time work on this began in the 1880s, Alfred Booth & Co. had a substantial annual turnover from both sides of the business. The absence from England entailed by this was also responsible for a rich seam of correspondence between the Booths over the 43 years of their marriage. Charles was away from Mary attending to it for several months each year. His letters to her are mainly given over to accounts of his travels, inquiries about the children and details about the business. The latter occupied much writing space, and this, together with Mary's detailed and considered replies, shows how much he depended on her to make a success of it.[27] When Charles's letters venture into self-reflection, they demonstrate his insecurity and the intensity of his dependence on his wife. Here he is writing to her from the S.S. Algeria en route to New York in March 1878: 'As I lie in bed thinking over all the mistakes & blunders I have made comes naturally to my mind the chorus. Bless my wife. Bless my dear dear wife, & then I think of all she has done for me & all she is ever doing for me & I am grateful – & then behind all that & bigger than all that comes up with my love for her ... Surely never man needed the help of a wise wife more than I did, or was so slow to admit it & take advantage of the wise wife by his side, for though your wisdom has been forced forward by these years you were always wise by side of me. I cannot say that I wish I had now more confidence in myself, for I evidently have plenty, but I wish it were of a firmer better grounded kind. Why should I be confident? What have I done that I lying here seasick should believe that I can pick up the disordered skein of a business & set it right? I say the future shall show – but at 37 a man should have something more than the future to point to. I know the words of encouragement you would speak if you were with me.'[28] From Boston, a few months later: 'Do you know you are always present with me – the companion & witness of all I say & do ... you are there helping & comforting & listening.' She has made him a new man, he says, both in his character and in the ways his eyes 'have been opened to the truth in me & round me'.[29]

After the ineffective stay in Switzerland, Charles's health was restored by a trip to Brazil in 1874. Mary, who never shared his fondness for travel, agreed to go with him. They left the children with Booth relatives in Liverpool and travelled on one of the Alfred Booth & Co. steamers to Pará (now Fortaleza) in northern Brazil. The object of the trip was to experiment with speed and coal using a new pressurised engine, and Charles and Mary and one or two passengers 'to whom the case had been explained' achieved the journey with an astonishingly small consumption of coal.[30] Mary, bored on the lengthy journey, took up the study of astronomy, and by the end of the trip had become so familiar with the night sky that she detected the failure of the ship's compass to keep it on the correct path. For the rest of her life she was prone to dragging family and friends out at night so they could marvel at the stars.

Her serious ambition

As a young woman, Mary Macaulay had performed all the usual duties that were expected of young Victorian ladies. These usually included philanthropic activities. Mary first met the renowned housing reformer Octavia Hill as a teenager through Miss Harriet Harrison, the Lady Superintendent of her school; Miss Harrison was a close friend of both Octavia and her sister Miranda. When Mary first met the Hills, she and her classmates enjoyed helping with festivities for Octavia's tenants and in the little playground Octavia had arranged for the tenants' children in the East End of London. It was probably also through Miss Harrison that Mary first met the Barnetts – Canon Samuel and Henrietta, who had established the renowned social settlement Toynbee Hall in the East End in 1884.[31] The connection with the Barnetts, which would prove tremendously important in the poverty inquiry, was Mary's well before it was Charles's. In June, 1878, she noted in a letter to him that, 'Yesterday evening I went down with Miss Harrison to the Barnetts. It seems funny too to be getting in a way quite intimate with these people who have never even seen you; & know me only as an apparition unconnected with anybody or anything coming down every now & then to Whitechapel to make myself useful or agreeable as the case may be.'[32]

But Mary's heart was not in philanthropy. In fact, she had developed a scepticism, which she would communicate to Charles, about its usefulness as a strategy for ameliorating the damages of poverty. If she had a serious ambition of her own, it was to be a writer. Traces of her independent early writing survive in the Booth archives: a clever philosophical dialogue featuring Bacon, Protagoras, Socrates and Aquinas; an essay on the development of European culture; a discourse on the relationship between the French literary celebrity Madame

Germaine de Staël and her mother, Madame Suzanne Necker; a highly scholarly account of the similarities and differences between the four New Testament gospels; a comparison between the nature of English and French political rebellions; various essays in French, short stories and poems. There are drafts, too, of a novel. This is about the large squabbling family of a doctor who was killed in a railway accident, leaving not much money and a very undomesticated wife. The narrative is told from the viewpoint of a daughter called Lucy. She had been her father's favourite; she had brought her lessons into his study while he wrote his letters; 'he would have her at his side at dinner, and her place in the library was always the footstool at his knee'.[33]

At some point after the Booths' return from Switzerland, Mary apparently submitted a full-length novel to a publisher who rejected it. She immediately burnt it.[34] There are references in Mary Booth's diaries to her getting rid of evidence about her personal writing life: on 21 May 1899, for example, she noted 'destroyed papers & writings,' and the next day, 'destroyed papers & writings again'.[35] A few papers were left behind: notes for a lecture on Goethe she gave in 1892; other notes for lectures on Faust and Dickens and the history of the public health movement; a thoughtful article on changes in the position of women; and the text of a speech – in her handwriting, though Charles probably gave it – for the Economic Club on methodological issues in the collection of family budget data.

It's hard to know how much importance should be assigned to this thwarted ambition of Mary Booth's, for thwarted it was, not only by unappreciative publishers, but by the whole panoply of life as Charles Booth's wife, the mother of seven children, and the orchestrator-in-chief of the dense network of social relations that supported all the Booth endeavours. She did worry about her future, sometimes. 'What shall I do when I have finished teaching Mary & Imogen to do fractions?' she asked Charles in November 1884. 'Set up a dancing academy I think ... in the drawing room ... while you with a set of intelligent & enlightened unwashed friends discuss positivism & social dynamics in the dining room.'[36] To their credit, both her father and her husband encouraged her to write. 'What a delight you are with ... all your dreams,' enthused Charles to her from Boston in August 1880. 'But you are right. Something more ought to be the outcome of such powers as yours. You seem to be a knife without the handle sometimes & when the handle is found – lo! The blade is different. I wish I could do as much for you as you can for me. What you can do for me is only limited by your power of being with me. I need you every hour. But for you it is only circumstances that can make you what you might be

– & those circumstances are hard to create. You might have stumbled into them – may still do so.'[37] He did make some practical suggestions; for example, in a letter from New York in 1887, that she set aside some time to write every day. 'It is a really capital plan;– your idea,' Mary responded, 'and I mean to stick to it! ... when I get up to Grenville Place, I shall start a writing table in my bedroom there, against the evenings when you will have to be away ... Mrs Sidgwick [probably the educationalist Eleanor Sidgwick] to whom I talked a little about my confused head in answer to some kind, sympathizing remarks of hers;– suggests writing as a likely cure for it;– writing for publication, I mean. She says she thinks it comes from being over-burdened with detail, & unable to shake off the presence of such to my mind;– and thinks that to write a good absorbing novel would relieve my head.'[38]

Evidently, the Simeys in their biography of Charles weren't entirely convinced that Mary was happy giving up her independent creative life in favour of her husband's craft of social investigation. Describing her as 'domesticated more from a sense of duty than from inclination', they saw her as someone who reluctantly gave up her claim to an independent life, a course of action that placed talents at Charles's disposal 'without which he would have been ill-equipped to undertake his work'.[39] Mary's children, confronted in the 1950s with the Simeys' draft book, took the view that Mary relinquished the serious ambition to be a writer after the first few years with Charles. Certainly by the time of Mrs Sidgwick's advice in 1887, Mary doubted the possibility of finding any time away from the cares of the household.

Mary's cousin, Beatrice Webb, saw the advantages for Charles of Mary's devotion to the domestic life. Visiting their country house, Gracedieu, in the summer of 1887, Beatrice found, 'The beautiful old place, filled to overflowing with happiness and youth ... Mary says her life is one continual sunshine. Charlie has the three sides of his existence complete – profession, home, intellectual interest. His business, he says, is the most important to him of the three, but I expect he under-rates the constant happiness of satisfied affection.'[40] The satisfied affection is demonstrated in the photo on page 44 of the Booth family on the steps of Gracedieu Manor. By 1895, when the Booths dined with the Webbs to discuss the London School of Economics, the ever-critical Beatrice found Mary's absorption in her children just too much: 'After dinner, when she and I retired, I listened for some twenty minutes to her account of the unsuccessful struggles to get Tom into the Guards and the successful compromise of the Black Watch. She was smartly dressed, her hair twisted into the last new knot, her face and figure looking singularly young, bright and charming, resembling much more her portrait as a girl than the highly-strung, worldly, dowdy "mother, friend and wife" that I knew and loved so well for fifteen years.' The family seemed 'strangely incongruous' to Beatrice: 'Charlie living most of the week in an artisan's house in a back street in Liverpool – not for the purpose of investigation but simply because "it suits him" – Mary carrying on a great house in London and one in the country entertaining the smart young friends of her children.'[41]

It was certainly unusual to have a husband who spent so much time lodging in other people's houses in poor districts, in both London and Liverpool, even claiming that their simple circumstances, including the basic food on offer, suited him better than the diet his own household provided. In addition, Charles was prone to take himself off for prolonged excursions in Europe, staying with local families, whenever he felt his health demanded it. 'I sometimes think you should have been a 16th Century person yourself, and have gone a-seeking for the El Dorado with Cortes or some such hero of romantic enterprise,' admitted Mary, when Charles was travelling in Spain in 1887. He'd been away so long she'd developed 'a sort of hazy feeling' about him, 'as though you were wandering out of our ken entirely'.[42] He must have been, in many ways, a difficult man to live with, working always long hours, at least eight a day whether at home or elsewhere, and normally beginning at 6 am with a cold bath.

Gracedieu

On the Booths' return from Brazil in 1874, Charles was well enough to open an office of the Booth steamship company in London, and Mary took a lease on the dark and draughty house in Grenville Place. Four more children were born, and the shipping business prospered. In 1886 Charles decided they needed a rural retreat, and he found Gracedieu Manor in Leicestershire, so named after a 13th-century priory on the edge of Charnwood Forest. The house was conveniently equidistant between London and Liverpool. It was leased to the Booths, who occupied it when they were not in London for the rest of their lives, with the exception of a year in 1896, when they experimented with a stay in Ightham Mote, a small well-preserved medieval moated manor house in Kent, now the property of the National Trust. Visiting friends there in December 1895, Mary had been overtaken by the 'poetic beauty' of the house, 'floating like a galleon on the moat, the water lapping and reflecting the walls and turrets above',[43] and so she moved the family there for a short but utterly memorable time.

Unlike Ightham Mote, Gracedieu was architecturally undistinguished; their son George, in a memoir of his childhood, recalls most people judging it 'remarkably bizarre' with its sprawling grey mixed Tudor-Gothic style, and anachronistic Pugin-designed chapel. It retained this curious aspect throughout its subsequent existence as an independent school. When the Booths found it, the house had 29 bedrooms but only one bathroom, was damp with a leaking roof and wore a generally 'decayed and dissipated appearance'. Its saving grace was the grounds, with acres of grassland, streams, trees and an 'island pond' on which the Booth family and their visitors skated every winter.[44] While Charles was away, either in London busy with the beginnings of the poverty survey, or in New York managing the business, or somewhere in Latin America investigating trading opportunities, Mary hired and supervised local workmen and tried to bring some order to the house, which she at first did not like at all. It wasn't an easy house to manage, being lit by candles and lamps until 1932. Cutting the lawns took three days and involved a pony pulling a machine. Despite these inconveniences, Gracedieu was the site of many key conversations, meetings and decisions about the work which made Charles Booth famous. Both Mary and Charles were to die at Gracedieu – he aged 76 in 1916 and she in 1939, aged 91.

Whereas Charles treated Gracedieu as a weekend cottage, Mary found herself quickly enmeshed in the community. The new establishment was in an old-established Midlands mining community, a neighbourhood which 'would not be a bad centre in some ways for the "personal observation" part of your scheme,' as Mary wrote to cousin Beatrice, the social investigator. 'We have a fearfully poverty-stricken population ... a violent Irish element, disorderly.'[45] The opening of Whitwick colliery in 1824 had set in train a major expansion of the coal-mining industry across north-west Leicestershire. Mining was still very much the local industry when the Booths moved to the area. Mary supported the women through various miners' strikes in the 1890s, and in April 1898 when there was a fire at Number Five Pit which killed 35 men, Mary and her son George went at once to see what they could do. Mary never forgot the silent waiting women with shawls over their heads. A committee, numbering Charles Booth among its members – but we can hear Mary Booth's voice behind him – was set up to fundraise for the widows and orphans.

Mary Booth's mistrust of much conventional middle-class philanthropy didn't prevent her from launching practical remedies of her own. The Whitwick and Thringstone Nursing Association was set up in 1899 to provide the villages with a nurse, and thus access to healthcare at a time well before the NHS. In 1910, the nurse in question, Nurse Ada Morley, attended a total of 180 cases and made 3,670 home visits, dispatching only three cases to hospital. In the 1920s and 1930s Mary Booth was still helping raise funds for the Association, which continued its good work until at least 1947. In 1910, also, Mary Booth founded a small nursing home for girls with lung diseases. St Andrew's Home at Cross Lane Cottages cared for these girls with a staff paid for by Mary Booth.[46] Mary's diaries feature many mentions of time spent on these ventures. She gave regular annual tea parties for all the Thringstone children – some three hundred of them – during which the children were served cake and buns by members of the Booth family, and sent home with a bag of sweets and two oranges each. Mary's daughter Meg developed philanthropic work of her own, as a volunteer for the Children's Country Holiday Fund (CCHF), travelling regularly to the Fund's London office from 1903 on. In this capacity she would certainly have come across Jeannette Tawney, whose work with the CCHF appears in Chapter 4. Unsurprisingly, one of the locations for the children's holidays was Thringstone, which received 85 of them in 1905. Both Meg and her mother also acted as managers for local schools, inspecting premises and checking the reasons for absences. Mary continued with this work until at least her early eighties.

The Charles Booth Centre is a smart white building in the village of Thringstone today, in a side turning next to a small local Co-op shop. It's a centre for local activities, a place where clubs can meet and social occasions can be held, the first community centre in Britain. It's also a repository of memories about the Booths' legacy to the area. On a cold day in February 2020 I went there to meet two women, Nita Pearson and Ann Petty, who through their work for the Centre are rich with information about Mary Booth. The building is, perhaps, a little unfairly named after Charles, rather than Charles and Mary, since Charles's purchase of the original building in 1901 rested on years of Mary's own contribution to local activities. In April 1887, the year after they took the lease on Gracedieu, she had started a 'Mothers' Meeting' which was held every Monday in Gracedieu: 'Work and reading from two to 3.30, then tea'. According to a memorandum on 'Women's Work in Thringstone', the objects of the Mothers' Meeting were originally to enable women to buy materials for clothing their families at the lowest possible price, paying for them in instalments. Mary Booth bought the materials and organised the reading.[47] During World the First World War, she got them all sewing and knitting and making bandages, and as soon as the deplorable condition of prisoners-of-war in Germany became known, she galvanised them into organising sales of work.

In 1919, after Charles had died, Mary Booth established a separate trust deed for a Thringstone Women's Trust. The deed describes the Trust's aims as 'the establishment equipment and maintenance of an Institute for Women and of a Social Club for Girls and also the provision of instruction in housewifery cooking needlework laundry work and the general welfare and improvement of the home to women and girls' plus elementary religious instruction for young children.[48] A handwritten note dated 28 September 1910 recorded 12 girls attending the housewifery class in a cottage 'kindly lent by Mrs Booth,' who also supplied the equipment. 'Absolute cottage conditions are to be adhered to,' the note instructs, 'the girls thus being brought face to face with the identical problems they may expect to deal with when cottage housekeepers later in life.'[49] In 1919, the Thringstone women decided to form themselves into a village institute; in 1950 it was taken over by Leicestershire County Council.

A woman's life

On one level there's nothing extraordinary about any of this – many upper-middle-class women would have led similar lives of philanthropic duty to poor neighbours. What isn't so ordinary is that Mary Booth's devotion to the welfare of the local community was combined with extensive labours on behalf of what was, and is, seen as her husband's work. Her diaries, an unbroken run from 1887 until 1939, are an unplundered mine of information about this and on many topics.[50] As she herself once wrote: 'It is sometimes said that we are so full of ourselves & so self important now-adays, we write so many memoirs of each other that our descendants, instead of wanting to know more, will be perfectly sick of us. But in our voluminous "lives & letters" we often omit matters that would interest our grandchildren more than a great deal we put in;– & our budgets, our glorified accounts books may well give them "metal [sic] more attractive" than descriptions of our sentiments ... We must put it all down, sure that the same things which we care to know about the past will never fail to be eagerly noted in the future.'[51] Not only do Mary's own diaries show how enmeshed she was in her husband's two main occupations: they record the books she was reading; details of annual income and expenditure, including servants' wages and the many charitable subscriptions the Booths made; the furnishing and maintenance of the Booth households; the kinds of clothing she and her family kept; recipes for food and remedies for illnesses; and many wrenching accounts of all the episodes of ill-health she and her family endured. The diaries paint a colourful and extensive landscape of social obligations and pleasures: calls made, parties given and attended, operas, concerts and plays enjoyed – all the cultural paraphernalia of an upper-middle-class Victorian and Edwardian life. Notably, for the focus of a later chapter, all the Booth family were dedicated 'Bernard Shawists' and went to see each of his plays as they came out.

Mixed in with these cultural events is the taxing level of responsibility their marriage had assigned to Mary for the infrastructure of their life together. There were problems with the drains at 6 Grenville Place, and then at Gracedieu: a pipe burst, causing water to pour out by the WC on the children's passage. In August 1887, Mary wrote to Charles: 'Dearest Boy' – many of Mary's letters to Charles begin like this – 'More cases of typhoid in village. Cesspools, want cleaning out? I am going to see Mr Crane [Edwin Samuel Crane, the Thringstone vicar] about the school children, & shall get in a little talk about sanitary affairs.'[52] Then there was the management of the servants, and not infrequently servant trouble, about which she would write to Charles and to her father. She was the one who paid the servants' wages. 'It may interest our biographers', observed her son George in the 1950s, 'to know that I never once saw my Father sign a cheque in the house.'[53] And of course there was Mary's expert care and thought for Charles's own health, a duty that extended to such missions as acquiring and posting him a new set of dentures.[54]

Throughout their life together, Mary was the domestic manager, administrator and accountant. She was extraordinarily busy with all forms of work all the time. Her busyness, and Charles's dependence on it, is illustrated in the photo on page 44 of him gazing reverentially at her while she sits doing something important at her desk in the Gracedieu drawing room. It helped, according to her grand-daughter Fanny Hugill, that she could read and write extremely fast. Fanny recalls the morning routine at Gracedieu when she was a small child staying with her grandmother. This was for 'the postman to deliver the morning post, probably about 10 o'clock. He then had a cup of tea in the kitchen, during which interlude MCB [Mary Catherine Booth] opened, read and sorted her large number of letters. I had the privilege of standing by her Partner's desk [an antique two-pedestal desk] and waiting while she wrote her replies, completed cheques … and addressed the envelopes and sealed the letters. I was then allowed to stick on the stamps from her stamp box. The bell was then rung and the postman, having finished his tea, perhaps about 20 minutes, took the letters away on his bicycle.'[55] In Mary's letters to Charles abroad, she took it as an important duty to keep him well informed about the condition of the household. A typical letter in June 1886 contains domestic news, admonitions about Charles's welfare, and selective information about her own: 'Make the proper time to do your work thoroughly,' Mary counsels, 'and be at ease about me & all here. Dodo's [Antonia, aged thirteen] cold is better;– & she is looking more herself;– but poor Meg [aged six] has gone in for one of her funny little feverish attacks, & has been very poorly all day. I have kept her on slops, and very quiet;– & have administered a dose of physic and trust she will be better tomorrow. George [aged eight] is very well and bright, enjoying himself hugely in the society of the plumbers and bricklayers with whom he is on the very best of terms … I hope I shan't have things in an utter mess for you to deal with when you come home to rest after Gloversville anxieties.'[56]

There were five children aged between four and 13 when she wrote this, and Mary was a few weeks away from giving birth to her last child (of their seven children, one had died aged six months). It's difficult to imagine what it was like, being left in sole charge of these demanding mansions and the staff needed to look after them, and the children, and their attendants, as well, of course. She was often lonely. In April 1878, she wrote to Charles, 'It sometimes comes across me now that I am here alone with a sort of horror that I can't bear. I can only try to shake it off, and determine not to think of it.'[57] It would be surprising if she hadn't complained to him sometimes about the circumstances of her life, having to live so much of it without him. From her parents' house in Southsea she wrote to Charles in the summer of 1880, displaying some impatience with his absorption in the shipbuilding business: 'I often get the longing that you should be out of it all, & wish that you were working away as some quiet professor of chemistry or applied mathematics, away from the feverish pursuit of gain.' She hastened to add that she didn't mean to sound ungracious: 'I am never more thoroughly in sympathy with you than when you talk about your work; & I wish you to stick to it & succeed in it; & be brave and honest as you can be.'[58]

That first summer in Gracedieu, Mary's father was especially conscious of the stress she was under. 'My darling child, I cannot bear to think of all your worries,' he wrote, 'Charlie unexpectedly torn from you, and you alone in that huge Grace Dieu with no one to share the responsibilities of in-door and out-door superintendence.'[59] She admitted to Charles that she felt cut off from the outside world, 'rather like a great lady of olden time in the baronial castle whilst her husband was on a crusade. I love my Boy ever so much; and want him so badly.'[60] The solitary responsibilities of her life brought stress to the marriage; there were outbursts, sometimes, for which Mary felt it was necessary to apologise. In March 1888, after such an episode involving an altercation with the Gracedieu builders, she was full of contrition in her letter to Charles: 'Mine own most dear, most good & tender of all Boys what ever was;– All my heart has been going out to you this afternoon and evening, wondering how I could bear to grieve you & give you pain by such outbursts;– longing to be able to soothe the pain away ... I made a fuss about nothing to day'. But it helped her, she said, to be able to release her feelings to him; thus 'my nervous irritability throws itself off ... [and I] feel a certain lightness of having got rid of it all, & am ready for life & work again'.[61]

The letters and diaries echo the family's perception of Mary Booth that she preferred a literary life to a domestic one. She managed the double role by being a superb administrator of domestic affairs. Her domestic role encompassed, as was usual at the time, much attendance on family illnesses. Many common childhood ones – whooping cough, scarlet fever, chickenpox – were more virulent and less treatable than they are now. The illnesses sometimes seemed constant. It was chicken pox in the summer of 1884: 'I do believe,' confessed her father, 'that you are qualifying for canonization. Such trials as your patience is subjected to can but be sent to you for no other purpose than to bring you out of the furnace pure as gold seven times refined ... I think that the minister who up above has charge of the trial department, might be reminded that he is overdoing it.'[62] It was to her father that she wrote about her problems in breastfeeding baby Meg in the summer of 1879; her father reassured her that 'hand-nursing' would probably be fine. Before she decided on this, she wore herself out looking for a wet nurse: 'I have been to Queen Charlotte's, to St George's; and to York Road, Westminster. Ugh! Such horrid women.'[63] But Queen Charlotte's kept some town cows especially for the purpose of providing clean milk for women who needed it, so that might be a solution.

The importance of domestic knowledge in looking after the sick at home was one of the rationales behind Mary's investment in the domestic education of girls and women in the community around Gracedieu. She herself appears to have been regularly ill. Her diary for 1901 computes 36 days in that year 'disabled from ordinary life & work', and 21 days spent wholly or partly in bed.[64] Her daughter Imogen, responding to the Simeys' mention of Mary Booth's 'vague ill-health', threw some rather angry light on this: 'She was rarely vague about anything! She picked up a malaria germ in Switzerland and was

With her family on the steps of Gracedieu Manor, 1902

With Charles Booth at her desk in the drawing room
at Gracedieu Manor, 1890

Drawing of Mary Booth by Vanessa Bell, 1904

With her grand-daughter Belinda Norman-Butler at Gracedieu Cottage, 1936

really ill with attacks of fever ... It was many years before this malaria left her for good. ... In spite of a Macaulay heart she was fundamentally strong and healthy, and always seemed to look on her illnesses as personal insults to be treated with contempt or slapped and stood in the corner.'[65]

'My Mother did everything for us, arranged our schooling, our holidays, our allowances,' said the Booths' son George.[66] In her *Memoir*, Mary herself is at pains to defend Charles's behaviour as a rather absent father. He 'was ever a most affectionate father, keenly interested in every step of his children's development, and their constant familiar friend and adviser'.[67] It must have been tricky to maintain such a role in the face of several months' absence abroad every year. Charles himself recognised this: 'The children I left are fading away & changing into the new children I shall find & soon make mine again when I get home,' he wrote to Mary from New York in 1878.[68] Men's easy assumption that their wives would always look after the children and the home, however much wandering they themselves decided to do, was an unremarked feature of such marriages at the time.

Mary Booth cared enormously about the condition of women, but she was no feminist. She knew Millicent Fawcett socially, and in 1890–91 she attended 11 of her lectures in London. Mrs Fawcett represented the conservative side of feminism. Mary herself had a good intellectual understanding of what the social and economic changes of the time were doing to the position of women. An undated essay of hers opens with, 'Perhaps there has never been a time since the world began when the mission & capabilities of women, and her true position in life social, domestic & political, have been so much pondered & discussed as they have been during the last twenty years. On all these points the most different and conflicting theories are maintained, and they are debated with a fierceness scarcely to be met with even in the disputes of rival theologians.' Mary goes through the changes that underlie these fierce deliberations and settles particularly on the transformations in manufacture and the retail trade that have taken women's traditional household work away: 'The ladies of two centuries ago had plenty to do,' observes Mary. 'They knitted the stockings, they stitched the shirts, they superintended the preserving, they marked the linen, they embroidered their collars, they worked their lace; they went to market, and if any of the family should chance to fall ill, they had to the ready possets and infusions and poultices for the relief of the invalid.' Mary Booth's opinion was that the loss of these functions meant that the middle-class woman 'must feel sometimes that if women ever had a mission in the world it is over, at least for a very large number of them'.[69]

This grand inquiry

It was by no means over for her, however. The move to Gracedieu happened at the same time as the start of the Booth poverty inquiry. No-one is quite sure when or how this originated. Charles's early work, apprenticed as a teenager to a firm of Liverpool shipbuilders, must have included a powerful introduction to the extreme poverty of the local Irish dock-labourers.[70] But for a man with his background and business interests, spending upwards of four million pounds on charting the living conditions of people in London certainly requires some explanation.[71] Perhaps the most remarkable feature of Charles Booth, who has come to be lauded as a pioneer social scientist, methodologist and poverty reformer, is the total absence of any relevant educational background. He *was* primarily a businessman; the Booth commercial business was, said Mary, 'a sort of romance to him'.[72] It was also a *moral* enterprise, with the purpose being profit to be used for the common good.

Charles shared with Mary, both in his work in the shipping industry and in his career as a social investigator, an enormous respect for facts – what people really did, how they lived, in what ways the circumstances of their lives shaped the contributions they were able to make to society. It's even possible that Mary is actually the main explanation for Charles's research on poverty – not just the initial commitment to doing it, but sufficient knowledge of the research methods needed. The methodological expertise didn't come from nowhere. Its most likely source is Mary's knowledge of her grandfather Zachary Macaulay's brilliant statistical work for William Wilberforce's campaign to abolish slavery.[73] That Mary had a keen appreciation of Zachary's work is clear from the account her son Charles wrote of Zachary Macaulay's life a few years before she died. In this Charles notes a heavy dependence on his mother's 'superlative memory' about Zachary's life and work.[74] Zachary would also have supplied a role model for Mary's husband's own divided business and social-statistical life, since he ran a trading business in West Africa (much less ably than Charles Booth), while simultaneously gaining his reputation as an encyclopaedic source of data on the slave trade.

The possibility that Charles Booth's grand inquiry might have been firmly rooted in Mary Booth's own life and experience doesn't seem to have been seriously entertained by any of those who have puzzled about its origins – and they *have* puzzled about what led him to become such a passionate and competent poverty researcher. Mary's acquaintance with the Barnetts is noted (though perhaps not sufficiently its closeness), and an account by her in 1878 describing a visit to the Barnetts in Whitechapel gets some attention: in this Mary reports a 'most interesting long talk with Mr. Barnett about work and waiting and enthusiasm', in which the respective merits of immediate if uninformed social action were balanced against the wisdom of 'holding your hand till you were quite sure'.[75] Mary was always strong on the crucial distinction between fact and opinion.

By the 1880s, and as Mary acknowledged in her *Memoir* of Charles, the problem of poverty was occupying much public attention in Britain: diverse opinions were expressed, and 'remedies of the most contradictory nature' were proposed.[76] The background to the Booth poverty inquiry was a changing view of how firm knowledge about social conditions could, when combined with intelligent action, effect a change in those conditions which were no longer seen as God-given. Darwin's revelations about the natural origins of human beings had destabilised traditional religious beliefs; the French philosopher Comte had come along with his alternative philosophy of positivism which offered a more rational brand of evangelism. Comte's alternative, especially as spread by the sociologist Harriet Martineau's 1853 English translation, proposed that knowledge combined with conscience would lead to a scheme of education and action that would effectively combat the economic and social crises of capitalism. It may be relevant that the Martineau and Booth families were interconnected; one of Charles's aunts was a Martineau and one of his and Mary's grand-daughters married another Martineau. The approach of a 'science of society' promoted by Comte and Martineau appealed to the circle in which the Booths moved. Charles's cousin, Alfred Crompton, had founded a Positivist Club in Liverpool in 1873 which Charles joined. Another cousin, Edward Spencer Beesly, a professor of history at University College, London, was a well-known positivist. Alfred Crompton and his brother Henry, Edward Beesly and his wife Emily, and other positivists such as Frederic Harrison are recurring figures in Mary Booth's diaries throughout the 1880s and 1890s. In old age, Mary Booth recalled that, 'the Benthamites, Mill, Comte and the abounding Utilitarians, Positivists and other faiths came to be as much part of breakfast as marmalade'.[77]

The first meeting of the Board of Statistical Inquiry, which was to oversee the grand inquiry into *Life and Labour*, was planned for early March 1886, though this was an ostentatious name for a meeting no one attended and an enterprise that had only three heads behind it – Charles and Mary Booth and cousin Beatrice Potter. Most people agree that the inquiry was conceptualised and shaped by these three, which means that the two women had plenty of opportunity to present Charles with their opinions about the methods to be used.[78] Sadly, the early conversations were not recorded, but in 1890 Beatrice noted in her diary a 'delightful evening' with the Booths when there was a return to 'the old sort of triangular discussions' of the early days.[79] The initial plan was to answer three questions: what proportion of the population of London lives in poverty; what causes poverty; and what could be done to alleviate it? A total of more than 120,000 households would eventually be surveyed, using various means: observation, covert ethnography, interviews, questionnaires and census data. The 17 published volumes fall into three series, dealing with poverty, industry and religious influences. It was the first series on poverty that made Charles Booth's name, and especially the famous coloured poverty maps, first produced in 1889 and updated in 1898. On these, every street was coloured according to the income and social class of its inhabitants. The colours ranged from black ('lowest class, vicious, semi-criminal') through dark and light blue (very poor or poor) to purple and pink (mixed, 'fairly comfortable') and finally to red (middle class, 'well-to-do') and yellow (the wealthy upper-middle and upper classes). The work that went into both the maps and the texts was of gigantic proportions, requiring enormous sustained commitment and enthusiasm from a large team of data-collectors at a time when the science of social investigation was in its infancy. Indeed, the importance of the Booth inquiry probably lies as much in the model it provided of how to organise large-scale social survey work as in the results it obtained and thrust on a world reluctant to confront the true extent of inequality.

At first the inquiry was run from the offices of the Booth shipping company. Then in 1893 the team was moved to some spare offices of the Royal Statistical Society at 8 Adelphi Terrace, and later to 11 Adelphi Terrace. These moves had the serendipitous consequence of locating the poverty project in close proximity to another key enterprise with which *Forgotten Wives* is concerned: the infant London School of Economics, which was housed at 10 Adelphi Terrace. This geographical connection, that has mostly passed unnoticed by other commentators, would have facilitated easy communication between the Booth outfit and the Webbs and the Shaws at number 10.

The inquiry started with the East End of London, because of its large working population, much of it casually employed. It focused on East End trade, particularly the docks and sweated industries (where workers were chronically underpaid, and laboured excessive hours in poor conditions). Information was collected during the autumn, winter and spring of 1886–87. Volume 1 was released in 1889, the same year as the Great Dock Strike when 100,000 striking workers paralysed the Port of London. The strike's successful non-violent resolution, and the transition to a strong trade union movement, may well owe something to the change of attitude towards the poor among dock-capitalists prompted by the wide circulation and enthusiastic reception of this first volume of *Life and Labour*. It was, said one typical review, 'as full of information as twenty Parliamentary Reports, and as full of life and movement as a dozen popular novels'.[80]

One aspect of the inquiry's methods that has received a lot of attention from Booth scholars is the use of information supplied by school board visitors – officials charged with ensuring children's attendance at school. The suggestion to depend on the visitors' accounts was apparently made by Beatrice Potter, on the advice of Liberal Party politician Joseph Chamberlain, the man she fell in love with before she met Sidney Webb. Mary Booth's diaries and letters from this period combine heavy-duty comments about the inquiry with admonitions about poor Beatrice and her unfortunate choice in men: 'You could never be happy and would be increasingly unhappy with that man,' observed Mary to Beatrice about Chamberlain in the summer of 1885; the following March, 'you are well rid of him'.[81] Five years later, when Beatrice informed the Booths that she was going to marry Sidney Webb, a 'curious little look of veiled determination' came over Mary's face, and she told Beatrice: 'You see, Charlie and I have *nothing* in common with Mr Webb. Charlie would never go to him for help, and he would never go to Charlie.'[82] Mary Booth wasn't alone in finding Sidney Webb – 'an undersized, underbred, and unendowed little socialist' in Beatrice's own words – an odd choice for Beatrice to make.[83] But Mary Booth's friendship, interrupted by periods of disagreement, was supremely important to Beatrice Potter in her transition to the well-known social research expert Beatrice Webb. Mary was a key academic adviser to Beatrice in her early work. Beatrice sent drafts of her first papers to Mary and Charles, and Mary was usually the first to respond. 'I wrote last night to Beatrice giving her a first draught of my view of her paper,' Mary informed Charles in September 1886. 'The more I think of that paper the more I like it, and feel that it has an inspiriting ring and force if its own;– which I hope it will not lose in the revision which I recommend.'[84]

Mrs Booth and the secretaries

By December 1886, according to Beatrice's diary, the inquiry was in full swing, with Charlie absorbed in it, working every evening with three paid secretaries. His helpers on the inquiry were usually referred to as 'secretaries'. The key players, apart from Mary and Beatrice Potter, were Jesse Argyle, Ernest Aves, Arthur Baxter, Clara Collet, George Duckworth, and Hubert Llewellyn Smith. Jesse Argyle, Mary's favourite, had originally been a clerk in the Booth steamship company, and had first started working with Charles on occupational census data in 1884; it was Argyle's name that appeared as 'secretary' on the official notepaper of the inquiry. Like Argyle, Ernest Aves came from a respectable working-class background; he was involved in the university settlement movement, and acted as sub-warden of Toynbee Hall from 1890 to 1897 (a few years before William Beveridge occupied the same role). At Toynbee Hall, Aves was deployed by Canon Barnett on researching the local population and he thus developed skills that made him an invaluable assistant to Charles Booth. Aves worked with Jeannette Tawney's husband in the National Anti-Sweating League, and with both R.H. Tawney and William Beveridge on the Mansion House Committee on the Relief of Distress; in 1903 when the news broke that Hewins was resigning as Director of LSE, Ernest Aves asked Charles to act as a referee for his (unsuccessful) application to be the next one.

Arthur Baxter, another stalwart researcher who spent much time at Gracedieu with the Booth family, had a legal background. Hubert Llewellyn Smith, a middle-class Quaker, contributed expertise on migration and social deprivation to the Booth inquiry, tried to marry one of the Booth daughters (Meg in 1895), and would go on to work with William Beveridge. Clara Collet, as has already been mentioned, researched women's work, and George Duckworth, the half-brother of the Bloomsbury set's Virginia Woolf and Vanessa Bell, spent a decade of his life as a Booth researcher. Mary Booth was a good friend to the entire Duckworth/Stephen/Bell/Woolf family, helping Vanessa and Virginia through the disasters of their sister Stella's death in 1897 and their brother Thoby's in 1906. Vanessa's sensitive and striking portrait of Mary, drawn on 16 December 1904, testifies to the affection in which the family held her (see page 45). Virginia's debut novel *The Voyage Out* is set on a steamship modelled on one of the Booth steamship company's. Like the Booths' cargo ships, Woolf's fictional *Euphrosyne* transports dry goods to the Amazon and brings rubber back. Virginia and her brother Adrian had taken a return trip to Lisbon in 1905 on a Booth cargo ship, so *The Voyage Out* was written from personal experience.[85]

Often Mary would see all the poverty enquiry secretaries and helpers independently of Charles – as she had to, given his prolonged absences attending to the business of Alfred Booth & Co. They all came to stay at Gracedieu, often for several days at a time; work was combined with family interaction. Mary's diary entries conjure up delightful pictures of the Booth secretaries ice-skating with the Booth children and walking or 'motoring' to visit local places and events. She evidently played a key role in encouraging the secretaries when Charles was away. In November 1895, for instance, Mary wrote to Charles to say that, 'I am posting to you to-day some more proof:- the Railway men. Not very bright;– who did it? I daresay it is as good as it could be made, but it is not up to the top level of crisp clearness. Arthur Baxter, who was here last Sunday, was very low about his butchers &c. I told him it was what you always felt after going over & over things again, & that I had much enjoyed the reading.'[86]

Some of what Mary did for Charles Booth's *Life and Labour of the People in London* was a consequence of her role as the wife of a public man. It was normal for wives to entertain their husbands' colleagues and associates, and, for the most part, Charles Booth's were simply included in the normal schedule of Boothian social intercourse. But there were also special occasions, as, for example, in November 1890, when Mary hosted a party for the school board visitors who had helped with the inquiry – a party to which 'over 500 people came'; or in July 1904 when she arranged for the whole team to celebrate the conclusion of the work by dining at the Savoy and then proceeding to a performance of Verdi's opera 'Un Ballo in Maschera'.[87]

But what did Mary REALLY do?

Biographers and historians have struggled with the formidable forensic task of arriving at a fair estimate of Mary Booth's part in Charles's work – both the poverty inquiry, and later work on the aged poor and old age pensions. Her family take a definitely partisan view that she did much more than is usually acknowledged. She read for him, discussed with him, took him to task for producing 'dull' texts – she complained of the 'dreariness that comes over one as one plods through the account of trade and trade' in the industry series, for example – and she wrote entire passages of the final manuscripts herself. Two of the family particularly have gone into print arguing for her rehabilitation as more than an 'informal helper'. Mary's daughter Meg, writing (30 years after her death) a new introduction to Mary's *Memoir* of Charles, talks about the need to recognise the part Mary played in everything Charles achieved. She was his 'chief consultant' for the *Life and Labour of the People in London*, and his 'main adviser' in the framing of his proposal for old age pensions and in the writing of other pamphlets. She 'gave her whole mind to the expression of his ideas, not only by rewriting sentences in order to clarify their meaning, but also by contributing her own words to convey that meaning'.[88] Meg's daughter, Belinda Norman-Butler, Mary's grand-daughter, repeats and underlines this message in her *Victorian Aspirations: The Life and Labour of Charles and Mary Booth*, published four years later in 1972: a touching photograph of Mary and Belinda together three years before Mary died appears on page 45. *Victorian Aspirations* was partly a response to the Simeys' biography, which Norman-Butler criticises for its failure to do Mary justice, and it draws heavily on Mary's correspondence and diaries. The notebook used for the book is in the Booth archives in London, thus rooting the re-evaluation of Mary's role firmly in the evidence. Both these family accounts observe that Mary's knowledge of her husband's other business – the multiple Booth & Co companies – meant that 'She was a partner in the business in all but name.'[89]

Biographers have certainly noted that Mary Booth and her daughter Meg sometimes accompanied Charles to meetings, and showed an interest in his work, but they have not observed how much and how independently Mary manifested intellectual and practical concerns for the issues with which it dealt. Nor have they, for the most part, acknowledged her extensive contacts with the team working on the inquiry and other similarly concerned individuals. Her diaries record the constant presence in one or other Booth house of many team members. The diaries tell us, too, of many contacts Mary had with other significant names in the circle of people around the Booths concerned with collecting information about the state of the poor. In Mary's diary for 1887, for example, we have several mentions of visits from Maggie Harkness, a researcher and writer of social realism novels (and yet another relative) who narrowly missed being hired by Charles as one of the Booth investigators.[90] On 16 separate days in that year Beatrice Potter is mentioned as a lunch or tea or dinner companion, or as an overnight visitor; in July, Mary also went to see her at the Argoed. On 13 March, Mary saw Beatrice in the morning and then went later to visit Canon Barnett; in September both Barnetts came to stay; in November Mary dined with Beatrice and the Barnetts, and in December both Booths attended a large party at the Barnetts' house. On 21 November, they dined with Beatrice in Bishopsgate Street, and then went on to a discussion at Toynbee Hall on 'Methods of Relief for the Poor'. The following day Mary returned to Whitechapel with her eldest daughter to see Constance Black, the sister of social researcher and writer Clementina Black, who is mentioned in Mary's diaries as coming to dinner 'to talk about docks'.[91] Constance Black was the librarian of the People's Palace in the East End, an educational and recreational establishment opened in 1887; she would later become a famous Russian translator whose work introduced Russian literature to English-speakers across the world.

We can't of course tell from a simple diary entry what was discussed, although sometimes there are clues:

> [5 July 1891] ... Mrs Bryant, Miss Collet, Mr Aves, Mr Hicks to supper. Budgets discussed.
>
> [23 February 1892] MCB [Mary Catherine Booth] all day at Labour Com: with Miss Collet. Worked at Pauper in the evening.
>
> [24 March 1892] [CB was away in the USA until 17 April] ... Went to the office to see Mr Argyle about the sketch for Pensions in the morning.
>
> [15 March 1892] In the Budget Committee in the evening: Mr Higgs, Mr Aves, Miss Collet & another lady and gentleman.
>
> [6 April 1892] Meeting of Budget Committee here, Mr Higgs, Aves & Miss Collet.
>
> [12 April 1892] Old Age Pensions in the Evening at the "Pernasnier". Miss Collet opened, Mr Loch & Mr Spender spoke.
>
> [13 February 1894] I to Economic to hear Mr Aves on the "Unemployed".
>
> [16 May 1893] To Statistical in evening, heard good paper on workmen's budgets from Mr Higgs. Saw Mr Barnett, Drage, Aves, Hooker, the Marshalls, Mr Llewelyn [sic] Smith, Mr Argyle.
>
> [8 June 1893] [Charles Booth was in Liverpool] Mr Aves, Mr Higgs ... Miss Dendy came in the evening to discuss what should be done with the budgets.[92]

[The 'Labour Com' is the Royal Commission on the Aged Poor, for which Mary read all the papers. The references to 'old age pensions' are to work that the Booth inquiry team took on in early 1892 between the poverty and the industry series of *Life and Labour* in order to collect information supporting the case Charles was working on for state-funded pensions. 'Pauper' refers to *Pauperism, a Picture, and Endowment of Old Age, an Argument* (1892); 'the Statistical' is The Royal Statistical Society. 'Mr Loch' is C.S. Loch, the economist and social reformer; 'Mr Spender' is J.A. Spender, a journalist and author of a book on old age pensions; 'Miss Dendy' is Helen Dendy, later the social theorist Helen Bosanquet.]

Mary's autonomous interest in the study of working-class life is evident in her correspondence with Charles and others. In June 1891, for example, she wrote to tell him that she had stayed the night in London 'to hear the debate at the Economic Club. 'Miss Collet opened it very well;– from her point of view, impartial & clear. Mr Loch followed. I thought his argument weak & the ground he took narrow. Then came Mr Spender, & with his quiet hesitating manner and perfect good humour;– ... made an excellent speech ... and was listened to with great interest & respect'.[93] There are signs of Mary's growing reputation as an expert on inquiry methods. Here she is in November 1895, writing to Charles from London about an interesting development: 'I assisted at a meeting of females yesterday who want to enquire into the views of women (working) about the new provisions of the Factory Act of 95. They desired my advice as to organization, but Lord! They were a foolish lot, and I had to throw cold or rather mildly tepid water on the meekest of deprecating ?? but with a liberal hand. They hadn't even read the Act, & wanted to get ladies to enquire all over England generally with no check;– & no arrangements for boiling down & arranging the vast material which they would get. I induced them to confine themselves to London & to one trade;– the Laundries;– but their only idea was to draw up a set of questions & give them to their laundresses to get answered. I suggested that employers' and employees' evidence needed to be taken separately. Also that much direct asking of questions ... which might bring people into trouble were undesirable. But for individual enquiry & work they all declared they had no time, so the question forms are to go to the laundresses, because a beginning must be made, & all information is worth something. "Worth a rotten apple" thought I, but was very polite;– declined to join the enquiry but should be happy to be of service in putting them in the way of any information to be got through the Labour Department and to let them know of any regular enquiries [that] had already been made.'[94] The methodological sophistication revealed in this advice was very advanced for the time.[95]

The diaries and letters are also replete with evidence about the work Mary and Charles did together. On 11 June 1892, for example, she and Charles entertained the communist trade union organiser, Tom Mann, at Gracedieu together, spending the whole of the next day talking to him. On 14 June they went to 'the Economic' to hear David Schloss, a collaborator on the poverty inquiry, lecture on a Labour Bureau: 'Miss Collet, Mr Clem Edwards, Mr Aves, Higgs ... Very interesting talk. Brought Miss Collet and Prof Foxwell [H.S. Foxwell, the Cambridge and London economist] home to supper. She stayed night.'[96] In November 1897, 'Went with CB to hear George Duckworth at the Economic (expenditure of an average young man)'; at the beginning of 1893, 'CB and MCB to Economic. First rate paper by Miss Dendy on the "Residuum economically considered"'; followed a few days later by 'went to the Statistical with CB and Miss Collet'.[97] Mary was privy to the discussions around this time between Charles and Mr Giffen of the Labour Department, which resulted in Clara Collet's pioneering appointment early in 1893 to the Board of Trade as a civil servant specialising in women's industries.

And then there is Mary's undisputed role as the reader in the family. Her diary entries allow us to guess how her reading might have directly informed her husband's work. In 1887, for example, she read *Industrial Peace* by L.F.R. Price; *Wealth and Welfare: Or, Our National Trade Policy and Its Cost* by Hastings Berkeley; a life of Charles Darwin; works by Tolstoy; and tales by Harriet Martineau. In 1890, there were *Free Trade in Capital* by A.E. Hake and O.E. Wesslau; F. Seebohm's *The English Village Community; The Function of Labour in the Production of Wealth* by A. Philip; *Socialism New and Old* by W. Graham; *Oxford Lectures* by F. Pollock; and *The Conflicts of Capital and Labour* by G. Howell. About these books she would write to Charles, in New York, or Manáos or Liverpool, sharing her ideas: 'I am reading Arnold Toynbee's *Industrial Revolution* & hope I am getting something at last about the facts of the prosperity in the first 60 years of last century,' she told him in the spring of 1891. 'The French cooperative books are very interesting, the two I have read are both by practical men who have been concerned in some of the undertakings. Productive cooperation has been much more successful with the French than with us;– mainly it seems to me owing to the absence of organised Trades Unionism; so that the young Societies were able to pass through their first terrible periods of non success & consequent suffering and semi-starvation without being interfered with by the Unions ... I suppose every nation must work out its own salvation in its own way'.[98] References to books in Charles's letters to Mary are much scarcer, but one in particular has been noted: in April 1878, writing from Gloversville, New York, the site of the Booth steamship office, he told her about his most faithful employee there, Mr Kuttner, who hailed from near Stuttgart, and was involved with working men's socialist movements, 'but he is not a red socialist & does not approve of Carl Marks (is that the name?)'.[99]

Mary finished Comte's *System of Positive Philosophy* in November, 1902. She had long been interested in Comtean ideas, and was familiar with the ongoing debates involving Herbert Spencer, a philosopher whose ideas about social Darwinism extensively penetrated Victorian thought and were expounded at great length in a ten-volume work on synthetic philosophy, which took him 40 years to write. 'Poor Mr Spencer is in great trouble, at loggerheads with Frederic Harrison,' Mary wrote to Charles in September 1884, 'who is bringing up with considerable cleverness & force his old charge against H Spencer of borrowing from Comte. Mr Spencer labours over the old ground, shewing that whatever is peculiar to Comte he detests and disowns & that what he upholds may be found indeed in Comte but is not peculiar to him. The dispute is growing embittered. It is a pity. It would be so much more dignified of Mr S to leave it alone, and say simply that he does not think he has borrowed from Comte, but will leave his readers to judge for themselves. F. Harrison's line is that H. S. who has never read Comte got his "idées mères" through talks with Lewes and George Eliot.'[100] (Frederic Harrison was a politician and historian, and the philosopher George Henry Lewes lived with the novelist George Eliot.) Such comments reveal Mary Booth's easy familiarity with intellectual debates of the time, a familiarity helped by her ability to read easily in French, and in Italian and German as well.

Star of the Star volume

As noted earlier, the reframing of Mary's role is part of a general revaluation of the Booth inquiry archives as showing just how many different individuals contributed not only data but opinions, analyses, interpretations and text. It's generally agreed that Mary Booth left a particular mark on the third series covering religious influences, especially the last, so-called Star, volume. Writing of this series, which covered education, health, housing, local government, family life, crime and policing, began in 1900. Mary read through all the collected materials, and made her own notes. At first she planned to work from Charles's own notes, but this wasn't satisfactory, as she told Charles in a letter dated 9 March 1900: 'I have reverted to the old plan of reading the interviews through, having come to the conclusion that the extremely concentrated form of nourishment of your notes is too much for my weak mental digestion. I make my own notes, now on bits of paper here & there, & if they are often only the same as some of yours, it doesn't matter, & I certainly get a more broad & definite impression, I think mainly from the mere length of time given to reading about each man.'[101] The advantages of this personal immersion in qualitative data – people's own narratives – are familiar to many social scientists.

In late March 1903 Charles departed for the US, leaving Mary and the team at the office in charge of the final stages of writing and publishing the Star volume – and with a strict injunction to make sure it was published by July when he planned to return. 'I have Charlie's words ringing in my ears,' Mary told Aves in order to hurry him up.[102] She and Jesse Argyle did most of the work, with help from Baxter, Aves, Arkell and Duckworth. The Booths' son-in-law Malcolm Macnaghten, later Mr Justice Macnaghten, was consulted by Mary about the sections on Licensing and the Police. At Adelphi Terrace, Mary established herself in Charles's room 'with pencil & india rubber, exactly after your model,' as she delighted to tell him.[103]

Whatever changes the secretaries in the office made, these all had to be approved by Mary. She herself engaged in significant relocations of material and reformulations of the argument, and persuaded Charles to modify the 'excessive colloquialism' of some of the interview quotations, in order to improve the flow of the text. She was, above all, after readability. To this end, also, she was in favour of omitting all the practical remedies Charles wanted to include. She advised him against passages which she read as diversion from the main argument, such as 'locomotion in the expansion chapter'. 'The matter is excellent,' Mary counselled carefully, 'but might it not come better as an article in one of the monthlies; only hinted at in this book? I have my doubts; & lay them before you, hoping they won't worry you. They are not things of supreme importance. Still, the Star volume does give me a certain sense of muddle & the pressing in of the extraneous; the suggestions of the statesman into the enquiries of a scientific man; & I am not sure whether science or statesmanship gain.'[104] To Ernest Aves, around the same time, she described the 'Economic Conditions of Life' chapter as 'a piece of writing not too easy for the ordinary reader to understand'. She would like one day for Charles to write an essay in which he could elaborate & make clearer his view of the functions of the various classes with respect to money employment.'[105]

These months, March to July 1903, were a pressured time for the team Charles had left behind. Revisions and re-revisions flew back and forth. 'Don't be frightened,' Mary wrote to Charles, always worried that the team might exceed the brief he had never clearly spelt out for them in the first place.[106] Her diary for 1903 is rich in mentions of her labours on the Star volume:

> [29 April] … MCB worked at book.
> [30 April] Book. Adelphi terrace in the afternoon. Saw them all.
> [2 May] Star book.

[3 May] Worked on Star book … talked over licensing with Malcolm … Charles & Helen Macaulay to supper & Arthur Baxter who stayed to go over 'Economic Conditions of Life' &c with me.

[4 May] … Star book.

[5 May] MCB worked at Star book in the morning, To Adelphi Terrace in the afternoon & later Mr Argyle came up to see me.

[6 May] Hair shampoo & later to Adelphi Terrace.

[7 May] Star book.

[8 May] Worked at Star book.

[9 May] Star book … Arthur Baxter came & took away the ? pieces of star book to look over & think about.

[12 May] To Adelphi Terrace to consult with Arthur Baxter & Mr Argyle.

[22 May] Adelphi Terrace.

[25 May] To Adelphi Terrace to do Star book with Mr Argyle.[107]

It would have been surprising if some of the revelations of *Life and Labour* hadn't incurred displeasure from those who found themselves in its pages. One of the additional tasks Mary took on in April 1903 was a threatened action for libel by the owner of 'the disgraceful tenement houses without backs on them in Miller's Avenue', which featured in Volume 1. Mr Miller, the owner of the said houses, wanted to get an injunction to stop the sale of the book. 'There seemed nothing for it but for us to employ a solicitor on our side,' wrote Mary to Charles in New York. 'Malcolm [Macnaghten] was a little anxious about having agreed with Arthur and Mr Argyle to do this because you had said before leaving that you wished, if anything of this sort should occur, that action should be delayed till your return. But in this case action could not be delayed'.[108] The judge rejected Miller's application, but he was a persistent man and his complaint grumbled on.

Despite, or maybe partly because of, these difficulties, 'I have enjoyed down to the ground all my little work at the book,' Mary told Charles self-deprecatingly.[109] In 1903, when work on the inquiry was coming to a close, Antonia wrote to her father: 'Mother is simply a marvel. It is quite clear that head-work regularly every morning is the thing for her! – but how is she to do it when the book is finished? She will never think anything important enough to give up housekeeping worries for, and she never will write that history of the French Revolution! … There is no doubt it's just the work she loves and it suits her so well.'[110]

The end of what the Booth children referred to as 'The Book' saw a curious episode of some cultural importance involving one of the most highly celebrated religious paintings. Mary, again, left a mark which has faded with time and the habit of wife-forgetting. The pre-Raphaelite painter William Holman Hunt and his wife Edith had been friends of the Booths for many years (there are references to social visits in Mary's diaries at least as early as 1888). In 1853, Hunt had finished an allegorical painting called 'The Light of the World'. The painting depicts Jesus knocking on an overgrown door, which Hunt explained stood for the closed human mind. Unhappy with the way his painting had been treated by its Oxford purchasers, Hunt produced two more versions, the third a considerably larger one, painted between 1900 and 1904. This was purchased by the Booths. Since Mary was a Christian, and Charles a Unitarian, investment in the painting is likely to have been her idea.[111] The Booths also paid for 'The Light of the World' to go on an expensive world tour as an icon of British colonial domination and an attempt at promoting imperial unity. The practical arrangements for the painting's journey were left to Mary. Some seven million people viewed it in Canada, Australia and New Zealand, and then finally South Africa. For this final leg of the tour Hunt wrote something called a 'special addendum', a catalogue document to accompany the painting. Evidently a sort of imperialist epistle, Hunt's manuscript is missing, but what is not missing is Mary Booth's distaste for Hunt's 'unfortunate jargon,' as a result of which the addendum did not form part of the South African exhibition.[112] 'The Light of the World' venture demonstrated the way the Booths worked: *he* had an idea or developed an enthusiasm: '*She* checked it out, challenged it, tested the logic ... and then ended up doing much of the work'.[113] In the case of this venture not the least of Mary's travails was the diplomatic negotiation needed to deal with the famously churlish Holman Hunt.

Today the final Booth version of Hunt's picture hangs in St Paul's Cathedral in its original classical frame, which was made by a forgotten woman frame-maker, Hilda Herbert. A condition of the gift by the Booths to the Cathedral was that no charge should ever be made for visitors to view it. The Booths' other joint commemoration in British art takes the form of two portraits by William Rothenstein painted in 1908. Charles Booth's hangs in the Victoria Gallery and Museum in Liverpool. Mary Booth's resides in the unofficial surroundings of a staircase wall in a flat in West London belonging to her great-grand-daughter Theresa Booth.

'My life is very much less important than yours'

Because of limited time and energy, I was able to read only a fraction of the mammoth Booth archives. Interrogating archives is rarely a simple matter, and those relating to Mary Booth's life and work share with others the complications of both omission and destruction. Another methodological issue with respect to reconstructing the life and work of Mary Booth is one she shares with Charlotte Shaw. Like Charlotte, Mary was constantly at pains to underplay the importance of her contributions to her husband's work, and was diplomatic in her critical exchanges with him. In September 1893, for example, she wrote to Charles to congratulate him on his resumé of a particular case in the draft text, and to propose that, 'If there is much of this sort of précis work;– your making abstracts of the detailed essays of your helpers, I think I might really help you, & take some of it off your hands. Of course they must never know that I did so, but I think it is work that falls within my powers.'[114] She once made the sad confession that 'my life is very much less important than yours'. But it does have 'a value, as you used to say of my arguments'.[115]

As with Charlotte Shaw, the motive for such modesty is obscure. The Simeys put it like this: '[Mary] did her utmost to keep hidden the fact that her husband submitted every page of the manuscript to her almost as he wrote it and that her disapproval was accepted by him as reason enough for changing or abandoning any doubtful passage. Perhaps even his staff never realised the extent to which he encouraged her to correct and even to re-write such portions of their work as she saw fit: "they must never know" was her strict injunction to her husband.'[116] It wasn't true, however, that Mary prevented the rest of the Booth inquiry team from understanding her importance to the enterprise. Here is Jesse Argyle writing to Mary in January 1915: 'You speak of not having taken an active part in what was accomplished, but I know of what inestimable value has been your ready sympathy & wise counsel to your husband in all his undertakings.'[117]

Old age pensions were another concern that Mary shared with her husband. In January 1892 she had interviewed John Spender, journalist and author of a book on the subject. When Charles served on the Royal Commission on the Aged Poor in 1893, Mary read the evidence for him: 'I am marking passages & noting down the pages on which those which you ought to read occur.'[118] The extent of her contribution to her husband's work in this area is suggested by one unguarded admission of joint authorship. In a letter to Charles in 1910, Mary congratulated him for having stuck so 'gloriously' to the pensions issue;

she went on to remind him of, 'the awful foggy night when one after another of the Statistical & Economic magnates rose amid the mists to tear at your impracticable scheme & demonstrate its absurdity; & we went down to Gracedieu next morning & wrote the book'.[119] The mists were real – the product of a London fog – and the arguments, in the Hall of the School of Mines where the Statistical Society held its meetings, had taken place in December 1891. The 'little book' was *Old Age Pensions and the Aged Poor: A Proposal*, and it had only one author. Charles did acknowledge the importance of Mary's intellectual work in various ways, including the famous dedication at the front of *Life and Labour*'s final volume: 'My work now completed has been from first to last dedicated to my wife without whose constant sympathy, help and criticism it could never have been begun, continued, or ended, at all.'[120] This doesn't really seem an adequate appreciation of Mary Booth's contribution, although (because) it fitted the spirit of the times with regard to assumptions about wifely labour.

Squandering the brilliance of her mind

Sometime in the late 1930s the English sociologist Jack Sprott was invited to tea by Mr Justice Macnaghten, who had married the Booths' daughter Antonia. The purpose of the tea invitation was for Sprott to meet Justice Macnaghten's mother-in-law. 'It was to be a memorable occasion,' recalled Sprott, 'because she was the niece of Lord Macaulay and had sat on the great man's knee. She was very old, very lively and full of charm, this niece of Lord Macaulay, but it was only after I had met her that I discovered that she had a far greater claim to fame in my eyes: she was the widow of Charles Booth, every page of whose celebrated inquiry into the *Life and Labour of the People in London* she had scrutinized. It was strange and significant that this fact was not mentioned.'[121]

It is significant but not especially strange that Mary Booth's claim to fame remains inescapably tied to her husband's life and work. She was an intimate part of this, but/and how much of it would have happened without her we will never know. This isn't really a question that's been asked, although, as Booth scholarship has progressed, Mary Booth's contribution has been increasingly recognised. Such recognition has mainly been confined to her direct intellectual and practical input into the poverty inquiry and the old age pensions work. Yet what strikes anyone reading through Mary's diaries and correspondence is the enormous edifice of domestic support her labours sustained. And, alone of the four wives who feature in this volume, her engagement in her husband's work was accompanied by the tireless care required for the successful rearing of many children.

When Mary Booth died, her obituary in *The Times* recorded that: 'For the last 20 years and more since the death of her husband Mrs Booth poured herself out in family life and squandered the brilliance of her mind, which had charmed and delighted great men and women of the past, on the babies, school children, undergraduates, and young married couples who trooped in and out of her book-lined drawing room. She would rise from her businesslike desk in the window to welcome them and lead them to the fire. There were copies of *Punch* on the table by the piano, a jig-saw puzzle laid out near the chintz-covered sofa, light and flowers everywhere, but above all the atmosphere was one of books and reading … To see her touch her treasured editions or to hear her enthusiastic reading of forgotten passages was to realize the greatest of English letters from which she could quote with astonishing ease.'[122]

In her 23 years of widowhood Mary Booth never relinquished her hold on Charles Booth's work. The American philanthropic fund that made possible the huge expansion of LSE during William Beveridge's reign as Director also funded a repeat of the Booth survey in the late 1920s and early 1930s; the *New Survey of London Life and Labour* was managed by Hubert Llewellyn Smith, who had worked on the original Booth inquiry. It drew a letter of congratulation from the 85-year-old Mary Booth, who would have recalled the talks about the unemployed she and Charles had enjoyed with William Beveridge, Ernest Aves, and Beatrice and Sidney Webb decades earlier. Mary didn't actually like Beveridge very much, describing him as 'self important & egotistic; & without the divine fire of love of the work & the people' that other people have.[123] No-one, after all, could compare on these measures with her Dearest Boy.

Mary Booth's body was laid to rest next to her husband's in a grave lined with evergreens and flowers in St Andrew's churchyard, Thringstone. The inscription above it, visible today, is fulsome with respect to Charles's life: 'During many years he devoted the leisure of an arduous life to a study of the condition of the poor in London. He diligently sought for a foundation on which remedies could be securely based; and he lived to see the fulfilment of a part of his hopes, in the lightening of the burden of old age and poverty. To those who lived under his immediate influence, he brought unfailing help and joy. He leaves them a precious example.' The precious example of Mary is recorded, however, only as his wife and as the daughter of Charles Zachary Macaulay.

FAMILY TREE OF MARY BOOTH

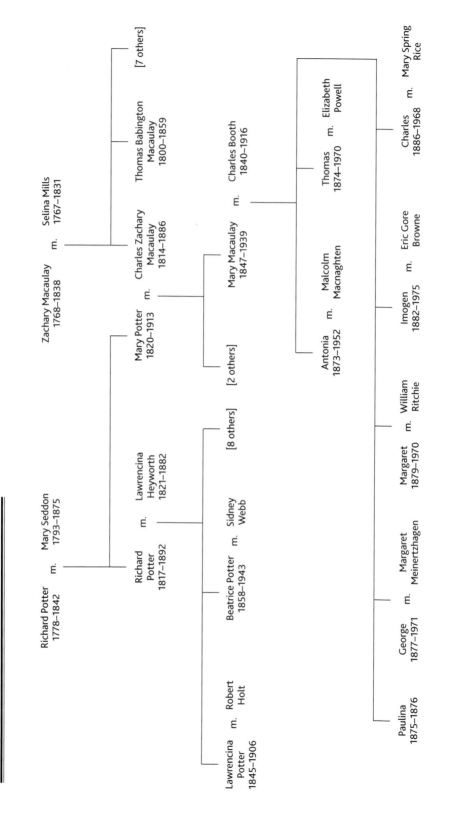

3

Charlotte Shaw

1857–1943

In 1897, Charlotte Payne-Townshend, an unmarried 40-year-old Irish heiress with radical ideas, wrote to an American friend she had met in Rome. Charlotte's financial wealth was matched by a rich resource of ideas about what she might do with her life, but she couldn't see any clear direction through these. She told her friend about her dilemma, which was typical of many middle-class women possessed of a social conscience at the time: 'Now it has occurred to me,' she wrote, 'that those who try to remedy the terrible evils we see round us by healing individual wounds and patching individual sores, by philanthropy in fact, are like the doctor who tries to cure his patients by rule of thumb … the social evil has gone too deep for mere surface palliation. We must have something else … Is what is wanted a new science? Something like the science of medicine applied collectively, and which will consist of the study of these social horrors we are talking of from the point of view of recent discovery; the study, in fact, of sociology … It is a study which has barely been attempted yet … and what I hope to do is this: with all my power, physical, financial and intellectual to study sociology as I describe it and to help and encourage others cleverer than myself to study it.'

In Charlotte's diagnosis of what was wrong, and what mere philanthropy couldn't cure, was the whole social system: vast inequalities in the ownership of property; the dehumanising commercial system; the struggle between capital and labour; marriage and the impoverished status of women. She felt particularly strongly about the latter; indeed, her feelings on this, she wrote to her friend, went as far and were as extreme as it was possible for them to go and be. She described herself as an independent woman with no family ties, she was perfectly free to do as she chose and perfectly aware that an accident of birth and social position had given her advantages that many people lacked. She'd come to the conclusion that a life that didn't try to remedy this in some modest way would be degrading. But what exactly should she do? She had made two 'small beginnings' she told her friend. The first was to visit the London School of Medicine for Women several times a week to study anatomy and physiology, chiefly in order to get to know the students and the staff and find out how best to help women get into medicine – perhaps by funding a scholarship there, or adding to the School's building fund. The second thing, she wrote, was 'more difficult to explain'. It concerned a revolutionary idea dreamed up by some of her friends to start a school of 'Economics and Political Science'. The country lacked any place of systematic instruction in these subjects; thus the average citizen knew nothing of the financial system or the social system to which it contributed such inequalities. So Charlotte saw that she might have a role in getting this new institution off the ground.[1]

Disappearing acts

In the London School of Economics and Political Science (LSE) today, there's a large room on the top floor of the oldest building called the Shaw Library. Its windows offer a good view of LSE's modern empire, a multi-million-pound construction project that's noisily accommodating LSE's expansion as a global centre for the social sciences. Whether this is quite what Charlotte Payne-Townshend had in mind when she conceived of the need for organised instruction in sociology and economics we will never know. What *I* did not know when I first encountered the Shaw Library as a child attending Christmas parties for the staff's children – my father taught at LSE – or later, as a teenager playing in the LSE orchestra, which used the Shaw Library for its rehearsals, or on my wedding day when the Shaw Library hosted our wedding party, was that the 'Shaw' commemorated in its name isn't the famous radical playwright George Bernard Shaw, the great friend of the Webbs, with whom the idea of LSE originated and to whom Charlotte Payne-Townshend referred in her letter, but Charlotte herself.

One problem with any narrative of Charlotte Shaw's life is that it's bound up with a number of other very famous stories. These have been told many times with differing links to the available facts. There's the story of the foundation of LSE itself, one in which Charlotte, as one of the founders, tends to melt away, or be assigned a limited role as simply its financial benefactor. She's an unfairly shadowy figure, too, in the history of the Fabian Society, and in accounts of the Fabian Women's Group, an enterprise which made a significant contribution to correcting the errors in women's history and in contributing political energy to the suffrage movement. Her work for the theatre, especially in translating the works of the realist French dramatist Eugène Brieux and campaigning for his extraordinary exposés of contemporary evils to reach the London stage, is often attributed to her husband. Then there's one outcome of her acquaintance with the Brieux texts, her work with an American doctor to write sex education materials for college students, at a time when ignorance of venereal disease was injuring many lives. And, of course through all the colourful biographies of her husband, George Bernard Shaw's, most entertaining life, various versions of Mrs Shaw weave their way in and out of anecdotes about this great man's creativity, political accomplishments, bodily adventures and spirited liaisons with other women.

Charlotte's main presence in the GBS panorama is as attentive wife, efficient house-manager, loyal supporter and helpmeet, even if at times a rather irritated one. Much of the work she did with and for GBS passes, as it tends to in all these forgotten wives' retold lives, as merely what is expected of a wife and therefore not worth remarking on. When, later in her life, Charlotte met and worked with the controversial British army officer and writer, T.E. Lawrence, leaving her considerable stamp on his *Seven Pillars of Wisdom* and other Lawrence projects, and developing a crucial intellectual and emotional relationship with him, it is sometimes, in the multitude of books and articles about Lawrence, impossible to see that she did anything very much at all.

A hellish childhood?

She was born Charlotte Frances Townsend on January 20, 1857, in Rosscarbery, a small market town in West Cork, Ireland. The Townsend home, a house called Derry which had been in the family for many years, was an impressive grey stone house outside the town, situated on rising ground with gardens sloping down to a lake and a view of the bay and its lighthouse from a south-facing terrace. Charlotte's father, Horatio, known as Horace, had trained in the law, but his main occupation was being a country gentleman. As

Charlotte explained in a letter about her childhood written when she was 70 years old and addressed 'to no one in particular', there was, in Ireland, no middle class.[2] They just had 'the People' and 'the Gentry'. Thus, when Horace Townsend married an English woman from a solidly middle-class Yorkshire family, Mary Susanna Kirby, certain tensions arose. Horace wanted to stay put in Ireland and go on being a country gentleman, surrounded by his books, and filling his days with riding, hunting and visiting the peasants on his estate, but Mary disliked the absence of fashion, entertainment and social connections in Rosscarbery and longed to move her family back to England.

Charlotte's sister Mary, known as Sissy, was born when Charlotte was two, and their mother's social aspirations were marked in the change of name from 'Townsend' to 'Payne-Townsend' in 1863 and then by the addition of an 'h' to 'Townsend' nine years later – Mary thought the 'h' made them sound more distinguished. An English governess was engaged for the children, and visiting language tutors ensured that they learned fluent French, Italian and German. Charlotte frequented her father's library, and learnt from him and his books much about the social and political condition of Ireland. As a teenager and young woman she filled many notebooks with synopses of great sweeps of history and swathes of religion and she dived eagerly into French and English literature and philosophy. In an effort to find husbands for the two young women, their mother took them to rented houses in Cork and then Dublin where there were more opportunities for attending balls, plays and suchlike, as well as riding, hunting and shooting. Charlotte became increasingly estranged from her mother and her mother's view of the kind of life she ought to lead. Sissy was the prettier of the two girls and she had a different temperament, which fitted much better with their mother's scheme of things. Charlotte, considered attractive in her own way, with startling green eyes, pale skin and masses of light-brown hair, was unrelentingly serious. She wanted to talk about books and politics and history, not dances and tea-parties. She announced that she would like to be a doctor but, because she knew this would never be allowed, she settled for a St John's Ambulance First Aid course, gaining her certificate when she was aged 23 in 1880.

The tensions in the family over class and location escalated after Mrs Payne-Townshend finally got what she wanted and moved the family to London when Charlotte was 20. Horace returned to Derry as much as he could. He became increasingly unhappy in the life his wife wanted him to lead with their daughters in London; he was no good at small talk and started to develop medical complaints. There were endless balls and dinner-parties and other social occasions and a great deal of travelling to France, Italy, Spain, Switzerland, Germany, Morocco and Scotland. In 1885, when Charlotte was 28, Horace died and her sister married, leaving Charlotte as her mother's sole companion. This was an experience she had to endure for six years – and it *was* a matter of endurance, as her letters make clear. She was able to assert herself in some respects. For example, she spent some useful time back in West Cork working to establish a local railway for the small farmers there; she joined The Royal Society of Antiquaries of Ireland, and The Cork Historical and Archeological Society. And she turned down at least four proposals of marriage, one from a Danish count her mother rather favoured – 'I do not wish to marry,' said Charlotte, quite determinedly and repeatedly.[3] But what should she do instead?

When Mrs Payne-Townshend died in 1891, Charlotte was liberated from the burden of accompanying her on world-travels and pretending to enjoy the social rounds, but she was never freed from the guilt she felt at having, simply, hated her mother – perhaps even enough to have caused her death. This admission she made in her letter 'to no one in particular': 'It is really awful to think how glad I was,' she says of her mother's death, 'I sometimes wondered if my constant longing for her death had anything to do with killing her.' Despite its superfluity of wealth, this was in Charlotte's eyes a 'terrible home' and a 'hellish childhood'. Her mother had been domineering and unable to bear any opposition: 'if it was offered she either became quite violent, or she cried. She constantly cried. She felt she had sacrificed her life for us and my father, my sister and myself and she never ceased telling us so.' Her father, on the other hand, was 'gentle and affectionate, well-educated and well-read; very, very good – honourable and straight' and he suffered at his wife's hands, from her snobbishness and emotional manipulations, so really her mother had killed him.[4]

The problem of marriage

On this contorted constellation of family relationships, or Charlotte's reaction to them, rested her personal objection to the institution of marriage and her distaste for the idea of children. She didn't wish to become embroiled in any such dramas as she had witnessed in her childhood home, and she especially resolved 'never to be the mother of a child who might suffer as I had suffered'.[5] But she couldn't resolve not to fall in love. She was tempted, yet not quite strongly enough, by her next suitor, General Clery, a top-ranking army officer. Then, in a state of despair about her prospects for personal happiness, there followed the stirringly sad episode of her liaison with the charismatic Swedish doctor, Axel Munthe.

They met in Rome. It was always Charlotte's habit to take off travelling when life got difficult or tedious – GBS would later take exception to this, calling it 'vagabondage'.[6] Rome in the 1890s was frequented by the English upper classes, rich Americans and aristocratic Europeans, and Dr Axel Munthe had built up a lucrative practice taking care of their medical complaints and being plied with social invitations in return. Having spent time with the French neurologist Jean-Martin Charcot at the Salpêtrière in Paris, he specialised in nervous disorders among women. Munthe was a complex character, not averse to making money out of rich idle women, and fond of careering round Rome in a smart red-wheeled hansom cab drawn by a pair of Hungarian horses, his Lapp dog on his knee. His position as Physician-in-Ordinary to the Swedish royal family, and Crown Princess Victoria's personal doctor, in whose company he was often seen, added to his flamboyant reputation. But he was also generous with his own time and money for good causes. He often treated the poor without charge, and he campaigned for animal rights, although he did keep an owl and a baboon as pets. Munthe's overwhelming obsession – an expensive one, for which he always needed money – was to build a house on the site of the Emperor Tiberius's villa on a cliff in Capri.

When Charlotte Payne-Townshend met Axel Munthe at a dinner party in the Grand Hotel in Rome in the spring of 1894 he was between two marriages – the first to a Scandinavian teenager, the second to an English aristocrat. Charlotte was immediately drawn to him. She took rooms at another hotel, and went to consult him about her own health. She wasn't feeling well; she still didn't know what to do with her life. Dr Munthe told her there was nothing really wrong with her. He prescribed valerian, a traditional herbal medicine used to treat nervous disorders. Their encounter as doctor and patient was probably typical of many between male doctors and women deprived of agency in their own lives by their social conditions. What followed was a relationship that grew increasingly intimate, but from which Munthe progressively withdrew as Charlotte fell more and more in love. He was rather more used to infatuated women than she was to really interesting and desirable men. In fact a procession of infatuated women beat at his door, drawn by his seductive doctoring and charming conversation and not apparently put off by his disdainful attitude to wealthy women with meaningless lives. Charlotte was only one of many women whose affections and purses were raided by Dr Munthe. 'Often it took only a single meeting for the women to be head over heels in love with Axel, whom they felt to be a Christ figure.'[7] He wasn't good for Charlotte or for her confidence in her project of choosing the right path among her various ambitions. Happily, new social contacts in the aftermath of the Munthe affair would help to solve the problem.

The story of LSE

Charlotte Payne-Townshend discovered her mission to advance the subject of sociology in the autumn of 1895 when she met Beatrice and Sidney Webb at a lunch party in London. They were at the centre of an exciting intellectual and political network of people and ideas. She heard the Webbs talk about their plans for a London School of Economics, and about the philosophy of Fabian socialism, both of which resonated with half-formed impressions of her own. Beatrice Webb, always the pragmatist, spotted the fact that the 'Irish lady's' wealth could be useful to their project of starting a School. Beatrice described Charlotte as 'a large graceful woman' who dressed well, but had been somewhat spoilt by her irresponsible wealth: 'She is romantic but thinks herself cynical. She is a socialist and a radical, not because she understands the collectivist standpoint, but because she is by nature a rebel ... She is fond of men and impatient of most women, bitterly resents her enforced celibacy but thinks she could not tolerate the matter-of-fact side of marriage. Sweet-tempered, sympathetic and genuinely anxious to increase the world's enjoyment and diminish the world's pain.'[8]

In the oft-repeated story of LSE's beginnings, the prime movers were the Webbs, whose social investigations had revealed with particular acuity the need for systematic training in the social sciences. But other people were important too: the young stockbroker, Edward Pease, in whose Regent's Park lodgings the Fabian Society began, the social psychologist Graham Wallas, and others in the Fabian circle. In one of his accounts of LSE's origins Sidney Webb named the following in order of importance as founders of that institution: '(1) Miss Payne Townshend ... She took to it from the first, and has been most generous; she must have given or spent on the School £3,000 during the first seven years';[9] (2) Sir Hickman Bacon, a wealthy Lincolnshire landowner; (3) Bertrand Russell, then a young fellow of Trinity College, who donated nearly the whole proceeds of his fellowship; (4) the economist W.A. Hewins, who became LSE's first Director;

then at number (5) Sidney and Beatrice themselves. This list, compiled in a letter to the Vice-Chancellor of London University, may have been coloured by Sidney's desire to dissociate the School from its socialist origins, but Charlotte should, indeed, be counted as one of the founders of LSE: she is 'one often overlooked key player', 'a constant presence in LSE's early home ... and a generous donor both of time and money.'[10]

Charlotte was one of LSE's first trustees, and a member of the advisory board which in 1901 applied to the Board of Trade to register the School as a company; she was also one of the School's first governors. Her role in establishing the LSE Library was critical: she provided the £1,000 with which it was able to open in November 1896, and she was one of its five trustees (the Library had a separate trust from the School). That she wasn't just a funder but played an active role in the Library's development is demonstrated by the archives of the Library Committee, which was set up in 1897 with 18 members. Charlotte was one of four regular attenders at its bi-monthly meetings. Over the years she was a regular source of vital funding whenever LSE funds were low; she endowed a scholarship there, and later provided further funds for what became the misunderstood Shaw Library in the Founders' Room on the top floor of the old building. Charlotte personally helped to choose the books the Library housed.

LSE began life in cramped quarters in John Adam Street in the Strand. Within months it had outgrown this first home. A house for rent was found in nearby Adelphi Terrace. A seven-year lease was available at a rent of £360 a year, but this was almost exactly the whole amount Sidney Webb had to cover the School's expenses for the first year. Charlotte provided a heavy subsidy by agreeing to pay £300 a year for the two upper floors. The house was conveniently located next door to the Statistical Society, and it had a pleasing aspect over the river, although the top floor study was pokey and it lacked a bathroom. Charlotte moved in sometime in 1896 and lived there alone above the expanding bustle of LSE teaching in the ground floor classrooms until she married George Bernard Shaw in the summer of 1898. (This history does not prevent the flat becoming in several accounts 'the Shaws' home' even before the LSE was founded.) Charlotte was a notable intellectual presence in the School's life. When an 'Economic Students' Union' was formed, for instance, Charlotte organised its first formal dinner in February 1898: a much grander affair than most student functions today, held at Frascati's sumptuous gold-and-silver restaurant with eight courses at a cost of 5s.6d. a head and 13 speeches on the toast list.

No-one was in any doubt that Charlotte was an excellent hostess – she had, after all, been skilfully schooled in this by her mother. But she wasn't just a hostess, any more than she was just a purveyor of money to good causes. Her proximity to the work of LSE in its pioneering years provided many opportunities for discussion: 'Sidney and I meet there [in Charlotte's flat] on Thursdays to dine sumptuously between our respective lectures,' noted Beatrice in her diary in October, 1899.[11] Charlotte was better at food than Beatrice, who was noted for her borderline anorexic diet. The two women led almost exactly contemporaneous lives, born a year apart and dying within months of each other. One of Charlotte Shaw's gifts to Beatrice was to supply funds for Beatrice's enquiry into the working of the Poor Law, which required salaries for investigators, and then to sit on the executive committee which was formed in 1909 to give effect to the recommendations of Beatrice's controversial Minority Report. A year before she died Beatrice reflected in her diary on the lives of these four eminent Fabians, the Webbs and the Shaws: 'Shall we four ever meet again?' For 50 years, Beatrice said, they had lived together 'in constant intercourse, sharing the same opinions and cooperating in spreading the same gospel'.[12] Among the many surviving photos of 'these four' is the one on page 82, which shows them setting off on a trip to Russia in 1932. Charlotte is smiling at someone, GBS is his usual congenial self, and Beatrice is looking a little askance at the camera. She never quite lost her perception of Charlotte as a 'bystander', but she did grow to be very fond of her: 'In our old age Charlotte and I have become affectionately intimate.'[13] Despite Charlotte's evident prominence in Beatrice Webb's life, and her key role in the early days of LSE, she doesn't feature much in the relevant histories and biographies. Royden Harrison's *The Life and Times of Sidney and Beatrice Webb*, for example contains only one reference to Charlotte as a source of money. (This book is also remarkable for its prurient interest in the details of Beatrice's menstrual cycle.)

'The writing machine and the typist'[14]

It has been argued that Charlotte's profound dilemma about what to do with her life was effectively solved by her marriage. Thereafter she could be known simply as 'Mrs G.B.S.' – the title of her only full-length biography. The Webbs introduced Charlotte Payne-Townshend to her future husband at the end of January 1896. Beatrice was in matchmaking mode, but initially she had her eye on Graham Wallas as a husband for Charlotte. In the summer of 1896 the Webbs rented a

Spartan rectory three miles from Saxmundham in Suffolk and invited their Fabian friends, Wallas, Charlotte and GBS included, to stay. Another Charlotte was also there – the American feminist activist and writer Charlotte Perkins Gilman (then Stetson). Both this second Charlotte and Beatrice left accounts of the Suffolk house party in their diaries. Gilman, fresh from the International Socialist Workers and Trade Union Congress in London and a big peace demonstration in Hyde Park, spent five days in Suffolk, writing letters in a tent in the rectory garden next to a summerhouse where George Bernard Shaw was labouring over his play *The Devil's Disciple*. They all worked in the mornings and socialised in the afternoons, with a bit more work before the evening. Gilman went for walks, read the group some of her poems, and tried to learn how to ride a bicycle. (There was a lot of cycling going on at the time.) Of one day in Suffolk she wrote, 'Nice little walk with Miss Townsend [*sic*]. Rather stupid evening. Mrs Webb's cold worse. All these men are funny all the time. Miss T listens.'[15] According to Beatrice's diary, Charlotte was bored by Graham Wallas's morality and learning, but, once everybody else had departed, and the house party had been reduced to the Webbs and Shaw only, and the Webbs were occupied with their work and each other, Charlotte and GBS took to cycling, 'scouring the country together and sitting up late at night. To all seeming,' wrote Beatrice, 'she is in love with the brilliant philanderer and he is taken, in his cold sort of way, with her.'[16]

Like the story of how LSE began, the origins and nature of Charlotte and George Bernard Shaw's 45-year long marriage are wrapped in the stuff of gossip and speculation, as well as a modicum of fact. Who actually pursued whom? Was it a marriage, in fact? What is a marriage, anyway? Here was a woman who had declared her intention never to marry and a man who literally made good drama out of his objections to marriage. When Charlotte, as Mrs Shaw, put together a compendium of extracts from his writings in 1915, she chose this one, from his play *Getting Married*: 'Family life will never be decent, much less ennobling,' declared GBS, 'until the central horror of the dependence of women on men is done away with. At present it reduces the difference between marriage and prostitution to the difference between Trade Unionism and unorganized casual labor: a huge difference, no doubt, as to order and comfort, but not a difference in kind.'[17]

The prelude to the marriage consisted of a good deal of vacillation, on both sides, giving rise to many entertaining stories, and even, in 2006, to a romantic comedy by the American writer John Morogiello called *Engaging Shaw* 'featuring four razor-sharp tongues' (Charlotte, GBS and the Webbs).[18] In real life, when these four left the rented Suffolk rectory in mid-September 1896, they cycled back to London, a journey which took four days. GBS told Charlotte not to fall in love with him, and to hang onto her independence. She tried, fled to Ireland, he urged her to come back. Back in London he found her flat above LSE a convenient place to deposit his manuscripts, and from which to take her out to theatres and dinners, and she trained her cook to prepare vegetarian food for him. Most accounts of the prelude to their marriage are distinctly misogynistic in tone. According to one, Charlotte set out to make herself indispensable to GBS, learning shorthand and typing, and helping him 'prepare his plays for the press'. But she 'struggled to make an occupation out of Shaw's work'; her decision to attend lectures at the London School of Medicine for Women, instead of being a logical and previous step for someone who had from childhood longed to be a doctor, is recast as her reaction to GBS's occupational busyness.[19] In the spring and early summer of 1897 there was a particularly unhappy episode in a house jointly rented by the Webbs and Charlotte near Dorking on the North Downs. The Webbs were over-occupied with their history of trade unionism, and Beatrice's perception was that Charlotte sat upstairs 'miserably' typing GBS's *Plays Unpleasant*, while the playwright himself strode around the garden forming his dramatic opinions but not showing much interest in his typist upstairs. Taking his protestations about women's necessary independence at face value, Charlotte proposed to him during this rural stay; he responded by asking for his fare to Australia.

GBS at this time was relatively unknown and quite poor, whereas Charlotte was rich. Indeed, she belonged to the same family as the Uniacke Townshends, the land agents in Dublin who had once employed GBS as an office boy. When, in the course of their troubled courtship, Charlotte started to make herself unavailable to him, he couldn't bear what he referred to as the loss of a secretary, but it was much more than that. Her departure for a stay in Rome, to study its municipal services in order to prepare a text for LSE students, disturbed him considerably. Then he injured his foot, wrote her exaggerated reports of its condition – it was as big as the Albert Hall – and lured her back to take care of him. She returned, arranged for an operation which revealed a bone necrosis, removed him from the squalor he lived in with his mother in Fitzroy Square, rented a house in Surrey for his convalescence, hired two nurses, and generally created a situation in which, as GBS put it in a letter to Beatrice Webb, his objection to his own marriage ceased with his objection to his own death. Charlotte bought the marriage licence and the ring (presumably because GBS wasn't mobile), and he deposited an announcement of the marriage in *The Star* newspaper: 'As a lady and gentlemen were out driving in Henrietta-st, Covent-garden yesterday, a heavy shower drove them to take shelter in the office of the Superintendent Registrar there, and in the confusion of the moment he married them.'[20] Shortly afterwards GBS secured more of Charlotte's attentions as a nurse in the Surrey house by falling downstairs on his crutches and breaking his arm. It is perhaps understandable, although it is also lamentable, that GBS's ODNB entry gives Charlotte's occupation at the time of her marriage solely as GBS's 'informal nurse'.[21]

The Shaws' marriage wasn't such a spur of the moment decision as he made out, being prefaced with lengthy discussions between the two of them about the contract they would enter into in marrying each other. One key matter was the financial inequality between them: GBS didn't want to be seen as a fortune hunter, and Charlotte was used to controlling her own money. This dilemma was settled by a legal agreement preserving their separate assets and Charlotte's financial independence as a married woman. Their attitudes to marital finances, unconventional at the time, would later lead to a famously spirited exchange of letters between GBS and the Income Tax Commissioners which was printed in *The Times* in 1910 under the heading 'The husband, the supertax and the suffragists'. The law at the time said that wives' money belonged to their husbands, and husbands therefore had to report and pay tax on this income. But what was to be done when wives refused to tell husbands what their income was? 'I go to my wife and tell her that I shall be put in prison if she does not tell me her income,' observed GBS. 'She replied that many women have gone to prison for the cause, and that it is time that the men should take their turn.'[22]

The other matter they discussed before they married was Charlotte's unwavering desire to avoid motherhood. She was 41, which would have brought additional risks to reproduction, still at the time an inherently risky business. Everyone writing about the Shaws' marriage agrees that the insistence on childlessness came from Charlotte, but GBS didn't put up much of a fight. There is more, and indeed, endless, fascination with the topic of whether or not the marriage was consummated. Surely, if not, it couldn't be considered 'real'? As Janet Dunbar, the author of Charlotte's biography, wrote: 'The short answer to that is simple. No one knows, and no one has ever been in a position to know.'[23] Charlotte was a very reserved person, and GBS, who wasn't, never said directly that his marriage was platonic.

His biographers attach some importance to Charlotte's refusal to have sex with him (if indeed she did refuse), seeing in this a handy excuse for his recurrent pursuit of other women, a source of much distress to Charlotte. The two main biographies of GBS, the one by Archibald Henderson who knew the Shaws, and Michael Holroyd's more recent mammoth volume, both decide that the Shaws' union was a '*mariage blanc*'.[24] Henderson sees their marriage as 'a business partnership, a true *contrat social*, by which the partners obligated themselves to devote their lives, severally and jointly, to world betterment. Affection, good will, and loyalty were the foundation stones of this form of modernistic life-union.'[25] Henderson was referring here to ideas that flourished among progressive thinkers in the late 19th century that proposed continence as a device for securing gender equality. Male desire subordinated women; women's liberation therefore entailed the denial of sexual intimacy. Charlotte and her husband would have been familiar with this current of thought.[26] Their friends, interestingly, thought them an ideal pair, 'a supreme example of married companionship on the highest plane' which transcended base sexual passions.[27] However their marriage began, it clearly matured with a great deal of affection on both sides. The embrace in the somewhat fuzzy photograph on page 83 is evidence of this.

The post-1898 GBS was in one important sense Charlotte's work. She retrieved him from his muddle of dirt and papers in Fitzroy Square and prepared a study for him in the pokey room on the third floor of 10 Adelphi Terrace where he would work for 30 years. The room consisted of a long, narrow space, with his desk at one end and a desk for his secretary, Blanche Patch, at the other. 'Miss Patch' performed secretarial and social services for both the Shaws for many years, wrote a book about her experience, and tempered the stereotype of Charlotte as GBS's secretary – Charlotte wasn't, Miss Patch was (see Chapter 6 for more on 'office wives'). Charlotte worked on GBS's texts, passing them to Miss Patch for typing. She is probably reading one of them in the photograph on page 82, comfortably on a sofa in a delightful Arts and Crafts setting. In 1906, Charlotte found the Shaws' country retreat, an eight-bedroom Arts and Crafts rectory, now known as 'Shaw's Corner', at Ayot St Lawrence in Hertfordshire. For GBS this was a place of comfort and productivity, but Charlotte found it cold and isolated. She organised both their households, catering carefully for GBS's needs both at home and away. Wherever they went, she took a menu, typed out by Blanche Patch, of what GBS was prepared to consume, handing it out to waiters in hotels and on boats: 'Mr. Bernard Shaw does not eat MEAT, GAME, FOWL, OR

FISH, or take TEA or COFFEE. Instead he will want one of the undermentioned dishes at lunch and dinner ... He likes oranges and salads and nuts – especially walnuts.'[28] Charlotte was, in short, 'the perfect wife'. 'The home life of the Shaws was one of the modern miracles of perfected domesticity and quiet congeniality,' opined Archibald Henderson.[29] GBS's role in the domestic division of labour was to see to the camera, the car, and his work. It's not surprising, then, that after Charlotte died, GBS complained about the change in his duties to their friend, the socialite politician Nancy Astor, 'I now have to housekeep as well as be a great author'.[30]

The Fabians and feminism

Hidden in these conventional approbations of Charlotte as 'Mrs GBS' are the enterprises she herself engaged in during the 45 years of their marriage. Among the topics Beatrice Webb enthused to Charlotte about at their first meeting in 1895 was the Fabian Society. Charlotte joined the Society in 1895, and, although Edward Pease did suggest that she should resign from the Society after her marriage – what need was there for a wife to belong as well as her husband? – she was a most faithful Fabian. The Fabian Society, formed in 1884, was – and continues to be – a group of left-wing political thinkers who argue for a gradualist approach to socialist reform. It was the foundation of the Independent Labour Party in 1893 and the Labour Party itself in 1900. Charlotte's role took various forms. She was a member of the Fabian Society Executive Committee for 17 years, the only woman of the period to hold office for such a long time. She was Vice-Chair of the Society's publishing committee, and the author of a Fabian tract called *Rent and Value*, based on an early Fabian essay. She was an organiser and the main funder of the Fabian summer schools, a visionary attempt to extend the reach of Fabianism to the provinces and provide intellectual stimulation and social events. Charlotte – and GBS – attended the first one in North Wales in 1907 where lectures included 'Socialists – their lives and ideals', 'Present problems of social reconstruction' and 'Modern dramatists'.[31]

One of the services Charlotte Shaw provided to the Fabian Society was to help them through an awkward storm in 1906 when the writer and social critic H.G. Wells wanted to abolish the 'old gang' and radically expand the Society's membership. Charlotte herself had tired of the long wranglings that went on in Society meetings, which were, in her view, increasingly staffed by 'a parcel of boys and old women thinking they are making history'.[32] At this crucial moment in its development when Wells was stirring dissension, she was one of three people appointed by the Society to determine future Fabian policy. 'I am married to the Exec[utive],' she told Wells in a conciliatory letter, 'I *am* the Executive'; therefore she was unable to support Wells' criticisms of it.[33] Her response was to produce a list of activities which would hopefully set the Society on a new and more useful course. These began with lectures on 'The faith I hold' by eminent Fabians who would each interpret socialism, relating it to their personal faith; continued with the production of simple tracts, a new version of the Society's *What to Read*, and a revamped quarterly magazine; and proposed the formation of groups to study specific subjects. The Executive ran with all Charlotte's ideas.

But the bulk of Charlotte Shaw's Fabian activity was devoted to a subject closer to her heart – the position of women. She was a founder member and a main funder of the Fabian Women's Group (FWG), which began life in 1908 in the drawing room of Maud Pember Reeves. The socialist suffragist Reeves was the author of what is probably the FWG's most famous product: *Round About a Pound a Week*, originally a Fabian tract. She joined Charlotte on the Fabian Executive in 1907, and the two women found they had the same ideas about the need for change. The photo on page 83 shows them in a (comically) dominant position either side of Maud's husband, the New Zealand politician William Pember Reeves, who was also Director of LSE from 1908 to 1919. Another new female Executive member was the social investigator and economic historian Bessie Hutchins.[34] These three women, plus Charlotte Wilson, anarchist, socialist and feminist, and an ex-postal clerk, actor and theatre producer called Millicent Murby, battled unsuccessfully against the resistances of Fabian men to the notion that the Society should support sex equality, and so decided to get on without the men. They set up the FWG to focus on the call of equal citizenship, provide publicity and undertake research on women's economic status in relation to socialism, and carry out related practical work in both socialist and feminist movements. The FWG had its own separate office and paid secretary (whose salary Charlotte covered when necessary) and it operated much like an independent organisation. One of its functions was to organise lectures on the presumed and real disabilities of women workers, on women as producers and consumers, and on women's economic circumstances in the family and the labour force.

Charlotte was a very involved member of the FWG and she worked closely on its programme of lectures, research and publications with a number of professional women historians and economists who made key contributions in this period to the reformulation of women's history. The group included women such as Marion Phillips, Labour Party activist and LSE lecturer and researcher, and Mabel Atkinson, economist, LSE researcher, later race relations activist in South Africa, the originator of Fabian summer schools, and the author of an influential Fabian tract on *The Economic Foundations of the Women's Movement*. Bessie Hutchins made her mark on the Fabian legacy with two FWG tracts on *Home Work and Sweating: The Causes and the Remedies*, and *The Working Life of Women*. Charlotte herself provided much of the information, and wrote the preface, for the FWG's tract on the discriminatory National Insurance Bill of 1911, and she helped to meet the expense of the publication that sold 10,000 copies. She also summarised for publication the results of the papers presented in the FWG's first lecture series. Charlotte was a prominent member of the FWG's Women's Studies Group Committee and played a major role in producing a compendium of essays on *Women Workers in Seven Professions*, based on FWG lectures. The book was edited by Edith Morley, the first British woman university professor.

The evidence-gathering role of the FWG made a significant contribution to the growing pile of data about the circumstances of women's lives assembled by (mainly women) researchers in this period.[35] Maud Pember Reeves' report, for example, was based on a four-year investigation carried out by the FWG into the lives of 42 poor families living in South London. Detailed and intimate data about domestic conditions and financial circumstances were collected during weekly research visits to each family over more than a year. *Round About a Pound a Week* is typical of many forgotten multi-method projects carried out by women researchers in these years. The FWG's research endeavours also encompassed a survey of women's earnings and caring responsibilities, and a report on *Women and Prisons* by Helen Blagg and Charlotte Wilson. This was the first such document to argue that women should be appointed to the medical staff of all prisons housing women, and that they should be recruited as prison governors, police officers and magistrates. An essential element in the FWG approach was to follow research with dissemination and publicity. One example is the conference the Group held in 1910 to discuss their research findings with the Associations of Headmistresses and of Women Sanitary Inspectors, the Salvation Army, the Women's Labour League and other groups.

The FWG participated directly in politics both inside and outside the Society. It pointed out that 600 of the Society's 2,000 members but only four out of the 21-strong Fabian Executive were women. It nominated women candidates for the Fabian Executive and worked to qualify its members as municipal electors and run as candidates for local bodies. The New Independent Party began its brief existence in December 1913 as a forum for representing women's interests in local government and electing more women candidates to the metropolitan borough councils and the London County Council: Charlotte was an elected member of its Council. All of this was entirely in line with her alertness to the underrepresentation of women in public life; in 1907, for example, she wrote to the Divorce Law Reform Union of which she was a contributing member to ask why there were no women on their Board of Directors.

The suffrage movement was, naturally, an important arena for the FWG's political work. The FWG's second meeting was held in the studio of the art nouveau sculptor Marion Wallace-Dunlop, the first suffragette hunger-striker; 11 FWG members were suffrage prisoners. Charlotte herself marched in all the major suffrage processions. *The Times'* Special Correspondent's report of the massive London demonstration held in 1908 – an event attended by some 500,000 people, with seven different processions and 3,000 banner-bearers – singled out for mention three Fabian women – 'Mrs. Pember Reeves', 'Mrs. Bernard Shaw' and 'Mrs. Grant Allen', noting that, 'Mr. George Bernard Shaw benevolently regarded the procession from the kerb'.[36] Two years later Charlotte convened an emergency meeting of the FWG in Trafalgar Square to consider the Women's Social and Political Union's (WSPU) invitation to join the Hyde Park rally planned for a fortnight later and 'woman' a platform there; this they decided to do, with the help of a few Fabian men. The FWG's support for the suffrage movement moved the Fabian Society out of its traditional muddled thinking about women to become the first socialist organisation officially to support the suffrage cause.

Charlotte Shaw, normally no self-publicist, felt so strongly about the suffrage issue that she wrote a long and impassioned letter to *The Times* in 1911 about the government's latest Manhood Suffrage Bill. The Bill proposed a very limited extension of the franchise to wealthy propertied women. 'It is the intolerable insult of being at last finally dismissed in the Oriental fashion as creatures of another and inferior species, without political souls, that rankles,' she declared. Her letter called the Prime Minister, Anthony Asquith's, personal conviction on the subject 'impenetrably unreasonable and atrociously insulting, besides being absurdly out of date ... Mr. Asquith says to me, in effect,' Charlotte wrote, 'that in 1912 the vilest male wretch who can contrive to keep a house of ill-fame for six months shall have a vote; and the

With George Bernard Shaw and Beatrice and Sidney Webb, 1932

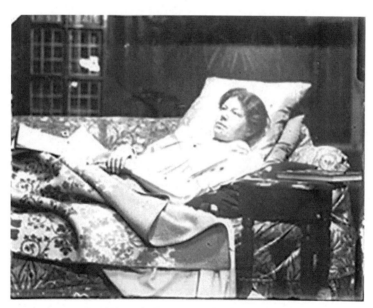

c. 1903 at Maybury Knoll, Woking, Surrey

With George Bernard Shaw, 1926

With Maud and William Pember Reeves, 1900

noblest woman in England shall not have one because she is a female. I wonder how Mr. Asquith would feel if a government of women offered such an outrage to him?'[37]

Charlotte's feminism was more central to her life than her socialism, and there are suggestions that she occasionally bartered more attention to women's issues in exchange for her financial support of LSE in her dealings with Sidney Webb. Her feminism took many organisational forms. She was among the 'distinguished suffragists' elected as a vice-president of the United Suffragists, and a Women's Labour League delegate to an International Congress in 1914. Her private account books show that she gave sizeable donations to all kinds of societies and groups of whose work she approved. These donations included, aside from the LSE and the FWG, the London School of Medicine for Women; various birth control clinics; the WSPU; the Anti-Sweating League (Charlotte was an Executive Committee member of this organisation, which campaigned to improve conditions in the 'sweated' trades of low-paid, arduous insanitary work); the weekly feminist magazine *The Freewoman*; and the Passmore Edwards Settlement in London, founded in 1890 and a major provider of services for poor children and their families.

The mystery of the Fabian window

The Fabian stained glass window is a very special cause célèbre and memento of these radical years. Today it hangs in the Shaw Library of LSE, but it's been there only since 2006 when Prime Minister Tony Blair unveiled it with some fine words about Fabian values surviving in the modern Labour Party. There are two versions of the window's provenance: in one it was designed by GBS, and in the other by Charlotte herself. Quite possibly they were both involved in commissioning (rather than designing) the window, but its purpose is unknown.[38] Whatever its origins, its artist was a cousin of Charlotte's, Caroline Townshend, a woman 20 years younger from a radical branch of the Townshend family. Caroline, her mother, Emily, and at least one of her sisters, Rachel, were active suffragettes; both Emily and Rachel spent some time in Holloway prison. They were also members of the Fabian Society, and Caroline was a member of the Citizenship Sub-Committee of the FWG. Emily Townshend wrote three Fabian tracts: one on William Morris, one on *The Case Against the Charity Organization Society*, and a third on *The Case for School Nurseries*, which proposed modern reforms such as free nursery education, free meals and playgrounds. Charlotte would have spent much time in the company of this other Townshend family, so it's odd that they do not feature in any of the relevant biographies.

Caroline Townshend made the Fabian window in 1910, probably in her studio in Fulham. Mysteriously, it appears to have stayed with its maker until 1944, when it was acquired by the Webb Memorial Trust (of which R.H. Tawney was a trustee) and hung in their conference centre in Surrey. In 1978 it was stolen from there, re-emerging briefly in Phoenix, Arizona, and then in a Sotheby's sale in 2005, at which point it was repurchased by the Webb Memorial Trust and given on loan to LSE.

The window is a political allegory about the Fabian Society's early years. Using the format of a Tudor family memorial, with the figures dressed accordingly, it shows at the top Sidney Webb and GBS energetically hammering out the shape of a new world beneath an emblem of a wolf in sheep's clothing (representing the gradualist approach of Fabianism). On their left is the Fabian Society secretary, Edward Pease, working the bellows, and across the bottom are ten other Fabian figures, five men and five women, kneeling around a central column of books to which most of them are praying. In the top pile are works by GBS, while the Webb collection beneath is topped by Beatrice's *Minority Report on the Poor Law*. There's less clarity about who the female figures are than the male ones, but they are probably: Maud Pember Reeves, Mary Hankinson, Mabel Atkinson, Frances Boyd Dawson, and the window maker Caroline Townshend herself. Frances Boyd Dawson was a sanitary inspector and long-term Fabian supporter. Mary Hankinson was a physical education teacher hired by Charlotte Shaw to provide Swedish drill and country dancing for the first Fabian summer school, a very active suffragette, and the model for GBS's Joan of Arc – the only woman, said GBS in an inscription to her, who didn't think she was, but the only one who actually was. Joan of Arc was also Charlotte Shaw's idea, and she researched the subject for him.

Scholarships for women

Among Charlotte's gifts to LSE was one that uniquely carries her name and thus can't be accused of being someone else's idea. In 1904, she endowed a 'Shaw scholarship' or 'studentship', which provided funds – £105 a year over two years – for research students. The first holder was the Fabian, Marion Phillips, but, after that, the awards from 1906 to 1910 were given to five men. Charlotte, deep in her work for the FWG, objected, and said that in future this studentship in her name must be given to women only, and it should fund work in women's history. When the studentship was re-advertised in 1911 the topic was defined as 'The social and economic position of women in England at some point before the Industrial Revolution'.[39] Applicants were expected to perfect their knowledge of investigative and research methods, and to prepare and publish an original monograph, afterwards donating all their research materials to LSE so as to make these available for other scholars. Charlotte's specification of the topics she wanted students to cover showed a keen and comprehensive interest in women's history. There were four sub-topics: women's position in agriculture during the Middle Ages and the influence of the break-up of the manorial system on women's economic position; women in their relation to the Guilds; trades partly or entirely carried on by women in the Middle Ages; and women's position in agriculture and other industries during 'the Tribal period' and early Middle Ages. Charlotte suggested one extra topic, which was especially close to her own heart: 'The effect upon the economic position of the married woman in Great Britain of the transition from tribal custom which placed her, in part at least, under the protection of her own kindred even during married life, to the theory developed by English Common Law during the Middle Ages that a wife was entirely subordinate to & dependent upon her husband'. 'What I want', said Charlotte, succinctly in a letter to the LSE secretary Miss Mactaggart, 'is a series of monographs on the position of women in England (or Britain?) from early days to the present which are to dovetail with one another finally.'[40] She wanted, in other words, to sponsor an entire sweep of women's history.

The first woman to get 'the Shaw' under this revised rubric was the economic historian and colleague of R.H. Tawney, Eileen Power. She held it from 1911 to 1913 during which time she worked on her history of medieval women, later expanded into several books and other publications. Power was a much-respected and brilliant medieval scholar, a feminist, pacifist and internationalist, and also a woman omitted from the canons of mainstream economic history, in part because of her status as a forgotten wife – her husband, Michael (known as Munia) Postan, her pupil and colleague, got more than his fair share of attention. A very different kind of researcher was the next holder of the Shaw studentship, in 1913–14: Alice Clark, a member of a prominent Quaker family, manager of the Clark shoe empire, and author of a book that has remained a much-read classic in the field of women's history *Working Life of Women in the Seventeenth Century*.

The LSE files on the Shaw studentship show that Charlotte kept a close eye on her scholars. When the war began, Alice Clark halted her studies in order to organise workrooms for unemployed women, and then asked for permission to take time off in order to train as a midwife. Her sister, Hilda, one of the early women doctors, had gone with a Quaker expeditionary force to run a maternity hospital in France. Neither Miss Mactaggart, LSE's secretary at the time, nor Charlotte, were happy about the interruption to Alice's work: 'What has happened to Miss Clark?' inquired Charlotte of Miss Mactaggart. 'I have heard nothing of her since she started her midwifery work. She promised to come & see me – but she never did! I think we ought to get into touch with her, as there are certainly limits to the amount of latitude I am inclined to give her.' Alice Clark wrote with a progress report relaying the huge amount of material she'd collected, and she was allowed to keep her studentship. 'With regard to the next student,' said Charlotte 'keep the 17th century for Miss Clark and keep Miss Power's period for her ... The new student might start on a fresh period.'[41] The new student was Aline Stirling, who became Aline Meyer, and who did research on the Romans and Anglo-Saxon women.

Sociology on the stage

The winter of 1906 when Charlotte found what would eventually became Shaw's Corner, the rural retreat where she could shiver and GBS could write his plays, she came across the works of another radical playwright, the French writer Eugène Brieux. Brieux had gained a name for himself as the writer of didactic 'thesis-plays', which tackled contemporary social issues involving inequality and abuses of power. Brieux wrote about corruption and injustices in the legal system, the oppression of married women, eugenics, 'fashionable' charity, and such controversial topics as wet-nursing and venereal disease. Unsurprisingly, he found it difficult to get his plays on the stage. The play Charlotte found in the winter of 1906 was called *Maternité*, and in it Brieux raged against the social treatment of unwed mothers. The play uses the characters of a wife called Lucie Brignac, her over-ambitious husband, and her younger unmarried sister, Annette, who is unexpectedly pregnant, to tell a moral tale. On learning of the pregnancy, Monsieur Brignac banishes Annette from the house, saying her pregnancy will harm his reputation and call into question the family's respectability. Lucie's response is to announce that she will leave as well, taking their children with her. The play is centrally a plea for women's control of their own bodies, an argument – like many Brieux put forward – with which Charlotte agreed. She read *Maternité* from cover to cover without a pause, 'and when I laid it down I felt an event had occurred, and a new possession come into my life. I knew at once that I must translate the play into English to make it accessible to those of my countrymen and women who could not read it in the original French.'[42] She wrote to Brieux and asked his permission to translate it, which she did, and then she worked with the Stage Society to get it performed.

The Stage Society's aim was to put on new and experimental plays, chiefly at the Royal Court Theatre in London – their first was a GBS play, *You Never Can Tell*. Charlotte was a member of the Stage Society's Executive Committee, a role she shared with many of the best-known actresses of the Edwardian stage, including Lena Ashwell, one of the greatest actresses of the period, and a close friend. The Society sent Charlotte's translation of *Maternité* to the censor to be licensed and were told that permission would never be granted for it to be staged in England. So in April 1906 they produced it anyway. 'I shall not easily forget,' wrote Charlotte, 'the zeal and devotion with which the artists worked; or the impression the play made upon many of them, even under the crushing circumstances of rehearsal morning after morning in an unwarmed and semi-lighted hall in a most depressing part of London.'[43] Another of Brieux's plays, *The Three Daughters of Monsieur Dupont*, translated by St John Hankin, had already been staged in London, and a third, *Damaged Goods*, had also been translated. Charlotte decided it would be a good idea to bring the three plays together in a book. Again she wrote to Brieux, who told her that he had already assigned his literary rights elsewhere, but Charlotte wasn't to be defeated, and she managed to acquire the rights to publish an English edition. Eugène Brieux's reputation for writing scandalous dramas meant that no publisher would touch the projected volume for several years. It was finally published in 1914 and speedily ran through several editions.

Damaged Goods is about a wealthy young man who contracts syphilis and marries without telling his wife because he's afraid of losing his inheritance: they go on to have a child with congenital syphilis. The play scandalised, particularly with its revelations of medical details about the disease, its symptoms and consequences. It was this that particularly attracted the attentions of an American doctor, Thomas Hepburn, who wrote to Charlotte in September 1911 in his capacity as Secretary of the Connecticut Society of Social Hygiene. (Thomas Hepburn's other claim to fame was that he was the father of the Hollywood actress Katharine Hepburn.) Dr Hepburn asked whether they might get several thousand copies of the play in pamphlet form 'to be used for general distribution among the youth of our Connecticut colleges ... We would be able to get men to read the matter placed before them in this dramatic form, which we could not get them to do in any other way.'[44] Charlotte arranged for 10,000 copies to be sent. Two years later Hepburn wrote again to report that every copy had been sold and Brieux's play had been one of the best pieces of propaganda they had ever come across. Now he had been approached by the American Federation for Sex Hygiene – he was a member of its Executive Committee, alongside 'some of the leading men and women of America' including Jane Addams of Hull-House, Chicago – to request a further edition.[45] *Damaged Goods* was performed on Broadway in the US in 1913, with a special showing for President Wilson, his cabinet, and members of Congress concerned with the social pathology of venereal disease. The play was finally performed in England in 1914.

In between reading *Maternité* and getting *Damaged Goods* into the limelight, Charlotte Shaw turned her attention to a third Brieux play, *La Femme Seule*. The play's protagonist, Thérèse, is cheated out of her inheritance by her lawyer, deceived by her lover, sexually harassed by her employer, and foiled in her attempt to organise women workers by the anger and physical assault of the male workers, who object to the influx of cheap female labour. Charlotte's translation, *Woman on her Own*, added for dramatic effect some scenes of 'free for all tongue and fist fights' to the original French text.[46] *Woman on her Own* was produced at the Coronet Theatre in London in December, 1913, by the Actresses' Franchise League as the inaugural performance of a Women's Theatre group. In the cast were Lena Ashwell, and another prominent feminist actor/writer Cicely Hamilton. (Hamilton's *Marriage as a Trade*, a spirited rant of Edwardian feminism, is mentioned in Chapter 1.) The play was favourably reviewed, both for the fine acting and 'the sentiments awakening responsive echoes in every New Womanly bosom'.[47] Through her engagement with Brieux's work, Charlotte thus enjoyed a close collaboration with feminist activism in the theatre. The purpose of the Actresses' Franchise League, to present women's point of view, give an outlet for women members and advance the cause of the vote, very much resonated with her own opinions.

There's no doubt about Charlotte's role in advancing the cause of French radical drama in the early part of the 20th century, but it is par for the course that this achievement is discarded from her biography by those whose only view of her is as the shadow behind the great man. One commentator on Brieux and GBS as 'iconoclasts of social reform' cattily remarks that Charlotte's translation of *Maternité* is 'one of the few instances of her active participation in her husband's literary endeavors'.[48] At the most, it is argued that Charlotte's absorption in Brieux could be interpreted as a response to her husband's philandering. By 1912, when they'd been married for 14 years, GBS had just emerged from his lengthy passion for the actress Ellen Terry to embark on a 'flamboyant courtship' with another great actress of the time, Stella (Mrs Patrick) Campbell.[49] This was an occupation that lasted at least two years, and which drove everyone, especially Charlotte, mad. He told her about his affair and read her his letters to Stella. These were addressed to 'Bellissima Stellissima', 'Ever blessedest darling', 'Belovedovedest', and so forth, and were written in terms that GBS knew would give 'the greatest pain' to Charlotte.[50] She heard the two of them talk on the telephone. She knew, sometimes, when they were meeting. The situation was, clearly, difficult for her (surely it would have been difficult for anyone). Charlotte's objections to GBS's affairs are noted rather unsympathetically by many biographers. The chapter on the Shaws in Jeffrey Meyers' *Married to Genius*, for instance, calls Charlotte's 'gross eating habits, her obsessive desire to travel and her violent jealousy' all manifestations of her rejection of sex. Her jealousy is deemed the Shaws' most serious problem, while GBS's serial 'flirtations' are deemed both 'natural and inevitable', given his 'enforced celibacy' and 'professional involvement with beautiful actresses'.[51]

GBS's relationship with 'Mrs Pat' became more difficult for Charlotte, so in the lead up to the first performance of Shaw's *Pygmalion* early in 1914, with the object of his passion playing the role of Eliza Doolittle, Charlotte went with Lena Ashwell to the US three days before the opening night in order to avoid having to witness it. This visit included someone in whose work Charlotte had become very interested: Dr James Porter Mills. He was an American paediatrician who, together with his wife, a self-titled 'healer', had developed a system of Christian Science thinking mixed with Eastern mysticism which they called 'the Teaching'. Mills had come into contact with an Indian Hindu monk called Swami Vivekananda, a key figure in the transformation of Hinduism into a world religion and the introduction of yoga to the Western world – and, coincidentally, an associate of the Indian philosopher Keshub Chandra Sen, who beguiled Jeannette Tawney's mother into sailing for India in 1872 (see Chapter 4). Charlotte met Mills first at Lena Ashwell's house and she started going to his lectures, determined to find out exactly what 'the Teaching' was all about. This led her to take on the task of condensing and editing one of Mills' texts and publishing it as *Knowledge is the Door*.

Michael Holroyd's biography of Shaw has this to say about this stage in Charlotte's life: 'Her earlier interest in medicine revived in the form of a hypochondriacal belief in spiritual healing.' It was 'the only way open to her' of being unfaithful to GBS, a way she sought as offering her the composure to survive the 'lacerating scenes' of their encounters over his devotion to the other woman.[52] Yet, coming from a long line of Protestant clergy in Ireland, Charlotte had always been interested in religion and spirituality. In her later correspondence with T.E. Lawrence, she made it clear that she ended up being far from uncritical of Mills' philosophy, describing him as an 'odd, uncomfortable, unaccountable, rather trying American man', not very clever, and rather stuffy, and unacceptably pro-militarism, a position which offended her own pacifism.[53] Another reason for Charlotte's openness to the matter of spiritual healing was her own ill-health. She endured recurrent bronchitis and asthma, and she suffered from a form of arthritis called Paget's disease. In this condition the processes of bone repair and renewal are disrupted throughout the body, resulting in weak deformed bones and damage to the joints: it can cause considerable debilitating pain in the bones, joints and nerves. Traditional medicine could do little about the pain and disability of Paget's disease. Later in life Charlotte would suffer fractures and deformities, become heavily hunchbacked and confined to an armoured corset before the disease killed her.

A pillar of wisdom

Charlotte Shaw's written biography is caught between the pillars of two extensively biographised men: her husband, and a much younger but equally notorious representative of masculinity, Thomas Edward Lawrence, alias Lawrence of Arabia. A host of biographies, television documentaries and a blockbuster Hollywood film starring Peter O'Toole celebrate this man who began as an archeologist, became an intelligence officer and UK government foreign policy adviser, identified, led, and documented the Arab uprising against the Ottoman Empire in the Middle East, and enjoyed a series of newsworthy sexual and sado-masochistic adventures along the way.

In his contradictory search for both fame and anonymity, Lawrence was a man of various names, including, oddly, that of T.E. Shaw, an identity he told the poet Robert Graves he had picked at random from the index of the army list, rather than because of either Charlotte or her husband.[54] The result (or the cause) of these name games was that no one, including Lawrence himself, was quite sure who he really was. The word most often used in his obituaries is 'enigma'.

Lawrence of Arabia was not an obvious candidate for a close relationship with the refined and intellectual Charlotte Shaw. When they met in 1922 she was a comfortably married lady of 65: the tensions of the earlier years with GBS had vaporised into what looked to everyone like a contented domesticity. Lawrence was 42, a war hero, nominally still an official at the Colonial Office where he was advising Winston Churchill on Arab affairs; his reputed role during the war in the Middle East had already turned him into a household name. But he wanted to be a great writer, and when he met Charlotte he was the author of (the third draft of) an unwieldy and as yet unpublished memoir of the Arab revolt, which he dreamed might one day rank among the great masterpieces of the world.

Charlotte Shaw and T.E. Lawrence had several important things in common. First, there was the Anglo-Irish background: Lawrence's father was an Anglo–Irish landowner, who maintained a wife and four daughters on his estate in Ireland while constructing a second family containing Thomas Edward and four more sons in Oxford. Lawrence was fascinated by his Irish inheritance and by Ireland. Then there was the decision both Charlotte and Lawrence had taken to avoid 'normal' heterosexual relationships and children. This was connected to the issue of 'The Mothers'. Both had mothers whom they regarded as unpleasantly domineering, greedy for their children's love and attention, and harsh in their treatment of their gentle husbands. Mrs Lawrence had given her son 'a terror of families and inquisitions', so Lawrence confided to Charlotte, and this was a legacy not unlike the one Charlotte felt she had received from *her* mother.[55] Both Charlotte and Lawrence were translators – Lawrence had published his translation of a novel by Adrien le Corbeau called *Le Gigantesque* (The Forest Giant) in 1924 (under the pseudonym John Hume Ross), and Charlotte tried to persuade him against doing another translation of the *Odyssey*, but instead ended up helping him with it. They both loved reading and music, especially the music of Edward Elgar.

Their first meeting was on Saturday 5 March 1922, in London. Lawrence had a financial problem he wanted to discuss with the museum curator and collector Sydney Cockerell. The two men lunched in the Grill Room at the Carlton Hotel, and Cockerell left at the end of the lunch to call at Adelphi Terrace in order to collect a portrait of GBS by Augustus John, which GBS was donating to the Fitzwilliam Museum in Cambridge. Lawrence went with him, meeting both Shaws for half an hour. In August, he wrote to the Shaws asking for their help with his manuscript. In September, the postman 'dumped a parcel of 300,000 words upon us,' as GBS's secretary, Blanche Patch, put it.[56] GBS treated the manuscript rather casually, but Charlotte devoured it. On the last day of 1922 she wrote an enthusiastic letter to Lawrence about it: 'Dear Mr Lawrence, if you've been "mad keen" to hear about your book I've been mad keen to write to you about it ever since I read it, or rather ever since I began to read it, and I simply haven't dared. I got from it an impression of you as an Immense Personality soaring in the blue (of the Arabian skies) far above my lowly sphere, and that anything I could say in the way of admiration, or comment, or question, could only be an impertinence ... 'How is it conceivable, imaginable that a man who could write *The Seven Pillars* can have any doubts about it? If you don't know it is a "a great book" what is the use of anyone telling you so ... I am an old woman, old enough at any rate to be your mother; I have met all sorts of men and women of the kind that are called distinguished; I have read their books and discussed them with them; but I have never read anything like this: I don't believe anything really like it has been written before.'[57]

She called it 'a poignant human document' and spent 18 months suggesting revisions, and working on the proofs. 'And what form should your corrections take?' Lawrence asked Charlotte in the summer of 1924. 'Any you please', he continued. 'My pleasure is bounded only by your pains. Do as much, in each batch, as comes easy to you, avoiding laborious drudgery ... I'll value most such corrections as affect the manner & matter of the expression of ideas: because they will tend to make the book better ... I'll be grateful for any corrected misprints: but the sense of the book is the thing. Do please try & knock out redundant paragraphs.'[58] Lawrence made most of the changes Charlotte suggested in all his manuscripts. She was evidently sometimes quite outspoken; for example, of a passage in *Seven Pillars*: 'Clean men. Clean is a very dangerous word. I remember you used it in one of your early letters to G.B.S. Do you really know, *à fond*, the sociology of one English village? Believe an old woman it is very exceptionally only that men make women glad: do you know the war story: "Mrs A, (just having received her week's pension money) 'This 'ere War's too good to larst, I says. Eighteen shillins a week, and no 'usban giving one at night. My it's eaven!'"'[59] Charlotte worked also on *Revolt in the Desert*, the abridged version of *Seven Pillars*, and then on his collection of brutal observations about service life, *The Mint*. When Lawrence first mentioned *The Mint* to Charlotte, she asked to see it, 'and instalments of the typed version came to her as Lawrence tapped them out,' recalled Blanche Patch.[60] While GBS did no more than 'sample' it rather primly, Charlotte read every word, considered it a marvellous achievement, and treated its conversational obscenities as merely incidental to the main theme; 'my builder's-yard of a book is most unfit for a lady's eyes,' Lawrence had sighed in a letter to GBS.[61] When Lawrence had corrected what he wrote, and corrected it again, he posted off the latest batch for suggestions from Charlotte.

Among the numerous academic treatments of Charlotte's, GBS's and T.E. Lawrence's lives, is an MA thesis by Mary Fernald at the University of Maine. She originally intended to research the literary relationship between GBS and T.E. Lawrence, drawing on the (then) unpublished correspondence between Charlotte and Lawrence. But when she read the letters she found that Charlotte was much more important than a mere connecting link between the two men. Charlotte, not GBS, was the person who worked and reworked Lawrence's manuscripts; it was thus she, not her husband, who must take at least some of the credit for the accessibility and success of *Seven Pillars of Wisdom* and the other Lawrence projects. But, in line with the general strategy of denying agency in wives, biographers have assigned with monotonous thoughtlessness Charlotte's influence over Lawrence's writings to her husband. GBS's comments about Lawrence were so often inaccurate that it seems unlikely he ever gave Lawrence much serious thought – aside from turning him into Private Napoleon Alexander Trotsky Meek in his play *Too True to be Good*. Lawrence himself was well aware of Charlotte's superior importance in both his and GBS's literary lives: referring to a flyleaf on which Lawrence had thanked both Shaws, he wrote to her, 'Apropos of my flyleaf, you took exception to my bracketing you & G.B.S. as having bettered my botch. Yet you can write the plays by yourself ... or parts of them. Don't imagine that by this I really mean that G.B.S. isn't a colossus, & us little mortals: but often you hold his hand.'[62]

Through her all-important editing ventures, Charlotte Shaw and T.E. Lawrence established a long correspondence, the most regular and intimate for both of them, a correspondence which lasted until his death, on a motor bike she bought him, in 1935. The surviving six hundred or so letters written over 13 years have been drawn on heavily by Lawrence biographers, who concur in seeing Charlotte as Lawrence's 'principal confidante and confessor', but who have shown little interest in studying them from Charlotte's point of view.[63] One problem – it was always a problem with the publicity-averse Charlotte Shaw – was that much less material survives from her side of the correspondence than from his. She kept his letters, and gave them after his death to the British Library, along with the manuscripts and other documents of his she had in her possession. Lawrence burnt most of her letters, partly, he said, because he had nowhere to store them in his British Army accommodation. Four volumes of letters between Lawrence and both the Shaws have been published, covering the years 1922–35. Out of the 417 letters contained in these volumes, 81 per cent are from Lawrence to Charlotte and 5 per cent are from her to him (the rest are exchanges with others in their networks).

Charlotte and Lawrence of Arabia wrote to each other about everyday life, health, families, childhoods, feelings, literature and music. The most frequent correspondence – weekly and sometimes more often – happened when Lawrence was in India as an RAF officer between 1926 and 1929. She sent him books – Brieux, Radclyffe Hall's *The Well of Loneliness*, John Masefield's *Lost Endeavour*, André Gide on Dostoevsky, James Joyce's *Ulysses*, Naomi Mitchison's *Cloud Cuckoo Land*, James Stephens' *The Crock of Gold*, Joseph Conrad's *Suspense*, H.G. Wells' *Christina Alberta's Father*, and dozens of lesser-known volumes. There were theatre programmes, copies of *L'Illustration* and *The Times Literary Supplement*, and of a spiritual journal called *The Quest*. There were food parcels – chocolates from Gunter's, a smart confectioner on Berkeley Square; china tea from Fortnum and Mason's; and foie gras and peach-fed ham at Christmas. When Lawrence's *Revolt in the Desert* was published, Charlotte took out an agency subscription to news cuttings about him, sending them to him in India. She bought him gramophone records – Elgar, Brahms, Delius, Bach, Beethoven, Franck and Handel – and then, to go with them, a fine scarlet and gold gramophone. When it arrived at Lawrence's camp in Karachi, he called it 'a lovely thing, everything the heart of any man in camp could wish … People who belong to the *News of the World* class discuss Bee-thoven and Mozzat at meals,' he reported with gratitude.[64]

When Lawrence was in England, he and Charlotte also met a good deal. For example, on 23 January 1926, Lawrence was at Shaw's Corner in the evening and talked to Charlotte while GBS read. The next day, a Sunday, they spent with the Shaws' neighbour, the Antarctic explorer Apsley Cherry-Garrard, and Charlotte and Lawrence passed the evening talking. He left on the Monday morning, and saw the Shaws again in London three days later. Sometimes he and Charlotte met without GBS. For example, on 4 November 1926 they had tea together with the novelist E.M. Forster; on 11 November she gave him lunch and they went to the Tate Gallery and then walked together through Westminster. The following Friday Lawrence called for her with the sculptor Eric Kennington and drove her to Kennington's house in Chiswick, lunching with her later at Adelphi Terrace. On one occasion, when Charlotte went alone to meet Lawrence in London, she offered him something rather precious, a 'commonplace book' in which she had written passages from works, mainly on mysticism, that interested her. (Such notebooks, personal to the creator, were popular ways of storing scraps of interesting information.) Charlotte's *Commonplace Book* survives today, a small thick volume bound in soft brown leather and kept in a locked wooden box in the Bodleian Library in Oxford. On the flyleaf is written 'T.E.S.' and under that, in a smaller hand, 'C.F.S., 1927.'[65]

This was obviously a relationship that meant a great deal to both of them. During the peak of their correspondence, in 1925–30, Charlotte noted in her diary the dates she sent and received Lawrence communications, which she did for no other correspondent. Their letters grew more personal after Lawrence sailed for India at the end of 1926. On 17 May 1927 she sent him the emotionally honest letter about her hellish childhood quoted earlier in this chapter. Lawrence's response was to tell her that it had 'exactly fitted a need I had'. 'We usually keep our family cupboards closed,' he remarked; so it can be very helpful 'when someone else with a cupboard is allowed to peer in.' The continuity of their 'tennis-game of a correspondence' was a miracle for Lawrence. 'I've not written any letters of this sort to anyone else, since I was born,' he admitted. 'Do you know,' he wrote, 'I think I treat you more confidently than you do me? At least I seem to tell you everything that happens to me every week.'[66]

It was on some level an extraordinary relationship: 'the strangest contact of my life,' Charlotte called it.[67] Here was a young-ish man who wrote openly about male rape and beatings and freely admitted to a somewhat tortured sexual identity; here was an old-ish woman who was not given to intimacy about such topics and who, as far as anyone knew, withdrew from the physical aspects of relationships. 'Are you writing history, or a fairy tale?' she asked him once.[68] This is a question that has been posed of Lawrence's *oeuvre* generally, and it also applies to the way in which biographers have treated their relationship. The dominant view is that she sought him out, driven by her frustration as a childless woman in a less-than-perfect marriage. Lawrence met some thwarted need in her, and in return she gave him the mother he never had. He was 'the perfect son' for her. 'She would have made an excellent mother,' declares Phillip Knightley in his *The Secret Lives of Lawrence of Arabia*. She 'directed onto Lawrence all the possessive maternal affection she had suppressed for years. In his turn, Lawrence found with Charlotte a tender understanding that had evaded him all his life.'[69]

Frustrated motherhood as a popular diagnosis of Charlotte's attraction to T.E. Lawrence is heavily contested by the evidence. 'Let me acquit you of all suspicion of "mothering" me,' wrote Lawrence himself to Charlotte in the summer of 1928. 'With you I have no seeking or suspicion of that at all … I talk to you exactly as I feel inclined, without any sense that I'm talking up, or you down. Which is very subtle and successful of you. I think it represents reality too, in your attitude, as well as mine.'[70] Admitting to a friend after Lawrence's death that he was 'an inexpressibly complicated person', Charlotte observed that, 'he would always have grinned at the idea of anyone "mothering" him.'[71] Blanche Patch, GBS's secretary who lived with the Shaws at Ayot St Lawrence, was in a position to see and understand more about Charlotte Shaw's life than most people; she acted as a postwoman, passing on phone messages and redirecting Lawrence's mail between Adelphi Terrace and Ayot St Lawrence or to Charlotte travelling abroad. In her account of *Thirty Years with GBS*, Patch talked about Charlotte's intimacy with Lawrence as bringing 'a glow to her later years', and about Lawrence as ignoring 'the gulf of time between them' and finding her 'the only woman with whom he was quite at ease', but she did not find in their connection anything resembling a mother-son relationship. Perhaps it was simply, 'one of those rare friendships where two questing minds find stimulus and help in sparking off against each other.' Undoubtedly too, what Lawrence most valued in Charlotte was her supply of wisdom. She was 'as wise as 10,000 of you and me,' he told Nancy Astor.[72]

Working in the dark

Charlotte Shaw moves fleetingly in and out of different versions of the stories this chapter has touched on – about the LSE, the Fabian Society, the Stage Society, avant-garde theatre, the suffrage movement, and the tortured lives of T.E. Lawrence: she is benefactor, editor, translator, networker, scholar, confidante, originator of ideas and schemes. But two factors impede any proper recognition of what she did, and the impact it had. The first is her legendary aversion to publicity. The second is the refusal of biographers to see Charlotte Shaw as anything more than a marginal figure, a woman connected to these stories almost wholly through her function as a wife: she was Mrs GBS for 45 of her 86 years, but Mrs GBS is what she has wholly become.

When she joined the Anti-Noise League in the 1930s one journalist inquired whether Charlotte was, 'Tired of hearing her husband blow his own trumpet'.[73] She was definitely not fond of blowing her own. Her shyness and intense dislike of publicity was well known, and this makes her a difficult subject for a biographer. Much of the material in this chapter has had to be ferreted out from dark places. She was much more concerned to preserve the documentary evidence of other people's lives than to leave any of her own. As the *Lancashire Evening Post* commented in December, 1931, 'Photographers appeal to her in vain ... the wife of one of the most photographed men in Europe ... is only known to the public by hasty snapshots.'[74] Newspaper reporters during the Shaws' South African trip in 1935 experienced the same frustration with a woman who persisted in remaining in the background. Frederick Whelan of the Stage Society, urging her to provide a photograph in 1911, was firmly told by Charlotte, 'I'm never photographed! It's a rule I never break.'[75] When both the Shaws went to see the first London performance of GBS's play *Too True to be Good* (the one that featured a version of T.E. Lawrence), 'Mrs. Shaw modestly concealed herself behind the curtains of her box ... She hurriedly left the theatre with her husband just before the final curtain, and together they walked back unrecognised to their flat in the Adelphi.'[76] And when it came to the naming of the Library on the top floor of LSE's old building, Charlotte resisted being acknowledged as its funder: 'Reward me by keeping my connection with it as absolutely private as is possible under the circumstances,' she pleaded to the Director. 'I have already had to excuse myself for refusing to have my portrait painted and hung in the Founders' Room at the School. I am abnormally & ridiculously averse from publicity and like to work in the dark, like a mole!'[77] She only gave way finally when she was told that people were calling it 'The Shaw Library' anyway.

Legacies

Charlotte Shaw's main legacy has to be a set of unanswered questions that hover around the narration of her life as a forgotten wife. How did Charlotte Shaw, the wife, and Charlotte Payne-Townshend/Shaw, the person, actually cohabit? Was it a harmonious union, or was it fraught with quarrels? What did she really want? What did this marriage to 'a great man' actually mean to her? Did she really define herself through the man she married, or was this something other people did for her, corralling her in that vast array of preconceptions about what it means to be the wife of a famous man – secretary, nursemaid, housekeeper, hostess, travelling companion, sounding-board, brave acceptor of male infidelity? Charlotte was herself an acute analyst of gender divisions in heteronormative relationships. Feminists beat at the closed door of man's determination to keep women enslaved, she said, and women, so very sadly, acquiesce in this. 'A man does not want the woman with whom he enters into personal relations to be either intellectual, original, independent, self-willed, courageous, or public-spirited; he likes her to be intelligent, conventional, dependent, submissive, timid, and private-spirited. He wants to feel in his home that he is not only master and owner, but lawgiver and deity.'[78]

We don't know if these remarks derive any of their force from her own personal life with GBS. But theirs was, undoubtedly, a conventionally gendered union, and in this it illustrated a common collision between radical ideology and traditional practice. In the case of gender, all small domestic revolutions must compete against the living pull of institutionalised patriarchy. But what we do know is that there's no need for these struggles to be overwritten by the gendered assumptions of biographers. Interestingly, the earlier biography of GBS by Archibald Henderson, who knew the Shaws, conveys a much less patronising view of Charlotte than the later one by Michael Holroyd. Henderson noted the 'efficiency and ability' with which Charlotte served as a member of the 'extremely important' Executive Committee of the Fabian Society; her commitment of time, 'directive thought, personal aid and means' to the Equal Suffrage cause and other movements aimed at women's betterment; her liberal contribution towards the founding of LSE; and her championing of the cause of the radical French playwright Brieux in England. 'How much I may have owed to her tact and diplomacy, in persuading her equally kindly but wayward and unmanageable husband, to attend to the requirements of his biographer,' concluded Henderson, 'I shall never know. ... What do I know about her anyhow?'[79] Much less humbly, and quite conversely, Michael Holroyd, reaching the story 42 years later, disposes nimbly and misogynistically of Charlotte's individual agency. Here he is talking about her position as GBS's wife: 'she treated him as her employer partly and partly as her child. It was the employer whose correspondence she dealt with, whose manuscripts she took to the typist. She also arranged lunches with people he should meet and protected him from other people who would worry him needlessly. It was on behalf of this employer, too, that she still sat on committees at the London School of Economics and the School of Medicine for Women, and had joined the play-reading committee of the Stage Society.'[80] Charlotte Shaw, the person who can make decisions about her own life, is thus smoothly dissolved into an appendage, a shadow, a puppet whose strings are manipulated by someone else.

When GBS read Charlotte's diary and correspondence with T.E. Lawrence after her death, he said he was astonished that he had never known the soul of his wife. She died in September 1943, at the age of 86, after having been painfully disabled for many years. GBS had cared well for her, reversing the relationship with which their union had started, when she, as his 'informal nurse', had rescued him from a septic foot. In the evenings he played the piano to her; it had been put in the hall in Shaw's Corner, so she could hear him playing and singing arias, Irish airs, childhood songs. Her body was cremated and her ashes kept until he died seven years later, when they were mixed together and scattered along the footpaths and around the statue of St Joan in the Shaw's Corner garden.

Charlotte Shaw's will was a controversial one. Aside from bequeathing most of her estate to GBS, there was a legacy for her niece and small sums for Sidney Webb and Frederick Whelan, and for her gardener and chauffeur and their wives, and her housemaid and parlour maid. Then she set up a large trust fund intended to benefit the cultural life of Ireland. Its stated purpose was both ambitiously specific – 'the bringing of the masterpieces of fine art within the reach of the Irish people of all classes' – and gratuitously vague – 'the teaching, promotion and encouragement in Ireland of self control, elocution, oratory, deportment, the arts of personal contact, of social intercourse, and the other arts of public, private, professional and business life'. This was to include something to which she had devoted much of her life – the endowment of university work.[81] But the phrasing of her benevolent intentions could have been more judicious. 'Mrs Shaw's Will annoys New York,' was one newspaper headline. A religious seismologist said, 'The Irish have always paid strict attention to the will of God, but they are not apt to pay much attention to the will of Mrs. George Bernard Shaw.' A Philadelphian even addressed a verse 'To Mrs GBS in Heaven': 'We Irish need manners? – the best of us/ And even the worst – cannot see/Why you should be judging the rest of us/ By what you observed in G.B.'[82]

Haunted by the inequities of wifehood even after death, Charlotte Shaw will remain, like her correspondent, Lawrence of Arabia, an enigmatic figure. But the story of her life will almost certainly endure as a classic example of how women's experiences and achievements can so easily sink into the sediment of marriage.

4

Jeannette Tawney

1880–1958

Annette Jeanie Beveridge, known as Jeannette, spent 49 of her 78 years married to the socialist historian Richard Henry Tawney. It's this marital persona that is remembered in the history and biography of the period; indeed, as the Labour MP Lena Jeger observed, Jeannette suffered from being taken as either Tawney's wife or William Beveridge's sister, or both. One historian even confuses the two, making her Tawney's sister and Beveridge's wife.[1] Such a mistake is perhaps to be expected in an *oeuvre* that pays so little attention to women's individual identity and agency.

Of the four women in this book, Jeannette Tawney is the one with whom I have had the closest personal connection. Although she died when I was 14, and I don't remember meeting her, her husband was a regular visitor to my childhood home. He and my father, Richard Titmuss, belonged to the same tradition of ethical socialism, and they shared the same post-mortem insignia of being seen as 'saints' who contributed much to Labour Party policy. Harry Tawney, as he was known, was old when I knew him, and immensely shabby – a more or less permanent characteristic, for which his wife never forgave him – and surrounded by a cloud of coltsfoot tobacco, another cause of marital disharmony. On the occasion of Tawney's 80th birthday, my father was enlisted to help write a celebratory pamphlet: 'We have said nothing about his wife. I do not think we should,' he noted in the correspondence with the editor.[2] Richard Titmuss transmitted his dismissive opinion of Jeannette Tawney to the more uniformly negative of the two existing full-length R.H. Tawney biographies: Ross Terrill's *R.H. Tawney and His Times: Socialism as Fellowship* (1974). Titmuss gave Terrill information about the Tawneys, and he read the manuscript of the biography and enthusiastically promoted its publication. He also sent some of the chapters with a strong recommendation to José Harris, William Beveridge's biographer, who repeats Terrill's negative evaluation of Jeannette in her own text.[3] These surreptitious pathways by which one person's evaluation colours others can have a major influence.

My mother, Kay Titmuss, was also dismissive about Jeannette as a poor housekeeper and a general hindrance to Tawney. These opinions echoed what I discovered, when doing the research for this book, to be the dominant characterisation of Jeannette Tawney in the biography and hagiography describing her husband's life and works. Jeannette's household arrangements were 'chaotic', condemning them both to a 'cult of squalor' and untidiness. The house was a mess, and their rural retreat was a complete tip because of her 'impulsive, distracted ways'. She emptied tea leaves into a stockpot, wore sprouting second-hand hats and clothes of colours that clashed like fighting cats. Her second great failing was her 'stunning extravagance': she wasted money on expensive trifles, threatening to impoverish her hard-working husband, and she drew heavily on her brother's generosity.[4] Tawney wrote a book called *The Acquisitive Society*, said the left-wing journalist Kingsley Martin in a much-cited remark, and Mrs Tawney illustrated it perfectly. Added to this was her constant ill-health, an invalidism and hypochondria of impressive proportions, which interfered with her husband's health, finances, and ability to work. She had, in short, hardly anything to recommend her (although the biographers do agree that she was loyal to Tawney and he did appear to be fond of her).

This is forgetting of a particular kind. It's not simply the refusal to look at what a wife as a separate individual did, thought and felt – because she is always eclipsed by the looming figure of her husband – but condemnation of her for not fitting a highly gendered stereotype. The view that was dominant in Jeannette Tawney's lifetime in Anglo-centric middle-class circles was of women as ideally uncomplaining, frugal housekeepers and devoted full-time carers of their husbands. Jeannette Tawney is not forgotten in the same way as Charlotte Shaw, Mary Booth and Janet Beveridge: she is remembered, even celebrated, for her derogation of wifehood.

In my childhood I saw Harry Tawney in the home he had shared with Jeannette for many decades in central London. 'By some good chance,' Jeannette wrote once of Mecklenburgh Square in Bloomsbury, 'sunrises exist in fact in this Square; a path has been left through the house-tops for the golden rays, here in the very heart of the metropolis is a silence so complete as to be audible. There is an atmosphere of past and present.'[5] It was a place she loved, walking round it on her husband's arm as she aged, remembering no doubt some of the many conversations that had taken place there with Harry's colleagues in the Workers' Educational Association, or in the LSE, and the sparring notes of all the young men and women in the labour movement, as she loved to entertain, despite the mess that accompanied Tawney wherever he was, and she loved showing off her cooking and her latest fashion in dress, and exchanging comments in German with Tawney on the mistaken premise that no one else would understand.

Getting inside the Tawneys' marriage

One thing no-one else did appear to understand was the texture of their relationship. In order to do this, one needs to envisage both Jeannette and Harry Tawney as separate personalities with histories, tastes, skills and inclinations all their own. As well as the two full-length biographies of Harry Tawney, there's a lengthy article in the *Oxford Dictionary of National Biography* (ODNB), and at least eight PhD theses,[6] besides many other accounts of his life and work. Jeannette enjoyed fleeting moments of media attention in her lifetime, but, apart from these and a few obituaries, there's no other published biographical memorial. How do you commemorate a wife who didn't appear to behave as wives were supposed to, and yet did nothing really salacious or shocking, and, although proud of what she did achieve beyond the domestic sphere, was never one to boast about what she did? Was she someone who, indeed, probably suffered from a chronic lack of self-confidence, nurtured partly by the lack of serious regard in which she was held by those around her? Fortunately for anyone who wishes to probe behind the conventional wisdom about Jeannette Tawney, a wealth of information about her is stored in the LSE archives. In correspondence with her husband, her parents, other family, and friends, in multiple drafts of fiction and autobiography, in records of housing, finances and legal matters, in faded black and white photographs, it is possible that the real Jeannette Tawney can be made to stand up.

A colonial childhood

As William Beveridge's sister, Jeannette shared a childhood with him, and the heritage of two upper-middle-class parents who spent many of their active years in the service of the British Empire in India. Jeannette and William's father, Henry Beveridge, joined the Indian Civil Service at the age of 21 in 1857. William wrote a book about their parents for which Jeannette supplied the title, *India Called Them*. Jeannette left her own account – well, several of them, as she wrote it up both as fiction and as semi-autobiography, under the stern guiding hand of the novelist Margaret Storm Jameson, who thought her a natural born writer, albeit one who needed steering in the right direction.

It's quite a remarkable story, the meeting of William and Jeannette Beveridge's parents, and it tells us something about the intersections of upper-middle-class femininity and 19th-century colonialism. The Beveridges' mother Annette Akroyd, a not-quite-so-young-woman of 29 in 1872, took a boat from Gravesend to India in order to open a school for the education of Hindu women. The local paper back in England, *The Brierley Hill Advertiser*, carried a headline about Miss Akroyd's 'school for Hindoo ladies', which taught a range of subjects from arithmetic to needlework 'on principles of the strictest theological neutrality', giving great attention to training 'in practical housework, and to the formation of orderly and industrious habits'.[7] Such an adventure was not all that unusual at the time among unmarried upper- and middle-class governesses and teachers in Britain. Jeannette's mother was an independent and feisty woman, one who had enjoyed some of the limited higher education then available to women at Bedford College in the early 1860s, and who, like many, had found the life of an idle unmarried woman stultifying. She had volunteered to teach in the College for Working Women in London, and enlisted in the movement for women's emancipation, and then was much taken by the proselytising of a handsome Indian philosopher called Keshub Chandra Sen who toured cities in England and Scotland in 1870 talking about problems of social reform and morality. Sen was especially keen on the importance to the moral fabric of society of women's contribution, who needed for this an appropriate education. Annette, whose flair for languages would lead her in middle age to pick up Persian and eastern Turkish and become a noted Oriental studies scholar, took lessons in Bengali and a course for governesses at the Home and Colonial School Society to prepare herself for her Indian project.

Annette's cabin companion on the boat to Calcutta was a Mrs Goldie who was travelling to visit her pregnant daughter in the swamps of eastern Bengal. Thus Annette Akroyd was led to Henry Beveridge. He was Mrs Goldie's son-in-law. He had married his first schoolgirl wife, Jeanie Goldie, Mrs Goldie's daughter, on his first furlough from India, and, soon after Annette and Mrs Goldie arrived in Calcutta in 1872, Jeanie and her baby both died. In the aftermath of this disaster, Henry and Annette got to know one another, with Henry providing much-needed support for Annette's educational experiment, although not enough to make it a success. In 1875, she left it all behind and married him: 'They were married, these two, the widower and the college woman without wedding bells or cake, at the Calcutta Registry Office,' recorded her daughter, adding that no 'white resident' had previously patronised this Office.[8]

Will and Tutu, as William and Jeannette were called, were the middle two children of the four to whom Annette gave birth in India. In childhoods constantly riddled with fevers, dysentery and various battles with death, two children did actually die, although not in India but in Eastbourne during the family's recurrent returns to England: Will and Tutu's baby brother, Herman, at the age of five in 1890, having been brain-damaged at birth, and their sister, Laetitia, of undiagnosed appendicitis at the age of 15 in 1893. Letty had been the Beveridge parents' first jewel, and neither Will nor Tutu would measure up, although Will had all Letty's brains and more. Jeannette had neither brains nor virtue: 'I had instead red-golden curls of the type associated with fast females, and an impish expression that I knew how to exploit from birth.' Her parents named her Annette Jeanie Beveridge, with one forename from each of her father's two wives, possibly a rather weighty emotional inheritance. 'My father's first wife, whom it was faintly hoped that I might a little re-incarnate if I were called after her,' wrote Jeannette, 'was religious, pretty, demonstrative and adoring. All the qualities she possessed my Father thought desirable in the trousseau of young wives. He must have sadly grieved that I did not develop as I might have done.'[9]

Jeannette's mother had already by the time of her marriage shown herself to be a different species of woman. Jeannette admired her 'masculine mind', which gave her 'an executive quality' that wasn't always easy to live with,[10] but was much needed in the effective management of the complex imperial life – not just the constant crossings between India and England, not just the children and the husband and the unavoidable dangers of the tropical life, but all the financial and practical arrangements of a colonial household containing as many as 39 servants, who together performed the functions the Beveridges' son would later assign to the welfare state. William

Beveridge is clear in *India Called Them* that his mother was an executive administrator rather than a housewife: 'She had a pen in her hands far more often than a frying-pan or a needle.'[11]

Jeannette Tawney, then, inherited two different models of wifehood from her father's two wives. She herself was very undecided about the whole issue of wifehood, and this vacillation is probably the most marked aspect of her correspondence with Harry both before and during their marriage. Her education was a mixture of conventionally gendered and less so: sent to England at the age of four with Will and Letty and their German 'Fraülein', she attended first a boys' school run 'by a middle-aged lady of mediocre proportions'; she then spent periods living with 'a General's family' and with her own in the country where her father taught her Latin, English literature and history, and she studied mathematics with a rector, which enabled her to scrape through London matriculation (the examination for university entry) at the age of 16. She attended a ladies' college in Eastbourne, leaving authorial traces in its school magazine, most notably an account of her travels in Italy and Switzerland with Will in the early 1900s: they climbed Monte Mottarone from Laveno on Lake Maggiore, found Lugano 'the dearest place', and much enjoyed the delightful drive from Chiavenna up to the Engadine valley, a place of retreat for many British upper-middle-class families at the time.[12] After the death of their brother and sister, Will and Tutu had drawn closer. They shared the climbing holidays, and he was also her protector and confidant, a role which could sometimes bring him into conflict with Harry Tawney.

It was in many ways a childhood typical of many upper-middle-class families of the period, but it wasn't without incidents that would call for some attention today. When she was a little girl, around five years old, Jeannette's father beat her for lying about the fact that she was eating bread and butter with jam, which was forbidden (you were allowed either butter or jam, but not both together). 'Without further delay I find myself in the night nursery … My position like my world has been inverted. I see only the floor. Then my panties are pulled down, my fat-padded behind lies bare to my Father's gaze. On to it descends one hard flat object with force … There is no sound from either of us. I do not flinch … Then I find myself pushed unceremoniously into bed.' Later, as a teenager, there was an experiment in self-harming with a broken tooth tumbler in her mother's bedroom. 'I desired to ascertain whether I were capable of causing myself bodily harm deliberately and for no other purpose but this of causing pain. I found myself acting under a compulsion that still seems to me inexplicable. I picked up the broken pieces of the glass.

I pressed it hard into my padded thumb until the blood spurted over my wounding hand. It was almost a loathing that I felt for the hand that had hurt me.'[13] These incidents occurred before the language of child abuse and self-harm had been invented, but they may well have signalled something important for Jeannette's adult identity.

When Jeannette was 13 in 1893 the Beveridge family bought a house in Surrey called Pitfold in Shottermill near Hindhead, 'a happily placed little house', although it wasn't so little, boasting two vine-houses with fine grapes, a barn which acted as a billiard and dancing room, and ten acres of land.[14] 'Pitfold' as an address features prominently in the Tawneys' correspondence and it was a place where Jeannette as an adult spent a good deal of time. The photo at the top of page 118 shows Jeannette and her brother William Beveridge side by side on what is presumably the Pitfold lawn, before her marriage and his fame. Hindhead, renamed 'Mindhead' by locals because of the number of intellectuals who gathered there, was the highest village in Surrey in an area classified as of Outstanding Natural Beauty.[15] George Eliot wrote most of *Middlemarch* there, Tennyson lived nearby, and Arthur Conan Doyle, the creator of Sherlock Holmes, chose its therapeutic climate for his sick wife. The novelist Grant Allen built himself a villa almost on the summit of Hindhead where he wrote *The Woman Who Did*, a novel which shocked Victorian morals with its sympathetic portrayal of a Girton-educated woman who rejected marriage in favour of cohabitation and motherhood. Allen befriended the young Jeannette Beveridge, but warned her not to read his books. The writer and Bloomsburyite Frances Partridge whose family lived in the area, recalled that all these 'first colonists' were seen as very eccentric and consumed by 'advanced ideas': she remembered the Beveridges' 'terrifying old mother' pointing a large ear-trumpet at every visitor.[16]

Then there was the Shaw connection, a serendipitous link between two of the case studies in this book. In the summer of 1898, when Jeannette was 18, the Beveridge parents followed a common Hindhead custom in deciding to let their house furnished and go for a change elsewhere. The prospective tenant was one Miss Payne-Townshend who, when all the arrangements had been made, 'admitted gracefully that she planned to take up the tenancy as Mrs. Bernard Shaw'.[17] Pitfold was thus where Charlotte Payne-Townshend and George Bernard Shaw spent their honeymoon. 'He and my Mother had heated arguments', recalled Jeannette. 'My Mother thought him a presumptuous, impertinent and very untidy young man.' Annette wasn't at all mollified when GBS inscribed a copy of his *The Perfect*

Wagnerite to her as 'perhaps the cleverest lady and the wickedest in her opinions that I have ever met' (she never forgave the 'perhaps'). In response, Henry Beveridge burnt a copy of Shaw's *Candida* under a copper beech on the Pitfold lawn. Later, as an Oxford undergraduate, Jeannette accompanied a group of friends to hear GBS speak. 'We went, most of us, to scoff. Some of us certainly came away humbled and resolute to challenge English hypocrisy.'[18] Pitfold's appropriately radical connections were resuscitated in 1924 when Jeannette's brother was Director of LSE. William Beveridge wrote to Sidney Webb, who had himself, with Beatrice, just bought Passfield Corner four miles from Hindhead, offering Pitfold as a country retreat for LSE staff and students. It would be a perfect place, he declared. The offer was declined. William never forgot the Shaw connection. After Jeannette died he wrote to Harry Tawney to inquire about the whereabouts of the book GBS had inscribed: 'I think I am the natural person to have such a book now.'[19] Unfortunately, Jeannette had sold it.

At the age of 16, Jeannette Beveridge was dispatched to a finishing school on the slopes of Lake Geneva in Switzerland, which charged exorbitant fees preparing girls for the London season. Girls 'of good family' were taught modern languages, music, singing, painting and drawing, and 'plain and fancy needlework'. 'It professed many things, did some of them, and failed to do more,' was Jeannette's estimation.[20] There she contracted the first of many serious illnesses, osteomyelitis, and was removed to a beautiful room with a view of the lake. Returning to England at 18, she found herself, like her mother, 'dissatisfied with a life of ease and comparative happiness'.[21] For a while she studied singing with the reputed Austrian lieder singer Marie Fillunger, and then in 1899 she joined Will at Oxford, to achieve a second-class degree in French, at Somerville College. Her presence in Oxford improved Will's life enormously. Jeannette was an excellent organiser of parties in his rooms, and on the river in punts, and she escorted him to commemoration balls, and she took care of his laundry. William Beveridge's biographer describes Jeannette at this time as 'a plump, fair, striking girl with an insatiable "appetite for seeing new things" – a good-natured scatterbrain with none of her brother's intensity or desire to change society'.[22] Throughout her life she excelled at having fun, a trait that biographers seem oddly to hold against her.

Being useful to others

'I was suffering from the adolescent urge to do something for someone,'[23] admits Jeannette of her teenage years. Some of Pitfold's radical connections did enable her to spread her wings. There was a keen social worker who knew Canon Barnett's work at Toynbee Hall, who encouraged Jeannette to think of earning her own living, and there was an 'odd little factory' in the village where factory legislation was disregarded and factory girls were paid miserly wages for 60 hours' work a week making the wick for candles and gold braid for military uniforms. In 1903, as a diversion from the tedium of typing her father's manuscripts, Jeannette started a club for the factory girls. She served as a self-appointed liaison officer between the workers and the factory inspectorate. The best case she helped to win was that of the young blouse machinist who accidentally ruined a blouse and had three weeks' wages deducted, which was in contravention of the Truck Acts (legislation which outlawed the practice of paying wages in the form of goods or tokens to be exchanged at employers' shops). 'We are going to teach them dancing and possibly later on morals,' she wrote to Harry about her club.' Will wants me to emigrate them [send them abroad], but I am so fond of them already that I don't feel at all inclined to do so.' Who the 'we' refers to isn't clear, but there was an active Mothers' Union in Shottermill and also a local suffrage association. In her fictionalised autobiography *A Learner's Life* Jeannette tells a story of how she opposed a motion at a Mother's Union meeting that divorce facilities should not be liberalised, submitting evidence to the effect that the poor deserved an equal chance to the rich. It was possibly with this same group that she embarked on a programme of ambitious reading. They studied The Fiscal Question, poring over official statistics and reading Adam Smith together, 'a society of us very select and only ladies, we bother all visitors with questions until they are glad to go away, and we feel we are doing our country good by going to the root of the matter and trying to lead the men in the right path'.[24] Jeannette worked directly for the suffrage movement and called herself a feminist. A main contact was Maude Royden, a theologian, pacifist and suffragist, the first woman to preach in an Anglican church, who was training women as speakers for The Cause. 'Our training was severe. Out of a roomful, any one of us was liable to be called upon to reply, audibly, clearly and tersely to a typical heckler's interjection.'[25] Jeannette herself, practising this art, was at least once moved on by a policeman for being an obstruction on the public highway.

At some point during these years, probably when she was an Oxford undergraduate, Jeannette did what young middle-class women from socially conscious families were prone to do, and she spent some time in a women's settlement. The one she chose was the Women's University Settlement in Blackfriars, with which Somerville had a link. Jeannette wrote to her mother at length about her experience, probably relieved to have something substantive to talk about for a change: 'I have now something to tell you that may interest you. I will recount my doings since my arrival ... The 16 ladies who live here seem all to have their respective work with the C.O.S. [Charity Organisation Society] & my first morning was spent in discovering & then inquiring of an old man his family history generally. It was very interesting & I was much surprised in his telling me – an entire stranger – his whole family affairs. His case was settled in the afternoon by the C.O.S. Committee & it was decided that with 10 children all earning money <u>some</u> ought to contribute towards his modest needs. He was such a nice old man. Then I spent the afternoon in writing luggage labels to be tied on to children going to the country. This morning I saw the children & after impressing it strongly on their minds to come punctually on the day assisted at their medical examinations. I felt most ignorant & when appealed to consider a certain child was at a loss what to say but felt sure – so I said – that a change would do him good. This seems to please parents & those interested in the children so I have adopted it as an answer to most questions concerning children.' After this she was sent to find four children who hadn't turned up for their medical examinations. 'I wandered among all sorts of back slums & into some very quaint old courts & alleys. I assure you it was most instructive ... It is certainly the best way to come & stay in the Settlement & to understand how things are done. I have been pleasantly surprised in finding the poorest people ever so civil when one asks the way or anything.'[26]

Marriage as a profession for women

'When academic successes are not forthcoming,' mused Jeannette in one of her many penetrating reflections on the institution of marriage, 'a female's direction seems to point to matrimony. Though this is indisputably the most difficult known profession, it has a surprising popularity. If statistics of broken contracts in it, as compared with other employment, were available, there would be a heavy percentage of failures to its discredit.'[27] It was obvious that, given her class and generation, she ought to marry. There were several suitors, and then there was Harry Tawney. He came on the scene sometime during Jeannette's Oxford years, probably in 1899, when she was 19. He was a close friend of Will's at Balliol, and after Oxford the two men did what more than a few Oxbridge men of the period did in going to live at the Barnetts' Toynbee Hall Settlement in East London.

Will was sub-warden and Harry was in charge of an outfit called the Children's Country Holidays Fund (CCHF), which had been started by Henrietta and Samuel Barnett in 1884 to arrange rural holidays for the children of London slums. (It still exists today.) Under the influence of Will or Harry, or perhaps it was even her own idea – the biographical commentaries are notable for stripping Jeannette of any agency in this and other matters – she applied for the secretaryship of the CCHF. This carried a stipend of £150 a year and turned her into a professional woman. She revelled in, 'the sense of expansion that independence brings'.[28] The job involved inspecting homes to which deserving children would be exported for an annual fortnight's holiday, and this entailed much travelling and interviewing. She lived with Will in his flat in South London and worked from the CCHF office in the Strand. It was a welcome change from typing for her father.

Common interests, running from the philosopher Spinoza to dogs, were what first attracted Jeannette Beveridge to Harry Tawney. According to the storyline of the 'fictional' *A Learner's Life*, his first act of courtship was to procure two tickets for a Bach Passion at St Paul's Cathedral. When they met again by chance one day on the Embankment, 'The gulls screeched to the screams of the trams that round the bend from the Kingsway tunnel. The water lapped the stone parapet idly and regularly ... No words came to them. They gazed into each other's eyes as though rehearsing Tristan and Isolde after the love potion has been taken.' She thought about her busy life, dashing about the country 'putting people right' and reporting their habits to groups of other people, and hurrying home at weekends to resent 'the obligations to be pleasant that parents require.' 'I had read little, and grown less,' she considered. 'Suddenly the adventure which I was asked to share became the one and only thing worthwhile. In it I saw a purpose, a fulfilment.'[29]

It took a tortuous nine years before they married. This period generated a rich correspondence enabling us to see (if we care to look) something of how these two individuals related to one another and what they each hoped to get out of life and marriage.

Harry Tawney, the socialist saint

Who, actually, was Richard Henry Tawney, this man who caused Jeannette Beveridge to be either castigated or forgotten? His writing and teaching united the moral principles of socialism and Christianity, and injected a heavy dose of ethics into Labour Party policy in the interwar years. By the time of his death, four years after Jeannette in

1962, Harry Tawney was 'practically canonised'; he was 'a socialist saint', 'the patron saint of twentieth century British socialism'. The Labour Party Leader, Hugh Gaitskell, called him simply 'the best person he had ever known'.[30] Tawney campaigned against the advantages and privileges of a social elite, condemned capitalism for its inegalitarianism and emphasis on material production and acquisition, and saw a practical socialism as an ethical duty. He argued for free education for all, and for an extended state role in the provision of social services. He was a member of the post-First World War's Ministry of Reconstruction's Adult Education Committee and largely wrote its report on the future development of adult education; he contributed to the Hadow Report, which laid down the principles embodied in the 1944 Education Act establishing free secondary education for all. Tawney's research and thinking about social class, equality, capitalism, religion and morality inspired his three most famous books: *The Acquisitive Society* (1920), *Religion and the Rise of Capitalism* (1926), and *Equality* (1931). These widely-read treatises represented significant milestones in the development of socialist thought and policy in Britain.

Like Jeannette Beveridge, Harry Tawney was born in India and in the same year as she was. He was one of eight children in a family dominated by their father's work in the Indian educational service. Tawney had a conventional gentlemanly education at a public school and Balliol College, Oxford. A close friend at Rugby school was William Temple, a future Archbishop of Canterbury who would later officiate at Harry and Jeannette's marriage. Harry's friendship with William Beveridge at Balliol provided a platform for the two men to have earnest discussions about social questions. Both at school and at Oxford Tawney was effortlessly a member of the late Victorian intellectual aristocracy. His post with the CCHF at Toynbee Hall was not an obvious career choice for a Balliol man, but it followed the disappointing result of a second-class degree (Jeannette used to embarrass her husband by remarking that this second-class degree was something the two of them had in common). At Toynbee Hall Tawney joined Beveridge in giving evening lectures on social and industrial questions. In 1906 he moved to the economics department at Glasgow University where he took up the craft of social investigation in order to study the education of working-class boys. By then he had discovered socialism and the Workers' Educational Association (WEA), two commitments he maintained for the rest of his life.

In 1908, when Harry Tawney was still negotiating the prospect of marriage to Jeannette, he was teaching adult education in Oxford, and beginning his first economic history book, *The Agrarian Problem in the Sixteenth Century* (1912). When the First World War began, he enlisted in the army, but, in line with his egalitarian principles, declined a commission, preferring the status of an ordinary sergeant. He was wounded severely by machine gun bullets at Fricourt on the first day of the Somme offensive in July, 1916, and cared for ably by Jeannette. When he recovered, he returned to his work for the WEA and for social reconstruction. This was funded partly by Charles Booth's businessman son George, at the request of a mutual friend.[31] From 1923, Harry Tawney's academic base was the LSE, where he became Professor of Economic History in 1931, enjoying a creative collaboration with another pioneering economic historian of the period, Eileen Power, a clever and elegant woman who also lived in Mecklenburgh Square and with whom he may or may not have had an intimate relationship.[32] It is interesting how often men's alliances with intellectual women are suspected of being primarily physical affairs – it's as though the women's brains can't possibly be enough.

Stories about marriage

At least three different versions of the Tawneys' marriage are available to us. The first, most accessible, one is the account rendered in the Harry Tawney biographies. The second and third are hers and his respectively, and these can only be reached, and then only partially, through the remaining archives.

'The marriage was always known to have been a difficult one,' says Lawrence Goldman, 'with the suggestion that Tawney was unfulfilled in it.' Goldman fleshes this statement out in his ODNB entry for Tawney: 'there were no children; Jeannette was often ill; her behaviour could be eccentric; and her disorganisation coupled to Tawney's untidiness rendered home life chaotic.'[33] According to Ross Terrill, Jeannette, 'hardly a distinguished woman' was a trial to Tawney.[34] 'Many of Tawney's friends regarded her as a liability rather than an asset,' says Dahrendorf in his history of LSE, 'and not just because she did so much of the talking in their untidy London household and the positive slum of a cottage in the Cotswolds.'[35] We are quickly returned to the theme of bad housewifery as proof of the bad marriage: 'Jeannette was not a housewife to go scrubbing in every corner,' offers Terrill. In addition, Jeannette was prone to trivial upper-middle-class anxieties: bother with servants, jewellery matters, where to store things, complications due to having two homes. These characteristics, combined with her financial extravagance, must surely, so these appraisals declare, have had a detrimental impact on Tawney's own health and work routines. Further, Jeannette's attachment to upper-middle-class ways would have interfered with something that was crucial to Tawney – opportunities for interacting with working-class people and intellectuals. Damning with faint praise, Terrill notes her kindness, loyalty to Tawney, and commitment to good causes, but condemns the latter as a 'do-goodism' of the 'paternalistic, individualistic, drawing-room kind'. There was 'something inconsequential about her flailing intelligence ... Scraps of fact she had, but her chatter seemed to hang suspended in the air like a feather without source or destination.'[36] Goldman withdraws from Terrill's uncompromising position somewhat, deciding that the problems of the Tawneys' marriage can't simply be blamed on her. Tawney did carry some responsibility; he chose to marry her. Goldman is quick to reassure his readers that this revised assessment in no way undermines Tawney as a public figure. He was just much more suited to education and politics than to matrimony, and 'the reasons for his ineptitude with Jeanette [sic] and with women more generally can probably be traced to his upbringing and early institutionalisation as much as anything else.'[37] We can, it seems, forgive him, but nothing about her background can exonerate her. In a later comment, Goldman is kinder to Jeannette, calling her a 'witty, funny, gay, charming young woman' who made a 'fatal error' in marrying Tawney.[38]

A different view of Jeannette's contribution to the marriage can be glimpsed in some of her obituaries. Here is an extract from one written by 'a younger kinswoman': 'To stay at the Tawneys' cottage near Stroud was an adventure of enchantment. [Jeannette] was creative in all her attitudes and attachments, but as an amateur refreshingly curious to learn more about the life of human beings, and always ready to praise and encourage what was genuine and charming, however unconventional it might be. It gave her as much pleasure to give a good cup of tea to the postman when he called at Rose Cottage on his early morning round as to the European or American savant in the drawing room at Mecklenburgh Square. ... She needed to live in a certain kind of ample disorder, as many artists do, from which the individual discipline can emerge ... The many illnesses, gallantly borne, interrupted any consecutive academic work of her own.'[39]

Arguing about marriage: gender, power, class and dirt

Harry Tawney and Jeannette Beveridge's prolonged courtship had gone like this: he pursued her; she rejected him; then she wasn't sure; he held on; her parents objected (which made her sure); finally, obstacles and objections were sufficiently diluted to allow a marriage to take place. Their correspondence, and that of other family members, is uniquely instructive about the requirements of Edwardian marriage as an institution, and about the yawning gender gap in the expectations applied to husband and wife.

The courtship years were dragged out for three main reasons. First of all, Jeannette was ambivalent about marriage. Second, she wasn't sure she wanted to marry *him*. And third, there was her parents' (particularly her mother's) resistance to the idea of their daughter marrying an impecunious socialist with a foul temper. There is widespread agreement about Harry's temper. About the wisdom of the marriage generally, Harry's father Charles joined the fray, counselling his son to understand Mrs Beveridge's point of view: 'I do to a certain limited extent, sympathize with the feelings of Mrs Beveridge. Mothers suppose that they have a kind of property in their daughters ... The position is an anxious one for a mother.'[40] Of great parental concern on both sides was Tawney's insufficient and insecure income as a lecturer and writer, which contrasted with the substantial financial settlement Annette proposed to bestow on Jeannette when she married. While Annette also worried that Harry wouldn't make her daughter happy, her son William's concern was the opposite of this: would Jeannette make his friend happy? William checked out Harry's health and his family medical history and joined his own plea to the chorus that filled the Pitfold air in the months before the marriage. 'I hope you will at least read what I have to say,' he wrote to his mother in the summer of 1908. 'You have not a pair of children to deal with but a pair of absolutely determined grown people. The parents cannot surely under such circumstances refuse assent because of their personal likes or dislikes.' Harry was a man of 'unimpeachable character' and 'great abilities', quite Jeannette's equal in standing and education, maintained William.[41]

For his part, Harry Tawney seems to have been absolutely determined right from the beginning to marry Jeannette. Writing from Toynbee Hall in the summer of 1900, he laid out his position: 'My dearest Jeannette, You don't mind my writing to you, do you? I know you said you wanted to be left alone ... What has been in my mind is something like this. I don't want you on any account to feel that I am waiting and expect you to make up your mind. I'm not ... I intend with the help of God to win your love sooner or later, if not now, next year, and if not next year, then the year after ... My love for you is not a fancy or an infatuation, but much stronger and more permanent than anything else in me. In spite of my folly, I believe that I could help you to be happy and your real self, for I love you and not your virtue or your cleverness or anything else, and I know that by being with you I am made more like what I wish to be ... I know I seem hard and flippant, and incapable of sympathy or tenderness, and I cannot expect you to think me other than I seem.'[42] This theme of her making him a better man is a recurrent one. R.H. Tawney, renowned throughout the world for injecting socialism into Christianity, admitted that he didn't know the meaning of charity until he met Jeannette Beveridge: 'You showed me ... that it is worthwhile to try and see people from their point of view, instead of only from my own, and by showing me that you have opened a new world to me'.[43]

Part of the attraction of this new world was that she had talents that could help him in his work: 'I also want you because I believe you will make me a better and more effective man in my work and all that belongs to it. You've got lots of ideas I haven't, and I shall steal them freely. I shall make you translate German & French books to me (I've got an enormous work called "Zwei Bücher zue Soziale Geschichte Englands" by a German called Adolphe Held which came yesterday & [with] which I want your help): and also accompany me when I go making inquiries from people who kick me downstairs. So you see you're going to be what my friends call "a wage-slave" – only there won't be any wages. Dear me, what nonsense all this sounds. Or rather it's not nonsense, for I want us to work together as well as live together, and to help each other as well as love each other.'[44]

Tawney's view of marriage was a mixture of misogyny and enlightenment. He wanted a partnership, like that of his friends Beatrice and Sidney Webb, but it was a partnership for which the ground rules were to be laid out by him. Jeannette rebelled against this, feeling that she had more to offer, and that he should respect her point of view: 'A true socialist like yourself will think he can love a person who is an ordinary woman, perhaps but he'll find he can't,' she observed. 'You don't mean to make your loving me conditional on my caring for your work & Fabianism but you can't keep it I fear ... I do see more & more that you want a comrade in all your work. I shall be no good so I feel I ought to leave you free to give the "best part of you" to your "main interest in life i.e. Special work". You'd have more money & more time for your work if I were not there. Do you wish me to feel this I wonder?'[45] Other people wondered what Harry Tawney wanted women to feel. His remark about the suffrage, that 'women are all fools' and 'all women over 30 are damned fools', is dismissed by Lawrence Goldman in his biography as 'knockabout student stuff'.[46] Yet Harry Tawney's derogatory attitude to women was well known. After a weekend with the Tawneys, the social historian Barbara Hammond wrote to her husband Lawrence about Harry's 'perpetual grumpiness' and rudeness to Jeannette. His contempt for women disgusted her.[47] Eileen Power was apparently an exception to this rule.

The imbalance of power between Jeannette Beveridge and Harry Tawney was reflected in his patronising attitude towards her. In 1907, she was working in the Edinburgh offices of the Charity Organisation Society, an organisation much involved at the time in the move towards state-sponsored school meals. She was also apparently helping Harry with some survey or other, but the main focus of her letter, a recent argument, caused her to dismiss him (temporarily) from her life. 'It is not fair to assume that everyone you meet is more ignorant or even as ignorant as you yourself!' she told him bluntly. 'Also you should wish to help those who are less gifted by the gods to feel happy & at ease & not make them go away feeling crushed – (now you can realise how I felt on Monday!) … Surely it is hard to expect all people you meet to be [an] appreciative audience for your theories! & to make them feel you talk to them as a favour. Of course if they are clever enough to convince you they are interested (or really are) you like them. Otherwise you put them down as bores … Well as this will be my final communication with you as of course I am not worthy to correspond with a (would-be) cultured Oxford man, may I thank you for past services & wish you well.' The sting in the tail of this letter is characteristic of the strength of emotion Jeannette sometimes poured into her missives: 'Please write <u>Edinburgh</u> twenty times to get your eye familiar with the spelling as your brain seems unequal to the task.'[48]

Jeannette emerges from these letters as a strong-minded but also cultured and thoughtful person who reads widely and engages easily in literary and political debate. She was elegant and refined in appearance, as young women emerging from finishing schools were supposed to be (see the photo on page 118). Her letters were sprinkled with cultured references. For example, writing from Pitfold before their marriage: 'My dearest Harry, just a line to give you news of your fiancée, last night I had a very successful Club meeting & the girls were in high spirits as I tried to dance Quadrilles & failed hopelessly. I read Newman's poems on the way down but could not find anything very fine except the Dream of Gerontius which I admire … It's very much like Dante in the point of view about "The longing for Him, when thou seest him not …" Do you remember how Dante feels when he sees Beatrice?' She reads Seligman on marginal utility – perhaps

Undated, with her brother William Beveridge

Aged 29 in 1909

With her dog at Rose Cottage,
Elcombe, Gloucestershire, undated

With R. H. Tawney on the deck of the *Queen Elizabeth*, 1948

because Harry is — and Arnold Toynbee, and Forster's *Room With a View*, and Jean Paul Richter, and Rabelais and 'Miss Thackeray'.[49]

Harry Tawney was famous for his neglect of middle-class conventions in dress and appearance. He padded around both his untidy homes in an old khaki sergeant's jacket and carpet slippers, emptying his pipe into the cuff of his neglected tweed trousers. Bits of half-eaten food nestled among his books, and 'now and then a mouse would hop over the one to get at the other'.[50] Far from encouraging these habits, Jeannette found them tiresome. They were going to a wedding, and she wanted him to be appropriately — that is, conventionally — dressed. He refused, citing his egalitarian principles. 'The idea that one should wear a frock coat and top hat at a wedding is connected in my mind with the idea that one must be a "gentleman", and live in a suburb, and have afternoon tea parties, and always be careful about money, and never do anything adventurous for fear of shocking the insignificant number of middle class people who call themselves society and earn a pension, & send their children to a public school, and be respectful to Lords and never call a spade a spade!' In the same letter he thanks her for sending 'Mary Woolentincrafts [*sic*] book' — he will read it in bed tonight.[51] She is trying to educate him. Later, after they're married, and she is in Italy for her health, she asks him to send her Olive Schreiner's book, which she finds deeply interesting. She tells him in a letter something of what Schreiner says: 'I am writing all this to you as you have a way of using no knowledge you have & of not believing me when I talk about these things. Perhaps you will believe Olive Schreiner then.'[52]

Dirt and disorder are regular themes in physical descriptions of Harry Tawney and life both in Mecklenburgh Square and Rose Cottage, the Tawney's rural retreat in the Cotswolds. The latter was undoubtedly primitive, with no running water or electricity until the early 1950s, and thus no toilet — a patch of ground near the dwelling was apt to give off terrible odours. There were also two dogs, who were treated like members of the family. On page 119 Jeannette sits comfortably with one of them on what looks like a table with a collection of junk underneath. The Tawneys' friends who stayed there found the place charming but uncomfortable. Yet, contrary to a great deal of supposition, the inattention to hygiene and order in both homes had a great deal to do with Harry Tawney's own orientation to the material world. 'I am always amazed at the view, probably less common than it was,' he announced to Jeannette, in the midst of their premarital correspondence in 1905, 'which regards the man sphere in work away from home, and the woman's business to be his housekeeper. Why, if one lives in these terms, one loses one's wife almost as soon as one marries her: it must be at least as hateful for the man as I should have thought it would be for the woman, and it is ruination for the children if there are any … To personify ones happiness in a person is degrading to the person, and I believe it is the death of real love … There's one subject, my dear, on which I shall put my foot down, and that is springcleaning. When our flat gets dirty, we will take another flat.'[53]

Jeannette's walking holiday with Will in Switzerland in August and September 1908 provided much space for her meditations on the wisdom of marrying Harry Tawney, which she spelt out in letters to him. Most important is his desire to improve and shape her: 'You are so keen to educate me & develop me – I know that's a fine way of caring but I want you to be a little more satisfied with what you've got if you're to have it.'[54] The next day's letter is equally decisive: 'You know you really are bad at judging character. You had absolutely no idea of Mother's & I wonder if you have of mine. You are hopelessly unobservant … We aren't machines to make bread or babies to please our husbands. I feel as though the selfishness of men is really awful. They give in in so many trivial ways but they insist in others without giving any choice. So many married women have told me that marriage means altogether serfdom but that you love your chains because you love your husband. That I believe is how they mostly interpret the "obey" in the marriage service. I hope you don't because I shall refuse to say it.'[55]

Marriage and after

Did she say it? Richard Henry Tawney and Annette Jeanie Beveridge were married by 'a full Canon and an embryo Archbishop' – Samuel Barnett of Toynbee Hall and Harry's childhood friend William Temple – on 28 June 1909 at St Stephen's Church at Shottermill. Like all long relationships, theirs passed subsequently through different phases of confrontation and accommodation, some of which are signalled in the surviving documentary evidence. But one thing does stand out: there is genuine affection here, on both sides, and a willingness to turn what might have started out as an ill-matched union into one which gave them both much comfort and satisfaction.

Tawney's disregard for hygiene and convention continues to occupy Jeannette, as do the displays of temper. He can see that his temper is a problem for her: 'My Dearest Jeannette, I am sorry for writing you such a cross letter this morning. …I really do apologize for my ill temper,' he writes from his lodgings in Ship Street, Oxford, before they marry.[56] He is still apologising to her for this decades later: 'I'm so sorry I was snappy yesterday, but you know I never really mean it,' insists a letter from Mecklenburgh Square in 1939.[57] Later that year he is forced to apologise again: 'Just a line to give you my love, and to say how sorry I am for making you unhappy with my bad temper. It grieves me to think of it: I get at times so depressed, and then I take it out on you. Please say you forgive me.'[58]

Harry's poor standards of personal hygiene proved no easier to tolerate after the marriage than before it. Here is Jeannette, writing from Italy in 1911: 'I know you don't really mean to improve your dirty habits & I know too that I never can be quite happy with a man who despises cleanliness & doesn't care if he vexes me with regard to it or not ... I feel ashamed of going anywhere with you as I know you are always so slovenly & I know that people – rightly – judge a man's principles by his practice. It is rather absurd to keep preaching social reform & better conditions when you, possessing them, still prefer to be dirty ... I don't believe you realise how I look at these things & I don't see why I should be made to conform entirely to your way of life. You point out often that women should be free etc & yet you ask your wife to live with you when you are a regular slut!'[59] In the next day's letter she announces her decision: 'If you simply refuse to be clean & shave etc I just shall not sleep with you. I suppose you will assert that you have a claim upon me but I hold it to be technical cruelty to be as dirty as you are...!!'[60]

And despite his vision of comradeship, Harry was soon causing Jeannette to feel she was slipping into the conventional role of a dutiful wife at home. In 1912 she was in Gibraltar for her health, and he wrote to say he was missing her. But, she responded, 'When I'm at home you take me so much as a matter of course – like your plate of porridge – that I often think you'd never miss me! ... You know you really are the most undemonstrative of husbands. No one would think you cared two straws about me. ...Still it does warm me up to see from your letters that you really want to see me again.'[61] He tells her that it's no good looking back except to go forward better. She agrees. 'I do so want to make things go more smoothly & better. I believe in you entirely in all matters not domestic. I think your notion of sacrificing us both to our common work is quite right but I do not see why we should both be sacrificed to your badness! ... I feel ashamed of myself for doubting our future. Forgive me, darling, I am afraid I am rather a trial & I know how hard it has been for you to put up with me. In fact, I'm bitterly disappointed to find myself still so much of an invalid as I did so want to be quite well ... I am greatly interested in what you say about Tolstoy. At present I am reading Anna Karenina & am deeply interested in it but it makes me feel wretched, it's so depressing. There is a character Leonie in it who is Tolstoy himself. His efforts at cooperation with the peasants are sadly futile. Would you like to read Anna Karenina?'[62]

Jeannette Tawney's papers are in a state of chaos not unlike, perhaps, the descriptions given of her and Harry's domestic interiors. As with many archives, they contain mysterious trails and hints whose accordance with the facts of Jeannette's life remain uncertain. The trail is further complicated by her various autobiographical and fictional narratives, which it is tempting to read as fact. What should we make, for example, of the strange scrap of a poem addressed to Jeannette and written by the feminist activist and abortion law reformer F.W. Stella Browne, who was known to be catholic in her sexual tastes? Stella and Jeannette were at Somerville College, Oxford, together in 1899–1902, and 'Miss Browne' is mentioned in Jeannette's letters to her mother. The poem, called 'Remembrance' was written on 1 November, 1914, and the second verse runs as follows:

> Remembering you, I still take courage, dear,
> Athwart the clamorous darkness of this place
> My heart still hears your voice, & sees the face
> I used to know.
> Ah, store of sweetness, hoarded year by year,
> From long ago.[63]

This was a time when emotional intimacy could still form part of female friendships without inevitable accusations of lesbianism, and Stella Browne was given to generally effusive correspondence with a number of women. Jeannette Tawney was known to talk publicly about sex – another unwifely trait. Ross Terrill in his biography of Harry says she had an obsession with the subject; apparently she once turned to the American writer Pearl Buck in Nanking to ask, 'Your husband; he looks as if he must be a beast in bed; is he?'[64] Speculations about Tawney's 'inefficiency' at the sexual act are countermanded by the evidence of the letters that they did sleep together. But there are various signs that whatever happened in bed did not quite satisfy Jeannette. A line in Jeannette's novel *Restitution* has one of the main characters ask the question, 'Were the happiest marriages those where sex relationships play a very small part?'[65]

Another unsolved question concerns children. Did Jeannette and Harry remain childless by choice? She is concerned, even before they marry, that he will not care for her if she fails to become a mother. Joan Wells, in *Restitution*, is unable to have children, and the cameo in chapter 13 of that manuscript may well be drawn from Jeannette's own life: 'The marriage of these two minds had been incomplete. What the trouble was, remained obscure. Neither knew just why they did not feel to each other as they had hoped and intended, when they had held hands on the Embankment. Everything had been propitious socially, financially and physically. What was the trouble? Each had longed for a baby. Perhaps unconsciously this was the trouble. Neither had sufficient courage to tackle the situation.' Joan makes an appointment on the anniversary of their wedding day to see a famous gynaecologist. The doctor says pregnancy is impossible in her case, and suggests she adopt. He says he usually insists on seeing the man as well, but in her case 'it is so obvious that the fault lies with you; it is, therefore, unnecessary to ask your husband to submit to the unpleasantness of being over-hauled'.[66]

Helping Harry

The biographers' fascination with Jeannette Tawney as a bad housewife and a scatterbrained pathetic hypochondriac allows them to neglect any proper account of her accomplishments. It's important to say that these achievements *did* include actively helping her husband with his work. Beatrice Webb noticed this, applying to it perhaps a little of the same formula she and Sidney used in their own partnership. 'My Dear Mrs Tawney,' she wrote to Jeannette in the summer of 1933, 'I was so glad to get your letter and to hear that you are so much better and are able to help your husband with his historical work. That must be a great joy to both of you.'[67] Researching, typing, discussing – manifold acts of taken-for-granted wifely assistance – lie behind the formulaic statements buried in the prefaces to Tawney's masterpieces. For his *Agrarian History of the Sixteenth Century*, he credits two research assistants for their help, and also his wife 'who has collaborated with me throughout'.[68] Thirteen years later she is thanked for contributing to his research on the puritans for *Religion and the Rise of Capitalism*. At this point Tawney declares that 'My obligation to the help given by my wife is beyond acknowledgment.'[69] Poignantly, and in the fictional guise of FloraNetta Smith in *A Learner's Life*, Jeannette reflects on the 'so-called intellectual pursuit of assisting my husband in his research work. I enjoyed this very much,' she says, 'but was always conscious of the handicap that I was not the person who would ultimately write up the results.'[70] In the same category of taken-for-granted labour was all the organising of Tawney's life – the meals, the two houses, the travels, the filing of all his notes and work materials. Jeannette accompanied Harry on most of his travels and made all the arrangements for these, which included their stay at the British Embassy in Washington in 1941–42 and journeying to China by train across Siberia in 1930. He depended on her to sort it all out. Anticipating a lecturing trip to Chicago early in 1939, for example, he asks her whether their boat will arrive in time for his first lecture, and does she have both the passports – he has forgotten where they are. One senses an aura of tight-lipped tiredness around Jeannette in the photo on page 119 as she stands next to Harry on the deck of the *Queen Elizabeth*, en route to the US in 1948, all arrangements made to his smiling satisfaction.

Jeannette as historian …

When she was not acting as Tawney's *aide-mémoire*, general assistant and domestic administrator, Jeannette was a factory inspector, a writer, a researcher and a serious historian. A volume called *A Bibliography of Female Economic Thought up to 1940* carries an entry for Jeannette Tawney, which includes an article she published in the *Economic Journal* in 1911 on 'Women and unemployment'. In its opening paragraph she asserts the problem: 'It is only within the last few years that public attention has been concentrated upon unemployment … As yet its special bearing upon women has been little considered or discussed; partly because of the preoccupation of Parliament with those who can voice their claims, and partly because of the prevalence of the old-fashioned notion that woman is exclusively a domestic animal – whether pet or drudge. In reality, of course, such a view is a survival from conditions existing before the industrial revolution took women's work from the home to the factory.' The article explores the extent of unemployment among women using three sources: figures for women registering at the Board of Trade Labour Exchanges; evidence given to the Royal Commission on the Poor Laws; and the returns collected by various Distress Committees. Jeannette concludes that a search for employment exists among women 'on a large scale, as among men': women and girls make up nearly one fifth of the total on the Board of Trade registers. Looking at the Royal Commission evidence, the special characteristics of women's unemployment 'come out with startling clearness' – very low wages, the prevalence of work in seasonal trades, the lack of trade union representation, the problem of childcare. Yet on a policy level, women's need for paid work is largely ignored. Serious attention needs to be given to these issues as well as to training, education and the relief of distress, she argues.[71]

As a historian, Jeannette also published a long article jointly with her husband in *The Economic History Review* in 1934 on 17th-century occupational statistics. At the time economic history was a relatively new branch of the subject, so Jeannette's work, along with Harry's, had a pioneering edge to it. Their article is recognised as 'an outstanding piece of scholarship'.[72] Of course it is impossible to tell from the label of a joint authorship who did exactly what (see Chapter 6); moreover, the Tawneys acknowledged the assistance of another social investigator, Mildred Bulkley, for help with the preparation of statistical material. Interestingly, Goldman's biography of Tawney doesn't mention this article. Terrill lists it as one of R.H. Tawney's publications ('with A.J. Tawney'), and he treats a pamphlet R.H. Tawney co-authored with Nettie Adler similarly, as one of Tawney's publications ('with N. Adler'). The Goldman biography calls Nettie 'Nathan'. These are small points, but they're indicative of a much larger problem. Similarly with the misspelling of names: 'Jeannette' is rendered as 'Jeanette' in the Goldman biography and by others.

The Tawneys' study analyses in painstaking detail data from a survey carried out in Gloucestershire in 1608 of men aged 20 to 60 who were fit to bear arms. These data (for 17,046 cases) enabled the Tawneys to get a handle on economic life in a prosperous part of England in the early 17th century. They were able to describe the proportions of people engaged in different occupations, and the relative numbers of employers, independent producers and wage workers, and could show that agriculture was less dominant than was usually supposed, employing only about half the adult male population. Most significantly, agriculture and industry were inextricably intertwined: 'Not only corn and cattle, but corn, wool and cloth, and even, in some districts, corn, coal and iron, were almost joint products.'[73] Many families were equally invested in farming and manufacturing, and, although a class of wage labourers was in the process of emerging, it had not yet really done so. Both this article and Jeannette's own on female unemployment display a real concern, shared by the Webbs and many of their circle, to root out the factual basis of the issues that occupied contemporary discussions about social questions.

Jeannette's independent editing of a volume of extracts from Richard Baxter's *Christian Directory* in 1925 is another omission from the Tawney biographies. Richard Baxter was an English Puritan Church leader, and his writings are said to have been a major inspiration for sociological treatises on Protestantism and capitalism, including those by Max Weber and Robert K. Merton. Jeannette's aim as editor was to bring out the economic ideas of a 17th-century Puritan, thus highlighting the survival in the 17th century of the medieval fusion of ethics and economics. The book delighted Harry Tawney's historian colleague at LSE, Eileen Power, and was said to deserve much wider recognition than it gained.

... and as social investigator

Buried in *A Learner's Life* is a glimpse of another career which Jeannette Beveridge might well have taken up, that of social investigator. In the early 1900s the problem of accommodation for 'vagrant females' was receiving considerable attention from women researchers such as Mary Higgs and Olive Malvery, both of whom used the strategy of covert ethnography to expose unsatisfactory social conditions.[74] Jeannette joined them in researching one particular lodging house for women. She describes what happened in *I Learn to Live*: 'In order further to investigate the place, an elementary school teacher and myself offered to dress like migrants and ask for a night's lodging … My companion merely impoverished her appearance. I … borrowed my husband's tweed fishing hat, and rammed it well down on my head after wetting my hair, thus giving me a hard stern look, almost a hungry one. I wore my Swiss hobnail boots and an ancient Burberry. Deliberately I had soiled my blouse but had forgotten to do the same to my underclothing, which was still of trousseau elegance … Our 4d bed tickets purchased, we were herded into a large mess-room of severe hygiene, in all particulars except that of the enamel cups. These were all chipped, some so badly that one feared adulteration from their use.' She suggested to her friend that the cups should be sterilised. 'My inept voicing of this pedantic word caught the ear of one of the women, who regarded us thereafter as objects of suspicion.' After a frugal meal Jeannette and her friend were escorted to an upstairs room with long benches and tables where they were further inspected by the inmates. One woman was friendly, and she gave them advice about how to get a job. She said, 'you'll never get a job with those dirty boots' and took Jeannette to the boot cleaning room, and then to the laundry room so she could wash her blouse. This meant that Jeannette had to strip off, thus revealing her elegantly clean underwear. 'She's not of our sort,' the women concluded.[75]

Becoming a civil servant

Jeannette Tawney's plea for unemployment among women to receive the same attention as male unemployment had a personal edge to it.

She was, herself, in many ways an unemployed, or at least under-employed, woman. While she knew that work was important to her, it was hard to settle on the nature of the work it would be best for her to do. When the First World War started, and Harry enlisted, Jeannette faced the unfortunately common dilemma of being effectively a separated wife with no separation allowance yet forthcoming. She needed to earn some money. The story of her search for work is told in both *A Learner's Life* and *Restitution*. She thought, with an Oxford degree, it would be no problem. But for ordinary secretarial jobs she was regarded as overqualified, and then there was the problem of her marriage: married women were not welcomed, and even definitely barred, from some sectors of the labour force.

Jeannette traced her desire to work as a factory inspector back to childhood, when she once watched the dissection of a kitten because she was told it would be a good preparation for slaughter-house inspection. Then there was her interest in the factory girls' club in Surrey, her knowledge of the work of Miss Rose Squire – 'the greatest of factory inspectors' – and her reading of *The History of Factory Legislation* by Amy Harrison and Bessie Hutchins, the first systematic treatment of the state's progressive intervention in regulating the conditions of work in factories and workshops.[76] The Beveridge family knew Miss Hutchins, who invited Jeannette to her house. Through her Jeannette gained an introduction to Rose Squire. Miss Squire, when she later saw her on a Sunday afternoon in St John's Wood, firmly pointed out the lack of precedent in the employment of a married woman factory inspector. 'The more I reflected on my failures, the more desperate I became,' lamented Jeannette. 'Those who have never tried to get work cannot fully realise just how one feels when one is turned down.'[77] But the War came to Jeannette's aid. As more and more men joined up, and their places in the labour force needed to be filled, Rose Squire suggested that Jeannette might send her particulars to the Home Office. Jeannette did so, and was taken on as a temporary factory inspector at a salary of £200 a year. Jeannette Tawney was the first married female factory inspector, an achievement which prompted a question about the propriety of this in the House of Commons.

Factory inspectors had extensive powers, including the right of entry by day or night into any factory or workshop. Jeannette wrote up her own experiences in an American magazine called *Life and Labour* in 1920. Discussing three of the cases with which she was personally involved, she began with a firm that employed a woman timekeeper in the women's toilets to limit the time employees spent there to two visits a day of three minutes each. Girls and women making more frequent visits were fined and, after three fines, dismissed. A formal complaint made by one victim resulted in a Home Office investigation and the abolition of the iniquitous system. In a second case, a married woman whose husband was in the trenches was asked to push a very heavy cask over an uneven surface in the yard. She had a serious miscarriage and nearly died. Jeannette Tawney visited the doctor and then the welfare supervisor, so when the woman went back to work she was given a light post.[78]

The third case came to the attention of *The Surrey Advertiser* on August 28, 1915, under the headline 'HOME OFFICE PROSECUTION at Godalming. Obstructing lady factory inspector. Laundry proprietor convicted.' Alfred Phillips, proprietor of the Hygienic Hand Laundry in Godalming, was summoned for 'having on July 29th, whilst the occupier of a workshop laundry within the meaning of the Factory and Workshop Acts of 1901 and 1907, obstructed an inspector, Annette Jeanie Tawney, in the execution of her duties under the above Acts'. The case was conducted by Rose Squire, who had a considerable reputation for successful prosecutions in such cases. The story of the event and the legal case appears in all of Jeannette's unpublished full-length manuscripts, but especially in the character of Sheila Johnstone in *Restitution*. Sheila is a factory inspector, and she visits a laundry in Godalming which had been reported for illegal working practices. 'There enters from the door facing me, a huge figure of a man. His hair is black and curly ... his eyes are bloodshot, and his mouth froths like a bit-champing horse. He does not sit down beside me for amiable converse as I had expected but stands towering over me leaning his forearms on the table and lets fly catapults of abuse of effervescent sequence.'[79] Sheila/Jeannette went to the police station, and a policeman accompanied her back to the laundry, where she was treated to further venom. The Home Office later praised her for her persistence. Jeannette was the chief witness in the case against the laundry owner, and was cross examined for three hours. They won the case; the laundry owner was sentenced and the laundry closed down.

Harry Tawney was 'pleased & proud though not surprised' when Jeannette got her factory inspector job, but he worried about the strains the job might impose on her. 'It is so hard for persons with energy & initiative to accommodate transition to the slow Civil Service stroke,' he told her, '& yet if they don't, they are almost certain to break down. Do, therefore, be wise & put a deliberate restraint upon your activities for the sake of the future.'[80] This protective attitude, which is apparent in many letters over the years, could be a cause of family tension. Now the War was on and Harry was away. Jeannette's parents and her brother Will thought that Jeannette should move back to Pitfold to live with her parents. Will put particular pressure on her, and Harry's response was rather critical of him: 'One must remember,' he counselled, 'that Will's complete absence of imagination & insight makes him not only an unsympathetic confidant, but often an extremely bad adviser, since he cannot see the facts which relate to personalities, temperaments, & the other matters of an imponderable kind ... he is dogmatizing ... quite unintelligently.' Yet Harry dogmatised as well: 'I absolutely <u>forbid</u> you to live with your parents, whether at Pitfold or anywhere.' Also under discussion was whether Jeannette's health was strong enough to withstand the strains of the factory inspector job. 'We must recognize,' inscribed Harry, 'that it may quite possibly be necessary for you to make the sacrifice [of the job], for the sake of your future welfare.'[81]

Jeannette's poor health did eventually lead her to give up her work as a civil servant. Dismissed as irritating hypochondria by most of those who have commented on her life,[82] there is no doubt that her health problems were real. A correspondence in the archives between Jeannette and two of her doctors in 1937 records her as having had 12 operations up to that point. The first was for tuberculous osteomyelitis, contracted when she was at school in Switzerland. Then there were injections for varicose veins, an appendicectomy, a cholecystectomy (gallbladder removal) and operations on both 'antra' (probably the nasal sinuses). In 1931 she had a large thrombosis of the leg with double pneumonia and pericarditis. Referred to a prominent cardiologist, Dr Strickland Goodall, who worked at the National Heart Hospital in London, she was diagnosed with heart disease in 1932. In 1944, she was in the Westminster Hospital for two months with phlebitis and heart disease. These problems intensified as she reached her seventies, and in 1956 she was admitted to the Royal Free Hospital in Gray's Inn Road, and then to a nursing home in Folkestone. However these diagnoses might be termed in more up-to-date medical language, they are evidence that Jeannette's ill-health was no psychological invention of hers. She really did have a misbehaving body.

Factory inspector, social worker, researcher, writer – which of these was Jeannette Tawney to be, if she could escape from the wifehood and sisterhood that linked her to two men remembered for the way they shaped the political and social landscape of the 20th century? The Tawney archives at LSE store files of Jeannette's short stories, and three full-length attempts at fiction/autobiography. It's not clear when these were originally written, but an exchange of letters between Jeannette and Margaret Storm Jameson, the writer and political activist, in 1935–37 reveals both Jeannette's strengths as a writer and the weaknesses of the texts she had so far managed to produce. Further insights into Jeannette's frustrated efforts to become a published writer languish in the papers of Lucia Turin, who was for many years William Beveridge's secretary. Among Lucia Turin's many roles (see Chapter 6), she was also a published fiction writer and Jeannette's confidante and friend. It was to her that Jeannette confessed her desperation not only to get into print but to make some money to help pay off her and Harry's debts.

Writing her life

Margaret Storm Jameson (1891–1986) was a leading figure in the literary, cultural, and political life of the interwar period and the 1940s. She was a novelist and a theorist of the novel who was much admired by peers, and she was also a political activist against fascism and injustice. The many novels she published from the 1930s through to the 1960s have their 'finger on the pulse of her generation' and are remarkable for their combination of political passion and imaginative writing.[83] Jameson was married to the historian Guy Chapman, and it was probably through him that she met Jeannette. Guy Chapman studied economic history at LSE in the 1930s. The two couples became friends, with Margaret and Guy becoming familiar with the acute discomforts of staying at Rose Cottage. Harry Tawney was Guy Chapman's hero. Margaret was also very fond of Tawney, and Tawney in turn admired her gift 'of endowing the recent past with "the permanence and significance of history"'.[84] Tawney has his own place in this history, or several of them, as characters based on him feature in at least three of Jameson's novels, *A Cup of Tea for Mr Thorgill*, *The Green Man* and *In the Second Year*. In the latter novel, Tawney appears as Robert Baxter Tower, a radical socialist intellectual and professor at London University. When the book's narrator, Andrew Hillier, first meets Tower, he is 'shown into a large room of heavenly disorder, books on the floor, on the mantelpiece, on the table with the coffee cups, on the bed, on all the chairs. In the middle of it, Tower, broad, shabby, shaggy, smiling. He cleared a chair for me by adding the books on it to the tottering pile on his desk, which fell down at once, breaking a glass and raising clouds of dust. ... He was astonishingly shabby. There was a large burnt hole in his jacket.' But Tower's eyes were 'bright and serene, the eyes of Socrates in the head of a professor of economics ... I had heard him spoken of as "a saint"'.[85]

Jameson was part of a network of professional women writers in the interwar period who turned to each other for support and encouragement. In 1935, Jeannette sent her novel *Restitution* to Jameson for advice. In the manuscript she disguised herself as the author by using the name Priscilla Westmacott, and claiming, when the manuscript was sent to various publishers, that she was acting on behalf of Priscilla, a friend who lived in the country. Jeannette could not have been very happy with Jameson's reaction to her manuscript, which was delivered with eight closely typed pages of criticism. 'I do not think you can do anything with this book,' concluded Jameson. Indeed, 'I am nearly in despair over it, because it shows so many rare and splendid qualities – wit, individuality of a high order, sharp knowledge of human motives – and yet as a <u>book</u> it is almost impossible. To a large extent, you have wasted your remarkable qualities in an incredible story, incredible situations and incredible characters.' Jameson's letter includes a summary of the plot (if indeed it can be called that): 'Let us begin with the story itself. It concerns Harold and Joan mainly, and begins on their honeymoon, with a dispute that starts over Harold's carelessness in nearly running over a child. It hints at a hitch that delayed their marriage for two years. And Joan, in resentment, decides to refuse herself to Harold that evening and arranges for them to have separate rooms at the hotel. We are then switched back more than two years, to give an account of the hitch. It appears that Harold had seduced or been seduced by a young woman called Rene who is about to have a child. He decides that he must break off his marriage plans at the last minute, and does so in the most incredible and farcical manner, with the help of a solicitor who is also both incredible and farcical. And he accepts a job that takes him out of England. Joan is overcome with grief, flies to the only sane character in the book, her friend Sheila (here come in some very interesting but entirely out-of-place accounts of Sheila's work as H M I) and departs to China with her. Harold returns, first rents Sheila's flat, then takes another in the same Square and lives there for <u>months</u> without daring to speak to Joan, until the solicitor, who is incredible even in death, gives him £2000 to marry on, the same sum he has spent in paying off Rene. They are reconciled. And the story ends on a scene two years later than the one it began with (which is left completely in the air and unfinished and so has no relevance for the book). Joan cannot have children, so they will adopt the one that caused all the trouble. ... This story is perfectly incredible. It is incredible even if it actually happened.'[86]

Jameson's advice to Jeannette was to take the good bits from *Restitution* and incorporate them into another book, which would present a more straightforward and coherent account of the life that constituted its subject. This eventually produced two further versions for Jameson to despair over, one called *A Learner's Life* and the other *I Learn to Live*. The author of these was FloraNetta Smith instead of Priscilla Westmacott. But, sadly, these manuscripts, which are somewhat intertwined in the Tawney archives, suffered from the same problems as the first: they told a true story dressed up as fiction, and the effort of doing this introduced all sorts of 'queernesses of construction'.[87] The plot still didn't make sense, there were multiple disconnected episodes, and the characters were essentially unbelievable. The publishers to whom Jameson suggested Jeannette should send the book were unconvinced, despite testimonials from such notables as Leonard Woolf and the writer Pearl Buck, whom Jeannette had met in China. Jeannette was, of course, dismayed. 'It's very hard to place ... I cannot say whether it will have any luck at all,' she wrote to Lucia Turin about her novel secretly during a weekend with the Webbs at Passfield Corner.[88] The publishers' reactions are summed up in this letter from Jonathan Cape addressed to Jameson: 'I cannot see how under its veil of anonymity this book is publishable. The author is clearly someone who has lived in interesting society, but since she is concealing her identity, the references to this society are obscured, and the people appear unimportant. So much trouble has been taken to conceal the identity of the characters, that they have lost their definition and the reader is baffled, feeling that there is something here which has been deliberately hidden ... Nobody wants to read a book whose author is mystifying them without giving them the clue to the reality.'[89]

Jameson held to her conviction that Jeannette Tawney was 'an original writer, a real writer,' who had simply not found the right medium of expression.[90] She thought Jeannette was essentially bored by novel writing and therefore didn't do it well. What she should do instead was write the life of Jeannette Beveridge up to the point where she becomes Jeannette Tawney, and after that to write the life of Jeannette Tawney. But this Jeannette adamantly could not do. She was absolutely convinced that Harry would hate any of these stories, especially the 'personal parts', as he couldn't abide any publicity. Indeed, it isn't clear whether Harry ever read any of the fictional manifestations of his wife's life. Her fiction writing was, she told Lucia Turin, 'a complete secret' from Harry, who did not believe that she was capable of writing a publishable novel.[91]

Jeannette Tawney's difficulty in finding an acceptable medium of expression for the story of her life both before and after her marriage reflects a much more fundamental dilemma. If we, studying the remaining documentary evidence, find it problematic to locate the real Jeannette Tawney, this may in part be because she never quite found this person herself. Caught between the demands of her own natal family, in an era where duty in daughters was expected, on the one hand, and the domineering behaviour of a husband, who also yoked her to him with sincere love and need, on the other, she remained perpetually unable to find a clear path for herself.

Richard Titmuss, my father, introducing a new edition of Tawney's *Equality* published in 1964, declared that, 'The social and moral case for equality, as stated by Tawney, cannot be more persuasively argued'.[92] He wasn't quite right, as Tawney's view of equality hinged on the brotherhood of man, and it hardly entertained the possibility, which his own wife laid before him, of women's entitlement to be treated on an equal footing with men. Whatever else Harry Tawney was, his behaviour as a husband was insensitive, and often thoughtless, and most of all it was drenched in heavily gendered expectations and demands. These have been copied and amplified by Tawney's biographers, who have not been able to free themselves from the screen such views erect in front of Jeannette Tawney's life as she experienced it. That so much responsibility for the 'failure' of their marriage should be deposited on her shoulders seems extraordinary. That the state of their homes was her fault and not his, that her habits interrupted his work and not his hers – these unarticulated assumptions do not give us at all an accurate picture of what was going on.

In any case, the marriage didn't fail; it merely joined those countless examples of marriages that depart from conventionally gendered norms but nonetheless manage to offer their occupants comfort, happiness, and a safe haven in that heartless world Harry Tawney so ably exposed in his writings on the injustices of capitalism. 'It all gives one to think how unjust is this our man-world,' sighs FloraNetta Smith, the author of one of Jeannette's Tawney's versions of her life.[93] Perhaps these fictional enterprises did enable her to find, at least intermittently, her own authentic voice.

5

Janet Beveridge

1876–1959

Janet Beveridge's career as a wife is the most complex of the four that form the focus of this book. It raises particular questions about the function of gender stereotyping in the description of wifely careers, and confronts any biographical historian with a jungle of plots and conspiracies that are hard to untangle. She was married twice: first to a taciturn civil servant and mathematician called David Beveridge Mair; and, second, to his cousin and Jeannette Tawney's brother, William Henry Beveridge, the man who is credited with founding the British welfare state. In the first capacity she was known as Mrs Jessy Mair; in the second as Lady Beveridge, with an accompanying change of forename to Janet. (William Beveridge in his writings about his wife solved the problem about which forename to use by simply calling her 'J.')

These changes in nomenclature signal a life divided into very different stages. As Mrs Jessy Mair, Janet Beveridge lived the life of a housewife in a small village in Surrey in the early 1900s. Her and David Mair's four children were born there, but raising them and cooking a three-course meal every night failed to absorb her abundant energy. Her engagement with the local Women's Institute was not a success; she railed against the role of 'professional hausfrau'; and she hated Banstead, which was still a village rather than the suburban conurbation it is now, although 'suburban' as a negative epithet probably did describe it. In her book about William Beveridge – unlike Mary Booth's, Janet's was written when her husband was still alive – she describes the moment she first met the man who would eventually become her second husband: 'One Sunday morning in the spring of 1904 he came down to Banstead, where we were living and raising our family. The first two of them were still at the perambulator stage. As I wheeled them home from their morning outing, I caught sight of a young man loping along the path towards me. He was loosely built and badly dressed, but he had an air which put him in the interesting class at first sight.'[1]

In 1904, too, Janet attended a gathering at LSE that marked a life-long interest of hers and presaged many efforts she would make, along with both her husbands, to alter the future course of British social science. The Sociological Society was a group of social reformers, theorists and investigators who came together to discuss problems and approaches to sociological work. It was a network of some importance and opportunity, bringing together directly or indirectly all the four households in this book. Janet attended its meetings, as did both David Mair and William Beveridge; other members included Clara Collet, who had worked with Charles and Mary Booth; the Barnetts of Toynbee Hall; George Bernard Shaw, and R.H. Tawney. Janet remembered the biostatistician and eugenicist Karl Pearson, a friend of both the Mairs, giving a rousing address at an early meeting of the Society in LSE. 'The occasion is fresh in my mind,' she wrote some 35 years later. 'It must have been a September afternoon, and the light filtered dustily through the crusted glass of that dreary room. The windows gave on the cat-ridden back yards of a row of small, ancient houses in Houghton Street, where the hour of five in the afternoon was struck to the sudden rich smell of kippers.'[2]

The conjunction of the two meetings – with William Beveridge and at LSE – anticipated two of the most important stories of Janet's life: her 18 years of work for LSE, and her dedication to the gestation and sponsorship of William's famous Report on the country's social insurance services. Yet these stories have been used to promote a devastatingly negative interpretation, discussed later in this chapter, of her personality, motives and contribution. In order to appreciate the injustice of this perspective we need first to review Janet's background and career as a public servant.

From Jessy Philip to Mrs Mair to Lady Beveridge

Janet Beveridge was born in Dundee to a long-established and prosperous Scottish family in 1876. She was named Jessie Thomson Philip – the 'Jessie' after her grandmother, who enthralled her as a child with stories going back to Napoleonic days (although named 'Jessie' she called herself 'Jessy'). Janet's father was a master joiner, who had met her mother when he went as a 'handsome young man' to help Janet's grandfather build a photographic studio with walls of glass like the Crystal Palace. There were six children, five girls and a boy. One girl died either at or shortly before birth; Janet was the fourth surviving child. Her parents, wrote Janet, 'regarded their son as a being apart. What was left over of my mother's devotion was lavished on Annie my youngest sister, the youngest of us all.'[3] This Annie became Anne Glenday Philip, Chief Woman Inspector of Schools for the English Board of Education after the Second World War, work for which she was given an OBE.

The family lived in one of the blocks of flats William Philip had built in Garland Place, Dundee. The five children, their parents, and a faithful servant called Jane squashed themselves into a two-bedroom flat with a 'bed recess' in the kitchen. This level of accommodation, a sign of the general ghastliness of late 19th-century housing stock, wasn't uncommon at the time. Two of Janet's earliest memories were of spilling onto herself a plate of boiling porridge, with a resulting scar that prevented her from ever wearing a low-fronted dress; and of the Tay Bridge disaster in 1879 when a tremendous gale brought both the bridge over the Firth of Tay and a busy train that was crossing it down into the water.

The Philip children were brought up with a strict moral code informed by their parents' membership of the Blue Ribbon Army, a gospel temperance movement imported from the US that was popular in Britain in the 1870s and 1880s. Janet went to a 'dame' school when she was five, where great importance was attached to sewing and crocheting: 'I sewed red wool hollyberries and bright green leaves on a soft roughish fabric known as crash for tray clothes, and blue silk forget-me-nots on a little black satin apron.'[4] Fortunately she did learn to read in preparation for rather more education from the age of seven to 16 at Dundee High School. With a 13th-century foundation, and many famous alumni, it was no ordinary high school. One of Janet's contemporaries there was Agnes Blackadder, later Dr Agnes Savill, a pioneering radiologist and suffragette. At Dundee High School Janet came top in every subject. She then went on to study mathematics and physics as one of the first women students at St Andrews University, where she was a leading light in the Women's Debating Society and where she again came (very nearly) top in everything.

'Of her many tales of her undergraduate days,' wrote her son Philip, 'she enjoyed telling her children that she had been one of the earliest of women to have flaunted convention; even though nobody today would raise an eyebrow at what she did ... she was sitting on a table swinging her legs and smoking a cigar when David Mair, sent as examiner from London, walked into the room'.[5] The examiner was much taken by the academic brilliance of this young woman (and perhaps her legs as well), and he persuaded her to marry him. He would not wait, so Janet had to shorten her academic career by giving up an honours degree in favour of a pass degree, and laying aside her ambition to take the mathematical tripos at Cambridge. 'He argued that he knew enough mathematics and physics for two at least,' she remarked, without giving us any sense of how she felt about it.[6]

Janet married for the first time at 20, and she was 28 when William Beveridge walked down the lane to the Mairs' house in Banstead. Thirty-eight years later David Mair died and Janet married William. As far as Janet was concerned, William's entry into the Mairs' lives 'opened out a new world for contemplation'.[7] He became a regular visitor to the Mair household, making 'an immediate conquest' of the children, and sharing with Janet, as David didn't, an interest in fiction, poetry and the theatre. She contributed enthusiastically to William's only journey into fiction, a rather strange book called *John and Irene: An Anthology of Thoughts on Women*. Publication day in 1909 of his book on unemployment coincided with the birth of her youngest child, Elspeth, and she devoted the postnatal period to reading it.

There were four children: Lucy in 1901, Marjory in 1903, Philip in 1905, and Elspeth in 1909. In 1913, the Mairs moved to London, to a house in Campden Hill Road, Kensington, round the corner from William Beveridge's own, 27 Bedford Gardens, which now sports a blue plaque in his memory as 'Architect of the Welfare State'. William's elderly parents moved into his house, and Janet made all the arrangements for their care. Once the First World War began, every evening after his parents had gone to bed, William would walk round to the Mairs' house, 'and lie on the drawing-room sofa discussing the events of the war and problems of civilian and military mobilization'.[8] Much collective socialising was engaged in, as Margaret Cole, writer and politician, recalled in a letter to William written after his wife's death: 'I remember Janet so well from very long ago, when I was a very raw young classical mistress at St Paul's teaching her daughter, & she was so kind to me, asking me round to Campden Hill Road to meet people. I met you there, during the first war; & I remember you arranging the evening picnic down the river, when we ate our meal on top of a barge off Wapping Old Stairs, & afterwards went up Limehouse Church Tower & saw St Paul's against the sunset.'[9]

Virginia Woolf recorded in her diary for 20 May 1920 dining with Margaret and G.D.H. Cole in Chelsea: 'Then there were Mr and Mrs Mair, from Government offices, jokes about Beveridge & Shaw, & David Mair subsiding into complete silence in the background.'[10] This first marriage, happy at first, wrestled with growing incompatibility. While Janet was a sociable extrovert, David hated social contacts except with a tiny band of male friends (including William Beveridge) who shared his mathematical and scientific interests, and he lacked Janet's interest in cultural and public affairs. David Mair's progressive withdrawal from the marriage was marked by periods of unspecified illness.[11] In 1925, Beatrice Webb noted in her unforgiving diary that 'the unfortunate man had taken to drink as a silencer of his mental agony'.[12] These were the circumstances in which Janet looked for companionship from her husband's second cousin. When David Mair retired from the Civil Service Commission in 1933, he left the family home for prolonged world travels during which he visited nudist health camps and pursued interests in meditation and vegetarianism. He was closest to his and Janet's daughter Marjory, in whose home he often stayed when back in Britain and in whose home and care he would eventually die.

The First World War saved many women from a narrow domestic existence, and so it was with Janet. On 26 May 1915, the government set up a Ministry of Munitions and appointed William Beveridge as Assistant General Secretary in charge of labour organisation. Janet started work a month later as an administrative assistant to deal with the thousands of letters that arrived daily from people who wanted to donate scrap metal or work in munitions. There was no space for her in the Whitehall building, so a tent was set up on the stone terrace facing the river, and furnished with a table, a light and a telephone. When William's two male secretaries joined up, Janet became his private secretary, and soon found herself 'acting on behalf of Mr Beveridge as a kind of reliable authority on the interpretation of the Munitions of War Act'.[13]

This arrangement, the beginning of Janet's 23 years in public administration, lasted a few months until another new ministry was created. In December 1916 William Beveridge moved to the Ministry of Food and Janet went with him to become Director of Bacon and Allied Fats, a post which gained her an OBE, like her sister, in the 1918 New Year Honours list. The pleasure this gave her is evident in the photo on page 154, taken with her four children the day she went to receive the award. The post for which she gained it was domesticated by the newspapers to the rather more lowly

'Woman larder chief'.[14] She was the first female civil servant to hold a responsible administrative position with no special connection to women's work. Most of her staff were men, some older than she was; they included a solicitor and two Rhodes scholars. Janet and her two female assistants, an actress and a parson's daughter, worked in the day nursery and William in the night nursery of a rather grand house that had been turned over to War work. Their official boss was Lord Devonport, the President of the Board of Trade, who was known for his insistence on gilded wastepaper baskets, had difficulty controlling anything, including his temper, and knew nothing about food. Janet's job entailed duties such as making financial bargains with packers in the Chicago meat industry, and attending debates in the House of Commons. This occasioned another first, with Janet being the first woman to be allowed to sit in the Official Gallery in order to give ministers advice: as *The Daily Mirror* reported, 'she wore a neat tight-fitting blue costume with a blue hat and ... gazed on the House with unruffled calm'.[15]

When the House met to debate a report issued by an interdepartmental committee on the high cost of food, Janet attended, along with William and Sir Hubert Llewellyn Smith, Permanent Secretary to the Board of Trade. The point of the debate was to allow members to voice the anger of housewives at the growing cost and scarcity of food, but the President of the Board of Trade's speech was instead about merchant shipping and the disastrous toll inflicted by German submarines. As a result, the housewives were forgotten. Afterwards, Janet walked with the two men to Westminster Bridge underground station. They were both talking about submarines; 'I said to them, "I think you are both missing the lesson of the debate. The immediate action which must be taken is the control of food." Sir Hubert was most contemptuous, indicating how like a woman I was.' On the way home to Kensington with William, Janet argued her point with him and finally he agreed. 'We set about at once framing a bill for the control by the Board of Trade of the distribution and prices of food.'[16] They began on Christmas Day by typing a plan for sugar rationing using an old typewriter belonging to William's mother. Later, Janet would claim that the first official letters written about the control of food in Britain were written by her.

After the First World War ended, Janet was invited, but declined, to become one of the new breed of women factory inspectors; there was also the possibility of an assistant secretaryship in the new Ministry of Health. She went instead to an administrative post at LSE. Sidney Webb had recruited William Beveridge to replace the New Zealand politician William Pember Reeves as the new Director of LSE. Beveridge took over the post in October 1919 and Janet joined him two months later as the School Secretary. They occupied these two roles together for 18 years. In 1937, William Beveridge left LSE to become Master of University College, Oxford. Janet stayed a year longer at LSE, during which she was dispatched by the governors on a fund-raising mission to the US. Then close to retirement age at 62, she moved to Oxford, first to a house in Headington and eventually into the Master's Lodgings at University College with William and her daughter Elspeth, who had been acting as his hostess and housekeeper. In 1942, two weeks after the Beveridge Report was published, and five months after David Mair died, she married William and became Lady Beveridge.

Building Houghton Street

When Janet and William went there, the LSE was already a unique institution, the only centre for the study of social science in England. The years of their sojourn at LSE saw a massive expansion of the School in every sense – buildings, staff, students, money, disciplines and ambitions. This 'second foundation',[17] set the School on its path to being the colossal structure it is today: well over 3,000 staff, 11,000 students, the world's largest social science library, an institution somewhere near the top for the study of economics and allied subjects worldwide. The beginnings of all this were an achievement almost entirely due to the efforts of the Beveridge-Mair collaboration. But LSE's second foundation was accompanied by a prolonged and nasty internecine battle between natural and social science models for the study of social subjects. This is a tale of intrigue and division that set British social science on a decisive path, away from the American model of experimentation and quantification towards a 'softer' and more qualitative exercise. It's a largely forgotten narrative that has somehow got mislaid in the interstices of the gossipy intrigue that settled around the figures of the new Director and Secretary of the School, an intrigue that has attracted an extraordinary amount of biographical attention.

When Janet joined William Beveridge at LSE, it was literally bursting at the seams. The student population had doubled since the War and teaching was accommodated by renting disused army huts. There were only three full-time teachers; most teaching took place in the evenings; there were just a few lecture rooms and no separate rooms for teachers, few graduate students or research facilities; and the library was tiny, providing space for less than 2 per cent of the student population at any one time. The School had been headed part time for the past 11 years by William Pember Reeves, whose main job was to direct the National Bank of New Zealand. It had effectively been run for 23 years by its Secretary, a Miss Mactaggart: 'the real seat of power'.[18]

The nature of Miss Mactaggart's role at LSE is important to an understanding of what Janet Beveridge did when she took over as the School Secretary. Christian Scipio Mactaggart was a highly efficient Scottish-Australian who had been recruited originally by the Webbs to housekeep at Charlotte Shaw's 10 Adelphi Terrace. As her job and LSE expanded, so Miss Mactaggart had taken to calling herself the School's 'Secretary' and 'Registrar'. The LSE archives for this period show that many diverse aspects of the School's life were in her hands: she appointed teachers, admitted students, managed the School's finances, and organised social functions. The statistician Arthur Bowley, connected with the School for more than 40 years, recalled her as 'Deputy director, hostess, accountant, and lady of all work'.[19] In May 1919, for example, in the interregnum between Pember Reeves' and Beveridge's directorships, Sidney Webb wrote to ask Miss Mactaggart if she could please make up at once 'the revised estimate for the current year (of receipts & expenditure)' for the Council of Management; and could she please let him 'know without scruple or delay anything that you think needs to be done.'[20] William Beveridge's first perception of LSE was also of 'a one-woman show'.[21] On Janet's arrival, Miss Mactaggart told her firmly that the administration of the School entailed preventing the governors, if possible, 'from knowing anything about what was actually going on: especially in the matter of finance'.[22]

Janet's appointment was initially as Business Secretary to help Miss Mactaggart, who was in poor health, and who left the School the following summer. From this point on, Janet found herself in charge of everything that had been Miss Mactaggart's domain, which was, in fact, everything. In January 1921 she was officially appointed Secretary and Dean. As her predecessor had done, Janet's responsibilities included running the School when the Director was absent, for example in 1925–26 when William was fully occupied with the Royal Commission on the Coal Industry, in 1926–28 when the Vice-Chancellorship of London University filled his time, and during his regular trips to the US for fund-raising and other academic purposes.

The first problem Janet and William had to solve in their professional partnership at LSE was buildings. There weren't enough of them. It was during their reign, and because of their efforts, that the School gained the world-famous address in Houghton Street it still has today. Among the Beveridge papers in LSE are a few pages by Janet Beveridge written in 1958 headed, 'The near loss of Houghton Street'. These record the train of events.[23] A start was made with the derelict Red Lion public house, which was purchased by the School in 1919. A few weeks after she joined LSE, Janet successfully negotiated with the London County Council (LCC) to license its demolition. In order to build on the site, both money and architectural ingenuity were needed to fit the new building onto an irregularly shaped bit of land squashed in between the old houses celebrated in Dickens' *Bleak House* and the tall office buildings in Kingsway and the Aldwych. (The Dickens legacy remains today in the form of the Old Curiosity Shop, which stands in the midst of LSE buildings in Portsmouth Street and is owned by LSE.) A body called the University Grants Committee set up in 1919 to advise the government on the distribution of money to universities was chaired by Sir William McCormick, who had taught Janet at the University of St Andrews, and had since become a good friend. It was this connection that led to McCormick visiting LSE and agreeing to provide £45,000 towards building costs. 'I do not suggest that the School would not have received a capital grant without this happy accident,' wrote William in his book about LSE, 'but certainly the chance of a grant was not lessened thereby.'[24]

That was only the beginning of the solution, however. St Clement's Press, run by the profit-hungry newspaper proprietor Sir William Berry, later Lord Camrose, was competing for Houghton Street space. Janet rang him up, 'very much in the spirit of the first wartime ministries in which I had served,' to explain why LSE needed to expand into Houghton Street. He was resistant. 'And then out of the blue came a stroke of good fortune' – an invitation from an old friend of her student days to attend a formal dinner at which her dinner neighbour turned out to be the legal adviser to the Board of Education.[25] Janet argued the School's case with him and invited him to visit the School the next day, as a result of which the LCC signed a compulsory requisition order for the Houghton Street houses.[26]

This story illustrates Janet's initiative in helping to get the 'second foundation' of LSE under way; it also underscores the perpetual importance of informal social networks in public life. The problem for Janet, taking over from Miss Mactaggart, was that, although Miss Mactaggart had been all-knowing and very competent, most of what she did was in her head and there were no proper systems in place. Here Janet drew on her civil service experience, and on the advice of David Mair – whose expertise, Janet stressed, she very much relied on – to bring the administrative systems of the School into the modern age. She introduced new procedures for student admissions, and appointed a special clerk to deal with these; David proposed one of his temporary clerks for this role, Eve Evans, who came in 1920 and stayed for 34 years, eventually taking over from Janet as the School Secretary. Janet started a typing pool on the Whitehall model, with a special room and noiseless typing machines, firm tables, each with its own light and the best chairs for the human frame; the head of the pool sat aloof in a glass-walled cubicle to survey the scene. In order to encourage high morale, each member of the typing staff was given the care of a special committee – preparing agendas, taking and circulating notes and so forth. More enduringly, it was Janet who was responsible for the motto LSE still uses today: 'Rerum cognoscere causas', 'To know the causes of things'. In 1922, she offered a guinea to any student who could come up with a good suggestion. In the end it was the economist Edwin Cannan who retrieved the successful entry from his memory of Book 2 of Virgil's *Georgics*. The motto accompanies a coat of arms showing books above the figure of a beaver, and this is still positioned above the entrance to the School today. Janet commissioned Arnold Plant, then President of the Student's Union, to design the coat of arms; according to her the beaver was a tribute to William whose surname means 'beaver island'.[27] Janet's legacy to the School also included sponsoring a modern languages department there in 1934–35 and a course for students wanting to take the civil services examinations in 1935–36.

LSE was the first higher education institution in the UK to introduce a system of family allowances for staff. This was an achievement urged by Janet and agreed to by William, both of whom were followers of Eleanor Rathbone's campaign for national family allowances. From 1925 all full-time teachers and senior administrators at LSE had £30 a year added to their salaries for each child aged between 13 and 23 while in full-time education. Staff salaries in general were raised, and a superannuation scheme started. Janet saw to it that the porters, an integrally important part of School management, should be included; she recalled that: 'With Miss Alder, then my chief accountant, and with Mr Raynes of the Legal and General Insurance Company, a Governor of the School, I worked out a pension scheme for them also, for they did not qualify under the F.S.S.U.' [the Federated Superannuation Scheme for Universities].[28] There were other improvements for the students also. As William wrote in his book about LSE: 'Janet and I had been intensely happy as university students and set ourselves to recreate the conditions of this student happiness at LSE.' They wanted 'to prove that a full University life did not depend upon living together in medieval buildings. These words, of course, were put into my mouth by Janet.'[29] In due course, students were supplied with proper space and facilities, an improved students' union, and better contact with teachers; and a system of advisers of studies for first-year students was introduced.

The LSE years were enhanced by Janet's purchase of a house on the Downs above Avebury in Wiltshire, which she called 'Green Street'. She and her younger daughter Elspeth found it in the summer of 1928; they tried it out by renting it and then Janet bought it. Green Street wasn't just a weekend and holiday retreat for the Mair family, but a source of delight for William who visited often. The photo on page 154 shows him happily ensconced there with the entire Mair family. Green Street wasn't, however, *his* house, as biographical legend typically has it.[30] He was put to work by Janet constructing a swimming pool and a tennis court, and she created a room for him and her son Philip in the hayloft of the coach-house where William wrote his book on the trade cycle together with the future Labour prime minister Harold Wilson in 1938. Wilson later recalled their routine: William would get up at 6 am, make a pot of tea, wake Wilson up with a cup, and then they settled down to two hours' work, William 'with a monstrous yard-long slide-rule made up of a series of slats, myself with a small cylindrical slide-rule, laboriously eliminating seasonal variations from the monthly unemployment figures for close on 100 industries'. It was a great moment when £300 of American grant money was found to hire a lady with a hand-worked calculating machine, in other words a 'calculating woman'.[31] Many distinguished visitors found their way to Green Street. Janet bought special curtains for the Webbs' bedroom, as Beatrice could sleep only in a completely dark room. LSE staff also spent time there; William's book about LSE contains photos of the economists Arnold Plant and Lionel Robbins, LSE founder Graham Wallas, and both Harry and Jeannette Tawney squinting in the sunshine at Green Street.

Janet made another unique contribution to the new life of LSE: music. She thought economics and political science needed an antidote. A friend of hers at the University of Leeds had started an experiment with lunch hour concerts, so Janet persuaded the governors to release £90 a year to pay professional musicians for one lunch-hour concert a term. LSE did have a piano, but it was 'a relic of the old days of the Adelphi', an upright cottage piano belonging to Charlotte Shaw. It was hardly up to the standards of professional pianists, so when the Founders' Room on the top floor was opened in 1928, Janet arranged for the installation of a pre-war Bechstein grand piano instead. The Prince of Wales presided over the formal opening of the room, choosing the musical programme for the evening which included a violin recital given by the Hungarian violinist Jelly d'Arányi. Janet knew her well. Together the two women arranged the decor of the room and chose the colour of d'Arányi's gown: 'It was the evening of the longest day in the year, and the scene was very beautiful,' reminisced Janet years later.[32] When she retired, she presented a silver cup to be given to each year to the student who did the most for the cause of music.

Both the Jessy Mair Cup for Music and the lunch-hour concerts continue to be part of LSE life today. There is also a Janet Beveridge prize for outstanding student achievement, which in 2016 was won by my grand-daughter Zoe Oakley. She wasn't alone among the students (or the staff) in wondering who Janet Beveridge was.

The Rockefeller connection

The LCC money, and various other smallish sums, were nowhere near enough to support the enormous expansion that LSE experienced after the end of the Second World War. As William Beveridge proudly quantified it in his book about LSE, the period from 1923 to 1937 witnessed a growth in the total space the School occupied from 51,000 to 134,000 square feet – an increase of 263 per cent. To finance this, a very large injection of money was obtained from an unexpected source: one of the American Rockefeller Foundation funds. Janet played a part in both securing the Rockefeller money, and in pursuing the scheme for which a major portion of the money was intended, something called 'the natural bases of the social sciences'.[33]

The story of the Rockefeller endowment carries with it this critical and more broadly important subplot about what kind of creature the social sciences are: sciences like the natural ones, depending on observation, experiment, and objective, empirical data; or enterprises consisting of theorising, philosophising, and the derivation of ideas about how society works much more from thinking about it than from engaging directly with it. This clash of models was already embedded in LSE's academic life, where empirical research was largely the province either of the social administration or the anthropology departments, and the economists and sociologists enjoyed creating grand theories.

In one of her unpublished autobiographical fragments, Janet described how the link between LSE and the Rockefeller Fund began: 'In 1923 the Annual Meeting of the British Association [for the Advancement of Science] took place at Liverpool. The Director of L.S.E. was acting as President of the Economics section and was being entertained for the duration of the meeting at a country house nearby. He found himself deeply involved in a controversy on the subject of population with his friend Lord Keynes, into which the unexpected interpolations of Dr. Marie Stopes may be said to have introduced an element of light comedy ... For myself, I was on holiday en famille in the Highlands of Scotland. An urgent message from the Director came to me there begging me to come to Liverpool for a few days to meet on behalf of L.S.E. an American named Mr. Beardsley Ruml who had been sent to Europe as the representative of the Laura Spelman Rockefeller Foundation ... Mr Ruml had been charged with the duty of discovering European institutions concerned with the Social Sciences in general rather than with the exclusive study of theoretic economics. It was a momentous meeting. Mr. Ruml was intrigued from the start by the description of a university institution devoted to the study of man in society from every angle, and one where it was proposed to develop study and research from the scientific as well as the philosophic approach. This was indeed what he was looking for. It was soon clear that he had found an institution to endow.'[34]

When William had finished arguing with Marie Stopes and Maynard Keynes, he took over the discussion with Ruml, and Janet went back to her family holiday. Beardsley Ruml, the grandson of a Czech labourer, was a brilliant germinator of ideas. He assumed the directorship of the Laura Spelman Rockefeller Memorial (LSRM) in 1922 at the age of 27 with a PhD in psychology. The LSRM had been set up in 1918 with sizeable capital of $74 million following the death of Laura Spelman, a philanthropist and abolitionist who had married into the wealthy Rockefeller family. The Fund had an undistinguished record in its early years, but Ruml injected it with a mission to advance the practice of social science in universities, which would then be able to make a practical contribution to policy development and the improvement of human welfare. This had already happened to a considerable extent in the US, but Europe lagged behind, and was thus potential fertile ground for these reformist plans. Under Ruml's direction, the smallest Rockefeller Foundation became the most important institution for advancing the social sciences in Europe as well as the US.

Although some of the historiography around the Rockefeller–LSE connection concocts it as an example of American imperialism, the desire to push the social sciences in a more scientific and more useful direction wasn't just ideological or political rhetoric. Many people, including the Director and Secretary of LSE, thought that society needed a more practical and empirically based social science. This was, indeed, in line with the attitude of the Webbs, Charlotte Shaw and other LSE founders. William Beveridge, who had studied mathematics at Oxford, saw himself as a natural scientist *manqué*. Janet, with her background in mathematics and physics, had little patience with armchair social theorising of the kind that was practised by some of the School's senior staff: she wanted 'a really scientific treatment of sociology and economics' focusing on 'tangible and verifiable realities'.[35]

The secret of the LSRM's success in its social science funding was that it was small and informally organised, and it kept the administrative burden down by giving large grants for programmes rather than small project grants, and then leaving the grant-holders to use the money more or less as they chose. This was a strategy that hugely benefited LSE. As a result of the first contact with Beardsley Ruml, the LSRM agreed grants to LSE early in 1924 of $25,000 for building work and $20,000 a year for four and a half years 'in aid of research by teachers'.[36] LSE's massive institutional growth in the years between 1923 and 1939 was largely financed by the LSRM, which covered 40 per cent of its total expenditure on land, buildings, books and equipment; overall, 25 per cent of LSE's total income came from this source, more than from all UK donors combined, including the Treasury and private benefactors. 'It is rather wonderful to feel,' wrote Janet to the LSRM in January 1926, 'that you are weighing our ideals and ambitions in the balance ... and liking our dreams and making them come true'.[37] In these years the much-quoted (and definitely still relevant) aphorism about LSE being an institution on which the concrete never sets was coined by William and Janet who, as crossword fans, were regular users of the *Oxford Dictionary of Quotations* and who found in it Christopher North's view of the British Empire in 1929 as the place on which the sun never sets.

Aside from its contribution to concrete, the Rockefeller money had a major impact on academic scholarship and the careers of many LSE academics who in turn had a transformative effect on their individual disciplines. Harry Tawney relied on LSRM money to support the research for his classic work on *Religion and the Rise of Capitalism*, as did he and Eileen Power for their *Tudor Economic Documents*. Power used Rockefeller money for a five-volume economic history of London and a register and depository of London business archives. The economist Lionel Robbins held a Rockefeller-endowed Chair of Political Economy at LSE. He, Friedrich Hayek and most of the senior economists at LSE drew on Rockefeller money to hire teaching assistants and finance their publications. Works on poverty and social conditions and the gold standard also benefited, and the American money enabled Hubert Llewellyn Smith to repeat Charles Booth's methodology in a *New Survey of London Life and Labour* based at LSE.

Rockefeller money transformed British social anthropology through the appointment at LSE of the Polish anthropologist Bronislaw Malinowski as a Laura Spelman Rockefeller Memorial Fellow, and his elevation with LSRM money to a Chair in Social Anthropology in 1927. Malinowski's commitment to fieldwork and the systematic collection of detailed empirical observations about different cultures resonated very well with Ruml and the LSRM's concern to encourage scientific approaches to social study. Janet and David Mair's daughter Lucy Mair, later Professor of Applied Anthropology at LSE, trained as an anthropologist under Malinowski, and her early fieldwork, resulting in her first book *An African People in the Twentieth Century* (1934), was carried out in Uganda with a Rockefeller grant arranged by him. The scale of the Rockefeller support for LSE in the late 1920s is illustrated by a reference in the administrative archives to the 13 'Rockefeller assistants' who were available to supervise the Founders' Room.[38]

Of mice and men

We come now to the forgotten subplot, in which Janet was intimately involved, of the internal conflict at LSE about what kind of subject social science is. Early discussions with Ruml of the LSRM had stressed the strategic value of a bridge between natural and social science models to include anthropology, genetics, the study of population and vital statistics, heredity, eugenics, physiology and public health, and geography as the study of natural resources. It was hoped that expanding these subjects would aid the importation of natural science methodology into that of social science and would establish a basis in biological knowledge for social policy. That, anyway, was the great idea.

The Ruml–Mair–Beveridge vision of a unified science led to further funding of $875,000 being agreed in 1927 (this is equivalent to about £9.7 million in 2020). A key part of the plan was the appointment of a Professor of Social Biology. Lancelot Hogben was personally recruited by William Beveridge for this post in 1930. He was a distinguished biologist who had held posts in Edinburgh, Montreal and Cape Town, a socialist, an environmentalist, a great believer in making science and mathematics accessible for ordinary citizens, and, what was to prove especially important at LSE, a man who made no secret of his scathing disregard for ivory tower academics. Beatrice Webb, in her inimitably critical style, found him 'undersized and colourless, unkempt and unhealthy-looking,' but 'extremely clever and ingenious', and 'full of original though imperfectly thought out ideas'.[39] Hogben laid down two conditions for accepting his LSE post, one predictable, the other less so. He wanted to be provided with proper laboratory facilities, and he wanted a position to be found for his wife, a population expert in her own right, Enid Charles. Both wishes were granted. Three floors of teaching and research space in Houghton Street were given over to the new Department of Social Biology. There was a laboratory with benches, chemicals, specialist equipment such as spectrographs and centrifuges, and basement accommodation for around 1,500 animals. There was a laboratory assistant and a distinguished team of researchers, including Enid Charles and other significant demographers such as the German émigré René Kuczynski and the young sociologist and demographer David Glass. The tradition of empirically based social mobility studies established by Glass and his colleagues was one extremely important consequence of the Beveridge-Mair-Ruml effort to get social biology established at LSE.

In its short life, the Department of Social Biology did two main sorts of work: statistical investigation and experimental biology. Most of the latter was on the physiology of reproduction. One serendipitous byproduct was a pregnancy test used worldwide for three decades. Hogben had worked on the endocrine physiology of the African clawed frog, Xenopus laevis, in South Africa, and he brought a collection of these frogs back to England with him. What became known as the Hogben pregnancy test, which involved injecting frogs with women's urine, was developed by Hogben and Charles at LSE. The Department of Social Biology's statistical projects included an early twin study involving more than four thousand school-age twins looking at the relationships between heredity, environment and intelligence. In fact, the Department did so much work that it published a collection of chapters reporting its demographic and statistical work in 1938. This volume, edited by Hogben, carried an unusual 'publisher's note' informing readers that any profits from the book would be devoted to the publication 'of other *factual* social studies'.[40]

Hogben and social biology didn't go down well at LSE. Some of the staff resented the virement of LSRM money to feed Hogben's animals: they complained that professors were asked to share rooms because Hogben was playing about with white mice. The emphasis on experiment, observation and number-crunching also proved an unwelcome diet for several influential senior figures. In her note on 'The chair in social biology', written in 1958, Janet chose her words carefully: 'It was found impossible,' she judged, 'to bring together into the same region of intellectual exploration some of the existing staff of the School with their traditional conceptions of the scope of the social sciences limited mainly to the study of the theory of economics and political science'. The more senior members of staff were perhaps open to the change, but in some of the younger members, appointed on promise, and promoted before their proper time, 'the dignity of professorial rank gave rise to an assumption of authority and a love of its exercise.'[41]

After seven years, Hogben abandoned his attempt at interdisciplinary work and he left LSE in 1937. That year, too, William Beveridge resigned as Director, tired of all the arguments about social biology and various other matters, and looking for new ground, and a year later Janet followed him. The cause of social biology wasn't helped by Ruml leaving the LSRM for a life in business, the Fund being absorbed into the overall Rockefeller charitable empire, and the general strain on financial resources occasioned by the 1930s Depression. In 1934, William, and probably Janet as well, had come up with a plan they wanted Rockefeller to fund for an Institute of Economic Research, which William would head while Janet would be its Secretary. The plan was turned down.

Years later, in his book about LSE, William recalled, 'the great adventure on which Janet and Beardsley Ruml and I embarked'.[42] He regretted that this great adventure didn't lead to a permanent result in transforming economics into the kind of science envisaged by the School's founders. Hogben published his own book *Retreat from Reason* the year after he left LSE, reviewing in it his fraught experience of being an experimental scientist in the midst of theory-addicted academics. Quoting Lionel Robbins on the nature of economics – 'The truth of a particular theory is a matter of logical derivation from the general assumptions of the subject' – Hogben deemed economics, 'the astrology of the Machine Age'. It provided, he said, the same kind of intellectual relief as chess, and had absolutely no right to be regarded as a science; its practitioners were 'permanently incapacitated for lucid discourse by prolonged preoccupation with the gold standard'.[43] Unsurprisingly, Lionel Robbins and Friedrich Hayek were two of the LSE academics who were most hostile to social biology and the general idea that the procedures of science proper should be applied to economics and other social subjects. The two first sociology professors at LSE, E.A. Westermarck and L.T. Hobhouse, had established a tradition of LSE sociology that was philosophical rather than empirical, with a bent towards abstract and speculative theory. Hobhouse died the year before Hogben went to LSE but not before he had voiced a strong objection to the introduction of social biology. But the sociologists at LSE, and also the economists, disliked the idea of interdisciplinary synthesis – of different subjects working together for a common goal – which was implicit in the plan for establishing the natural bases of the social sciences at LSE.

Mal-de-Mair

Differences of opinion among LSE staff about what social science ought to be and how the Rockefeller money should be spent proliferated in the mid-1930s. As these intensified, Janet became caught up in a whirlpool of accusations framing her as an arch-demon, the she-devil who was somehow held accountable for everything that was going wrong: she was overbearing, she interfered, she didn't know her place. The phrase 'Mal-de-Mair' – a play on the French term for seasickness – entered the local lexicon.[44] LSE was littered with allegations and counter-allegations about personalities and principles and behaviour, and especially about what the Director and the Secretary might be getting up to in Room 500, which Mrs Mair had appropriated as her own. Known as 'the bathroom' it had been built as a restroom for senior female staff; Janet would withdraw to it, and have her lunch there, and the room even had a divan in it. The mind boggles, and many did.

What caused all these ructions? Some of the 'old stagers', especially the Fabian socialist Graham Wallas and the economist Edwin Cannan who had both joined the School in 1895, found all the new ideas unsettling. One became hysterical and accused Janet of a serious misuse of School funds, a charge from which she was later exonerated. Harold Laski and Eileen Power gave particular trouble, watching Janet's every move and waiting, like one of Hogben's animals, to pounce. Beatrice Webb took to her diaries to record the progress of what she called, 'The Beveridge-Mair entanglement'. By January 1935 she judged that LSE had become 'a hot-bed of intrigue and scandal' stirred by Mrs Mair's "dangerous state of mind' and bad behavior. The only solution, judged Beatrice, was for Beveridge to leave LSE and take Mrs Mair with him. In July 1936 Beatrice recorded a weekend visit from Josiah Stamp, the Chair of the Governors, and his wife Olive to discuss the LSE 'crisis'.[45] Stamp reported a violent upheaval among the professors, led by Laski and Power, who threatened wholesale resignation if Mrs Mair wasn't discharged from the School immediately. She was nearing 60 and could therefore safely be retired, but the Director was resistant. In the end Sidney Webb had a word with William Beveridge and it was agreed that Janet should get a year's extension and a further year's salary to work under the new Director, Alexander Carr-Saunders, which, in the event, she didn't much enjoy as Carr-Saunders quietly ousted her from all sorts of jobs she had been used to doing for many years.

Plenty of people did, however, appreciate Janet's work for the School. When Laura Spelman Rockefeller's grandson David came to the LSE to study economics in 1937, it was Janet who sorted out his application, found accommodation, replete with cook and cleaner, for him and the friend with whom he came, took him to her house in Avebury, to the State Opening of Parliament and the Edinburgh Tattoo, and generally under her wing. The success of his year in London was, said David, largely due to her. The extent of Janet's social aspirations is marked in her writing (unsuccessfully) to St James's Palace in an effort to get David Rockefeller invited to meet King George VI.[46] When Janet visited New York in 1938, David's mother Abby Rockefeller told her how happy she and her husband were for all Janet had done for David: 'It has meant a great deal to us to realise that he has had such a kind and wise friend in London'.[47] While a cynical view of Janet's connection with the Rockefellers might be that it was part of her strategy for encouraging the flow of American money to LSE, the David Rockefeller episode came *after* the crisis over social biology.

The anthropologist Malinowski was grateful for her support and her commitment to empirically based study. As Lancelot Hogben, who also appreciated Janet's encouragement of the social biology experiment, told Janet later, Malinowski had a 'very real affection for you & always used Jessie as a pet name'.[48] Malinowski's respect for her and her opinions, as well as the authority she, à la Miss Mactaggart, exercised over LSE's academic affairs, is evident in a missive he sent her in early 1932. Malinowski explained that he had bad rheumatism and would need more assistance in his work at LSE. 'I am therefore extremely anxious to have a really efficient helper or two in my own subject. I would like to ask your opinion before I write to the Director – and this is a strictly private matter – whether you think there would be any chance of a Readership, let us call it in Cultural Anthropology, and perhaps a permanent Assistantship. Please treat this last part of my letter as purely private and unofficial, because I do not like to approach the Director before knowing your opinion.'[49]

With her children receiving her OBE in 1918

With her family and William Beveridge at Green Street,
Avebury, Wiltshire, undated, 1930s

With the LSE Army Class 1928–29

With William Beveridge, 1952

Choosing which stories to tell

Janet Beveridge was an accomplished writer of letters, memos, and official and unofficial records of all kinds, and she had a concern for the preservation of accurate archival facts, which of course doesn't itself rule out a process of selective preservation. But she never got round to finishing the autobiography, which exists in fragmented form in the Beveridge papers tucked away in LSE. Parts were written in the 1930s and the 1940s, and then the project was returned to a few years before she died in the 1950s. These somewhat scrappy and jumbled files are annotated in William's handwriting; he noted that some were found by him only after her death. Aspects of her life can also be derived from the books they both wrote: William's own autobiography, *Power and Influence*, published in 1953; hers on *Beveridge and His Plan*, which appeared in 1954; and the two they wrote about LSE and their work together there: his *The London School of Economics and Its Problems*, and her *An Epic of Clare Market*, both published after Janet died in 1960. The Beveridges' *Antipodes Notebook*, an account of their travels in Australia and New Zealand in 1948, was co-authored, with chapters written by each of them, and is probably a good example of the collaborative way in which they worked.

The main channel of information about Janet's life is historian José Harris's biography of William Beveridge, which was first published in 1977. A second edition followed in 1997. In both editions Harris's description of Janet's personality, her work, and her relationship to Beveridge, is unflattering in the extreme. She calls Janet 'forceful', 'formidable', 'bossy', 'domineering', 'self-centred', 'insecure' and 'histrionic', and says she resembled 'a deranged Hedda Gabler or a manic, raging Medusa'. Through her connection with William, says Harris, Janet was able 'to live vicariously in the world of administrative and social reform'. She was someone who 'craved a professional career and public recognition' but 'was unable to achieve either of those things without the unquestioning support of a powerful male partner'.[50] Harris maintains that Janet's position at LSE was controversial from the start. She was considered dictatorial and judgemental, going beyond her official remit in telling Beveridge and other LSE staff what to do. Harris interviewed two retired members of staff who recalled Janet as a 'wicked woman' and Beveridge's 'bad angel', 'who had effectively destroyed his chances of personal happiness and done untold harm to his professional life'.[51] To William, Janet attached herself 'like a limpet'; her obsessive jealousy and interference in his life was 'monstrous' and 'the degree of emotional blackmail seems at times to have bordered on mental imbalance.'[52] Harris finds in Janet's jealousy the reason for the Mairs' move to London in 1913: William Beveridge had become interested in a woman called Mary Sanders, a mountaineer and writer who published travel books and detective fiction under the name Ann Bridge; this, says Harris, was one of William Beveridge's recurrent and desperate attempts to escape Mrs Mair's clutches and find a wife/life of his own.

In other words, Janet ruined William Beveridge's personal life. But additionally, argues Harris, she added nothing to his professional life as the second founder of LSE and the father of the welfare state. Hard evidence of Janet's influence on his social thought 'or indeed of serious engagement with intellectual questions at any stage of her life' is difficult to find, argues Harris: insofar as Janet and William shared opinions, she merely echoed his. The Harris biography also caricatures Janet's 'ill-informed contempt for what she regarded as "soft disciplines"' and her 'rather crude devotion to the "hard" sciences' as partly responsible for William's intellectual feuds with other LSE staff – never mind that he championed scientific methods for social subjects all his life. 'It is difficult to avoid the conclusion,' Harris declares, 'that, although many of Beveridge's troubles at the School were in substance of his own making, the cataclysmic decline of his popularity as Director – from the soaring successes of the 1920s through to the conflicts and traumas of the 1930s – was closely linked to his ever-growing encirclement by Jessy Mair. That encirclement constantly coloured his personal relations with his colleagues, and added fuel to many of the controversies that reigned at the School, even if it did not actually cause them.'[53]

This does seem like an extraordinary condemnation. José Harris's biography of William Beveridge is the source for most other historical/biographical accounts of these fraught years. Ralf Dahrendorf's voluminous history of LSE, for example, draws its own narrative from what he terms Harris's 'tactful and plausible' text.[54] Maxine Berg's biography of the LSE historian Eileen Power in turns refers to Dahrendorf's 'careful assessment' of the Beveridge-Mair relationship, and describes Jessy Mair as 'the thorn in otherwise harmonious memories many held of the LSE'.[55] Many other accounts footnote the Harris and Dahrendorf histories as sources for dismissive, hostile and moralising remarks. One such talks about Janet's unfortunate role in William's life as an 'opinionated' woman reputedly motivated 'largely on the basis of personal prejudices'.[56] Biographies and memoirs by LSE staff who were antagonistic to Janet elevate personal views to the status of fact. The economist Friedrich Hayek mentions 'the extraordinary lady' who later became Lady Beveridge: 'She really dominated affairs. She was a crude, energetic woman who knew what she wanted.'[57] John Hall's biography of the social philosopher Ernest Gellner refers to 'the scandal' of LSE being run by Beveridge 'while under the thumb of the School's administrator, Mrs Mair, who may or may not have been his mistress'.[58]

Janet and David Mair's son Philip was moved to put together a very different account of his mother and William Beveridge's time together after reading José Harris's interpretation of Janet's part in William's life. As William Beveridge's stepson, Philip Mair enjoyed a close relationship with both him and his mother. Mair's book *Shared Enthusiasm: The Story of Lord and Lady Beveridge by Her Son Philip Beveridge Mair*, published in 1982, records the 'disbelief' with which he read the original Harris account. 'Much is so much at variance with what I know of them both' he wrote, 'that I could not let it pass into history without adding my story.'[59] Philip Mair's rebuttal of Harris's portrait of Janet in turn prompted further commentary by Harris in the revised edition of her Beveridge biography published 20 years after the first. This second edition, while clearly aiming to find a middle path between the negative picture of Janet in the earlier edition and her son's alternative view, does actually have the consequence of damning Janet completely.[60] In the second edition of her biography Harris is unable to find any evidence that Janet was really any good either with paper or with people; uncovering new information that William had a tendency to depression, she adds this to the list of problems for which Janet was purportedly responsible.

Philip Mair makes an important methodological point in drawing attention to Harris's heavy reliance on Beatrice Webb's diaries. Beatrice was notorious for disliking people and saying so; she was a well-known moraliser and very fond of gossip. He notes that Beatrice Webb and Janet Beveridge were poles apart in temperament, suggesting that Janet's 'generous warmth', obvious affection for her children and grandchildren and her unabashed enjoyment of the good things in life might have offended Beatrice's austere and childless life-style.[61] In May 1922, both Mairs, one of their daughters, and William Beveridge went to stay with the Webbs in Sussex. Beatrice and Sidney wanted to find out what had happened to their progeny, LSE. 'What interested and perturbed us was the hatred of Mrs. Mair, the secretary of the School,' wrote Beatrice, moving on quickly to note Janet's 'ambitious and domineering temperament' though observing, inconsistently, that, 'To us she is as sweet as can be.' Beatrice sympathised with David Mair's position – 'quite clearly suffering mentally from the intimate companionship of his wife and his cousin … How near the relationship borders on a domestic tragedy I do not know: Sidney pooh-poohs my concern. But Mrs Tawney, Beveridge's sister, burst out with expressions of hot dislike, and the dislike is shared by Tawney … and apparently by the great majority of the staff'.[62] Some of Beatrice's guests asked her if she could stop 'it' or get Mrs Mair transferred somewhere else. Beatrice replied that every institution has a devil and Mrs Mair was probably as harmless a one as they would get. Beveridge had great qualities but also defects, and Mrs Mair needed to be treated as one of his defects.

Like most of those who occupied themselves with the question, 'did they or didn't they?', Beatrice was pretty certain they didn't. For her, the 'essential wrongness of the whole business' lay in the pretence that there was nothing going on. William Beveridge and Jessy Mair ought to be man and wife, 'but then neither their domestic nor their professional status could be what it was.' 'I do not know exactly where the wrong conduct begins or ends: with the husband, the wife or the friend,' admitted Beatrice honestly.[63] There were other rumours that William entirely lacked sexual feelings for women. The economist Friedrich Hayek, responding to chatter about the Beveridges' premarital relationship, denied any suggestion of physical intimacy and cited an occasion on which Janet had come up to him in the Senior Common Room at LSE, indignant about William not making up his mind about something and bursting out with, 'He isn't man enough; he isn't man enough, I know.'[64] There's possibly another subterranean plot here involving both William Beveridge and Harry Tawney, during their Oxford undergraduate years, in a close homoerotic association with a clever young classicist called Arthur Collings Carré who died of opium poisoning. Carré was a focus for cult worship among a generation of Balliol College undergraduates, and William Beveridge was closer than most of them to the centre of the cult. He clearly loved Carré.[65]

We have here, then, in other words, a tangled web of different viewpoints: Janet's own on her life, relationships and work; William's version; Philip Mair's account of his mother and her collaboration with William; and the interpretations of a professional historian, whose account forms the basis for most other commentaries about the history of social science, LSE and William Beveridge. Extracting a single authentic narrative from all this is an impossible task. But trying to excavate from the layers of myth, rumour, gossip, and prejudice more about what Janet Beveridge actually did must be counted a worthwhile enterprise, especially in view of her intimate association with some of the most important social and policy developments of the 20th century.

Beveridge and his plan

The Beveridge Report on *Social Insurance and Allied Services* was published on 2 December 1942. Its euphoric public reception – mile-long queues outside the government bookshop and half a million copies sold – was quite unexpected. The Report was greeted by many around the world as the dawn of new age, which would replace the pre-war horrors of mass unemployment, unaffordable healthcare, and poverty in sickness, widowhood and old age. It was seen as creating the framework for Britain's welfare state, and thus its author, William Beveridge, became known as its father. Such an enormous institution as a welfare state is, of course, hardly likely to be created by one person at one moment, and modern scholarship shows how many of the Report's proposals drew on long-standing liberal ideas. But the Beveridge Report was extremely important internationally for what it said could be done by governments everywhere to protect the welfare of their populations in a modern post-war age.

David Mair died on 21 July and on 15 December, two weeks after the Report came out, William Beveridge and Jessy Mair were married in London, bringing, as he said, their more than thirty years of work together to a logical conclusion. Letters of congratulation on the marriage from friends and family got mixed up with letters about the Beveridge Report and William took them all on honeymoon to answer. Janet joked that she didn't know if she had married William or the Beveridge Report. She also let it be known that she wanted to be called 'Janet', rather than 'Jessy', from then on. Their intention of a quiet ceremony was somewhat defeated by the media attention, which celebrated different ways of defining Janet's identity: 'To marry his former secretary'; 'Sir William Beveridge married. Bride grandmother'; 'Sir William Beveridge at 63 to marry a lifelong friend'.[66] And so on and so forth. Janet's book about *Beveridge and His Plan* recalled the 'fantastic limelight' that followed the Report's publication. One day when she was trying to find a taxi in Bond Street an empty one passed and its driver leant over to inquire, 'Do you want a taxi, Your Ladyship?' Janet asked how he knew who she was, and he told her that everybody knew that, and when they reached her destination he refused to accept payment: 'It is an honour to drive the wife of the Beveridge Report.'[67] She hugely enjoyed such moments.

In the summer of 1941 William had been asked to chair a commission looking at the existing social insurance system with a view to possible improvements. He felt little enthusiasm for this task. Janet was able to persuade him. As he put it: 'She saw ... a chance for my earlier ambitions, of abolishing want and poverty, to be realised'. In his estimation, Janet 'was, and always will be, as much to blame for the making of the Beveridge Report as I was'; thus it was 'a partnership of two that had devised social security for Britain and set an example to the world'.[68] Much of the Beveridge Report was written on long train journeys to and from Northumberland and Scotland, where William was 'joined and advised continually by J.' [Janet].[69] One of Charles Booth's great-grandsons, Mark Stephens, remembers being told by Richard Burn, who married Janet's daughter Elspeth, about how Janet and William worked on the Report together at Carrycoats Hall in Hexham, Northumberland, the Burns' family home. Janet and William stayed there for long periods during the War. 'They often walked to the furthest end of the garden,' said Mark Stephens, 'and spent hours sitting on a bench overlooking the moors protected by a dry stone wall which the Burns had built.' There, 'on a warm day they spent hours in conversation'.[70]

The 200,000 words of the Beveridge Report were full of technical details, and would have made tedious and unimpressive reading were it not for Janet's intervention. As one historian has concluded: 'the document could so easily have offered all the excitement of a garden marrow rather than the striking bloom it turned out to be. Left to Beveridge the Report would probably have been confined to the kitchen garden.' Janet was the 'unsung heroine', sharing with William the responsibility of making a very ambitious interpretation of the Committee's terms of reference, which were merely to make a survey of existing schemes. Instead the Report offered a panoramic review of national social policy. Janet encouraged William to lay down long-term goals in many areas of social policy and to focus on three main policy objectives: prevention, education and treating the future as a gradual process leading to ultimate policy goals. 'Without Mrs Mair and her pleadings for a Cromwellian tone, the Beveridge Report, almost certainly, would have been indistinguishable from the dry-as-dust jargon-laden, statistics-ridden standard productions on social security, and would have been treated accordingly.'[71] Even Harris admits that, without Janet's influence, William's practical proposals would never have been wrapped in the grand vision of a new social order, which the public found so attractive. A sense of cataclysmic social change and an ethic of disinterested public service are part of the Report's rhetoric because Janet put them there. But her contribution is not formally acknowledged in the Report.

The four years between leaving LSE and life as Lady Beveridge were spent mainly in Oxford, where William had relocated as Master of University College to a house in the suitably named Logic Lane. Janet and David's daughter Elspeth had gone there to act as housekeeper and hostess. Jeannette Tawney, on hearing this, was most upset, as she had promised her and William's mother, Annette Beveridge, who tended to patrol fiercely all William's lady friends (as she did her daughter Jeannette's male friends), never to have anything to do with the Mair family. Jeannette had it all out with William, but he merely thought his sister was 'keeping up a feud'.[72] Janet moved first to a house in Headington and tried a reconciliation with David, from whom she had been living separately. The reconciliation failed. William was ill in hospital and she joined Elspeth in the Master's Lodgings, compounding Jeannette's problem about visiting her brother in Oxford. Then Janet broke a leg and so stayed there, taking over the hostess/housekeeper role, and eventually, with her customary domestic efficiency, modernising the house to her own standards: its 20 rooms, all made 'fireless, dustless, and drudgeless', as an admiring journalist reported. There was central heating and electrical devices abounded, though Lady Beveridge had further aspirations: 'an interior light in my refrigerator. Also I should like transparent doors and large thermometers with coloured figures.'[73] This (almost) perfect house was the setting for splendid entertaining. Mary Wilson, poet and wife of the Labour Prime Minister Harold Wilson, who had calculated prices in Janet's Green Street attic, remembered Scottish country dancing in the dining room, and a steaming bowl of punch in the hall: 'She did give *lovely* parties.'[74]

Janet's interest in domestic architecture and engineering overflowed into the further aspiration of taking over the duties of the Butler and the Domestic Bursar at University College. William canvassed for her appointment as Estates Bursar but her reputation for disturbingly formidable administrative powers had apparently preceded her, and he was foiled by G.D.H. Cole who got someone else to apply.[75] Nonetheless, Janet did have some domestic successes, for instance, in managing to get electric fires installed in all the College rooms. Some of the staff called her 'the Old Grey Mair' (after the children's song 'the Old Grey Mare'), and thought she was the Master's sister.[76] In these Oxford years, Janet occupied herself with various worthy public works: chairing a new branch of the Electrical Association for Women; becoming President of the Oxford Business and Professional

Women's Club. But these activities were nothing compared to what would come next.

The road to Lady Beveridge

After the two dramatic events of December 1942 – the marriage and the Report – Janet's life took another decisive turn in the direction of conventional wifehood. She became, for a time, a political wife. Senior academic staff at University College had been unimpressed by the amount of time their Master was spending away from his collegiate duties, and in 1944 William decided to go into politics instead. There was the electioneering, which Janet engaged in enthusiastically, and then there were the ten months William spent in parliament as Liberal MP for Berwick-upon-Tweed. Janet shared his disappointment when he, ironically, lost his seat to the Conservative candidate in the 1945 election whose results would prove so crucial to the final implementation of his Report.

Janet sold Green Street and they moved to a large house in Northumberland, Tuggal Hall, in 1945 in anticipation of many years in the constituency; when William was given a peerage in 1946, he chose the title 'Baron Beveridge of Tuggal'. The house stood in seven acres and boasted nine bedrooms, three bathrooms and an all-electric kitchen, which must have pleased Janet greatly. She found living in the quiet countryside 'a great change at my time of life', but it took her back to the stories her father used to tell her of Fife in his grandmother's time in the 18th century.[77] The house was well set up for the grandchildren's visits – there were four of them by 1945, and many warm letters in a childish hand repose in the Beveridge archives. John Gwilt, Marjory's son, wrote to thank Janet for the wonderful holiday at Tuggal, and to say he missed all the fruit and eggs immensely. Could she perhaps spare some jam? He and his brother George, at their boarding school, didn't have any left of this particular wartime luxury. John, George, and their siblings David and Lucy, were all skilled musicians whose musical careers benefited from Janet's help and enthusiasm. David Burn, Elspeth's son, recalls pleasurable childhood times at Tuggal Hall, with his grandmother 'an adoring granny … always smiling' and never a cross word from either her or William. Other family memories confirm this perception of Janet.[78] Grandchildren may be prejudiced, but perhaps the opposite description of Janet as a harridan owes something to prejudice too.

There were multiple public services performed as 'the wife of the Beveridge Report'; for example, opening exhibitions of child portraiture and electrical kitchens and a Pioneer Community Association Centre. Much of Janet's time was spent publicising the Report. In so doing, she made two important modifications to it. The first was to add a sixth freedom to William's list of five: his freedoms from idleness, want, squalor, ignorance and disease were extended by her to include 'freedom from war'. For women everywhere war is a hateful thing, opposed as it is to the preservation and fostering of life, contended Janet; war is an anachronistic survival from a world in which women have little or no voice.[79] Second, Janet directed attention away from the welfare state to the concept of a welfare society built around citizens' voluntary service to the community. 'In trying to abolish want, squalor, ignorance, ill health and idleness, have we produced other giants even more difficult to tackle?' she asked. 'Have we rushed into a Welfare State, instead of proceeding in a seemly manner into a welfare society? The claiming of rights under the Welfare State is widespread. The performance of duties within the welfare society is the other side of the shield.'[80] The Cromwellian tones injected by Janet into the Beveridge Report are echoed in her speeches. Talking to a large meeting held in the Coliseum Theatre in London on International Women's Day in the spring of 1944, she said: 'We and all the world have been shown more clearly than ever before that the women of this country, of China, of America, of all countries represent a power which, if it is properly used, can achieve anything … That is our great responsibility. Women can take responsibility. Let us get clearly into our minds that we want a new Britain …'. Reports of this event noted that the meeting was attended by a crowd of 2,300, including William Beveridge in an obscure seat at the back.[81]

Janet Beveridge was clearly committed to feminism. She believed that women were, and should be treated as, the equals of men, and she was inordinately proud of all the 'firsts' for women she could point to in her own life. She supported the suffrage agitation, but not its violence, and was unhappy about credit being given to the Pankhursts and other well-known names. When in 1958 it was suggested that the new women life peeresses should be marked by a memorial to Christabel Pankhurst, Janet wrote to *The Times* objecting that this was entirely wrong, as it was the work of ordinary women during the war, not suffragette activity, which had produced the 1919 Sex Disqualification Act.[82] But Janet notably failed to comment on something that subsequent feminist scholarship has made much of – the Beveridge Report's treatment of married women, or housewives, as it called them, as a separate class. It argued this special status on the grounds that housewives were entitled always to their husbands' financial support, they had 'vital duties' in the home to perform, and they were much less likely to be 'gainfully employed'. The concept of 'the family wage' and the essential dependence of wives was thus built into the structure of the British welfare state. But in her publicising of the Report around the country, Janet considered the recognition of housewives as a distinct insurance class to be an improvement, and she echoed the Report's ideological insistence on its treatment of man and wife as a team.[83]

Janet and *her* plan

But Janet Beveridge had yet another vision, one which her husband William didn't share. She wanted to write and publish fiction. This was an ambition she had in common with two of the other forgotten wives in this book – Mary Booth and Jeannette Tawney; like them, Janet's ambition was one she was never able to realise, although she came a good deal closer to it than they did. And were it not for William Beveridge's intervention, she might have succeeded.

Her first novel was called *Joanna's Family*, and it was written in the two years 1942–44. It no longer exists among her papers, but a short story does survive, called 'A storm in a teacup, or the country totalitarians', featuring a woman called Joanna. Joanna is married to Henry and she has just moved to a new house in the countryside: 'Neither Henry nor she had ever in their furthest flung plans included the possibility that he would stand for Parliament and actually win a seat. Events had followed one another after the manner of cataracts ...' [waterfalls, not eye conditions]. 'Joanna had thrown herself into the election campaign and had traversed the length and breadth of the constituency, holding meetings and canvassing votes.'[84]

The transparently autobiographical writing is competent, although not very exciting. Janet used all her contacts to get the novel about Joanna into print. While on a visit to the US with William as the guests of the Rockefeller Foundation, she contacted an American literary agent, Gertrude Algase, who wrote to her enthusiastically in June 1943 saying that the Viking Press was extremely interested both in Janet's novel, and in a possible memoir. 'If the novel turns out to be all that I think it is, it may easily carry film rights, which as you know can run into a small fortune.'[85] Janet wasn't able to send the manuscript until January 1944, and its dispatch was something of an effort in wartime when all transatlantic packages had to pass through the Censor's Department in the Ministry of Information. Janet also posted it to the British publisher Jonathan Cape, who read it 'with enormous interest'. 'It really is a delightful picture,' reported their reader, 'and I particularly enjoyed the delicious portrait of Joanna in the opening pages. Breaking all the rules I shall say "But surely I recognise Joanna"...!'[86] Unfortunately Cape wouldn't do the book as they had run out of paper for large-edition fiction. As a result of the Algase agency's pushy efforts (they were known for representing the great and the powerful, including the Kennedy family) it was the US publishing firm D. Appleton-Century Company who sent Janet a contract, which she signed. This contract was a generous one, offering $1,000 on delivery and acceptance of the manuscript, and a further $1,000 on publication (totalling about £28,000 in 2020 currency). The contract gave the company an option on a further book by Janet called, *On Top of Whitehall: Reminiscences of Diplomatic and Political Circles during Two World Wars in England and America* or some similar title'.[87] Although this would probably have covered some of the material Janet later put into her books about LSE and the Beveridge Report, we might have been treated to some entertaining 'Yes, Prime Minister' episodes.[88]

Janet seemed rather unconfident in the value of her work as a fiction writer; she self-deprecatingly called *Joanna's Family* 'a volume of tripe'; 'I am not at all proud of it'; 'in fact I think it is terribly bad'.[89] She became increasingly nervous about its publication. In January 1944 she wrote to her American agent explaining that she had used a nom de plume on the manuscript because her husband was very anxious that the book shouldn't appear in England under her own name. In America it didn't matter 'because no-one would be in the position to connect any of the characters with any living person, but in England this might he thinks, be possible and unfortunate'.[90] But even this solution wasn't sufficient to quell whatever it was that William was anxious about. Janet wrote again to the agent to say that he really didn't want the novel appearing anywhere under her own name and so she had decided 'that it should not appear in its present form even under a pseudonym'.[91] Please would they return the manuscript.

And that, seemingly, was the end of that. It wasn't the end of Janet's writing, however, as this burst out everywhere – not just in the two books about LSE and the Beveridge Report she wrote, and the one she co-authored with William about their trip to the Antipodes in 1948, but in multiple articles and broadcasting scripts. She was the correspondent for London University affairs on *The Sunday Times* for many years, delivering 30 columns a year. Her broadcasting correspondence in the Beveridge archives is considerable, and some of her broadcasts were published in *The Listener*. Topics included, predictably, 'The London School of Economics', and 'Grandmothers: asset or liability?'; less predictably, 'Is Latin really necessary?' and 'Living in a new town'.[92]

Housework without tears

Janet had always been interested in housing. The design of houses and the materials and equipment they contained had an enormous impact on the work of women in the home, and this was something whose importance, she, like many women before and since, had celebrated all her life as a most understudied subject. When William addressed the Wellington Institute of Public Administration in New Zealand on the 'Planning of New Towns for Housewives', a Wellington journal's headline 'Lady Beveridge steals the show' described Janet standing up and talking about the working hours of housewives, having sat there 'in agony' at the inadequacy of some of William's answers to audience questions.[93] Here she is talking at a public meeting in Salford in May 1944: 'It has long been said that the woman's sphere is the home. Well, let us rise to that particular challenge, for it is true, and refuse to permit the existence of slums, using the force of our knowledge and expertise to obtain dwellings for all, free of the inconveniences and frustrations of the man-made house, erected haphazard and for profit. We want to see great changes in such towns as Salford, where in the midst of factory life the homes should be conceived more than anywhere else with a view to garden spaces, wide open green parks and leisure centres. Both young and old need sunshine and beauty in their lives, and we want no more dark satanic mills.'[94]

This concern with good housing for all fertilised a rumour that Janet had written a book, which she didn't write, called *Housework without Tears* under the pseudonym of Priscilla Novy.[95] Priscilla Novy was a real person who worked for an organisation called Mass Observation and wrote children's books as well as her engagingly practical guide to housework. Janet did, however, supply the foreword to Novy's book. In it she argued that, 'There is no other device of any kind at all which can compete in curing the decline in the birthrate, or in lowering the rate of infant mortality.' She also proffered practical suggestions; for example, that, 'The abolition of the chimney-piece is a gain in space and in constructional expense, which could be set against extra power-wiring, introducing plugs into a number of places in all large rooms for movable electric fires on long flexes.'[96]

The 1947 Town and Country Planning Act was part of the post-war legislation designed to usher in the Beveridgean welfare state.

Newton Aycliffe in County Durham, in an area already desolated by pit closures, was designated as one of the first sites for a new town in 1947, at the same time as others such as Crawley and Hemel Hempstead. The Newton Aycliffe site housed a large industrial estate that had grown up at the end of the Second World War, replacing a top-secret munitions factory, whose women workers were known as the 'Aycliffe Angels' for their wartime production of millions of bullets, shells and mines. William Beveridge decided to make Newton Aycliffe his flagship new town: a place (and here we can pick up echoes of Janet's voice) 'in which every housewife will want to live if she possibly can'.[97] An Aycliffe Development Corporation was set up, which William chaired. The plan was to build houses around open grass-covered spaces, as in traditional villages, to provide nearby schools, playgrounds, health clinics, shops and a community centre, and centralised domestic facilities such as heating systems and electric laundries. These utopian plans were being copied in many other post-war developments.

The Beveridges took the Newton Aycliffe initiative personally. They bought a plot there at the top of the town, built a new four-bedroomed terraced house on it, and lived there for about a year in the early 1950s. Tuggal Hall had become too expensive to run; ironically for someone renowned for his promotion of pensions, William had been refused one for his years in the civil service and he received no fee for writing the bestselling Beveridge Report. Janet had tried her hand at market gardening to bridge the income gap, but this didn't solve the problem. Janet called Newton Aycliffe 'my new town', and she took to the airwaves talking about it in distinctly novelistic tones: 'Day comes gently with us. We are not disturbed in the early morning by clanking trams or by hooters calling in the factory workers. The quiet of each night begins to break between seven and eight ... Here and there, the quiet figure of the man of the house emerges, to proceed by bus, or car, or bicycle to his job at a distance, and from this house and that steps out on tapping heels a young wife, or a daughter, also making an income by working at an office or shop.'[98] But what she most liked to watch were the children and the babies. Newton Aycliffe was a town of young people; Janet Beveridge was its first resident grandmother.

The last years

After the Newton Aycliffe interlude, Janet and William moved in with Janet's surviving sister Florence in Edinburgh, but the arrangement wasn't harmonious. An appeal to University College, Oxford, produced their final home, a first-floor flat in Woodstock Road owned by the College to which they moved in 1953. Whatever the tensions that had penetrated the first thirty-odd years of their relationship – and what long relationship isn't marked by any of these? – Janet and William had by then settled comfortably into a close, affectionate and mutually supportive mode of relating to one another. Take these two notes, for example, written to each other on the same day in March 1946 when William was away: 'My darling I bought your silk yesterday, and whenever I have nothing else to do I take it out of its paper and think how nice it will look in its proper place on you.'[99] Janet was listening to music in Tuggal Hall: 'The fifth symphony is just booming to the last chord – there it is – the very last ... the important thing is that another day of my solitude is over. It has been a heavenly day – sunshine baking the house ... You'll soon be home and we'll walk in our own sunshine together, getting fat with being so happy.'[100] This connubial happiness shines out of the photo on page 155, taken seven years before Janet died. In their last years, the Beveridges exchanged few letters since they were living close together, but in 1956 when they were both admitted with respiratory problems to the Acland Nursing Home in Oxford for a few weeks in separate rooms, staff ferried their fond exchanges down the corridor.

In these later years in Oxford, they both specialised in annoying University College staff by perpetually complaining about dry rot, unfair rents, the cold, lack of garage space, noise from other tenants, weeds in the grass and similar matters. This fascinating correspondence, found only in the basement of University College by the archivist, Robin Darwall-Smith, in 2017, does show how bossy behaviour was as much William's sphere as Janet's. In fact, of the two of them, William was probably bossier than Janet, in the sense that he wished to impose his opinions on other people. But he was castigated for this rather less than was Janet. The newly excavated correspondence is also informative about another woman in William's life, Lucia Turin. Turin, a Russian émigré, had originally been a student at LSE and had then in the 1920s acted as Harold Laski's research assistant and as William Beveridge's secretary. Lucia Turin is the person who encouraged Jeannette Tawney's fiction writing. She worked devotedly for, or with, William for much of her life and nursed him in the last months of his life when Janet's death had left him grieving and wifeless (for more on Lucia Turin see Chapter 6).

Age often brings a reconsideration of past events and relationships. As she grew older and had more time on her hands, Janet Beveridge was keenly aware that her demeanour might have been a source of stress for some people. This included Lucia Turin to whom she wrote from the Master's Lodgings in Oxford one evening in 1938 when William and Elspeth were in London and she was all alone: 'I have been thinking so sadly of how I may have made things less easy for you in my own unhappiness this year at the School you and I have so much loved to serve', she wrote. 'You must try to forgive me ... No one knows better than I do how you have striven in the past, giving all your heart to the work. I have an endless respect for that, and I hope your devotion will be given the credit it deserves. Will you find some comfort in the reflection that all fair minded persons would wish that this should be the case.'[101] Reading an article penned by her old adversary Lionel Robbins in April 1949, Janet repeated her view, but now 'without any bitterness', that the plan for a Science of Economics at LSE had been thwarted by non-cooperative staff. 'Don't let us revive old disputes,' replied Robbins sagely. 'You know there are always two sides to any matters about which sincere people differ strongly or debate passionately.'[102]

Janet Beveridge died aged 83 in Hexham General Hospital, near the home of her daughter Elspeth and Elspeth's husband Richard Burn in Northumberland, where she'd been staying when she had the stroke that killed her. She was buried in the churchyard of one of Britain's oldest and tiniest churches, St Aidan's, in Throckington on the Northumbrian moors, just over the fells from the garden where she and William had discussed the Beveridge Report. Her grave was next to one of her grandchildren who had died as an infant. William joined them almost four years later, but, consistent with the historical disregard of Janet's role, most articles and websites mention only his presence in the graveyard and not hers.

Forgetting and remembering

The texts William Beveridge wrote about his wife both before and after she died are almost reverential in their admiration and praise for her as an individual and for her role in his life. 'Janet was a creature of outstanding ability and originality, shown in one public position after another.' She was endlessly hospitable and a perfect hostess, a perfect cook, a wonderful mother, and in her public duties she never had the publicity she ought to have had: 'It would be idle to attempt to separate what came from her mind and what from mine, of most of the new things that between us we invented'.[103]

Are we to accuse William of delusion and self-deception, or did he actually know what he was talking about? Like her husband, Janet

Beveridge could undoubtedly be incredibly annoying, judgemental and inconsiderate at certain times and with certain people. She liked to associate with famous and powerful people, to exploit her social connections. What Janet Beveridge actually did is, of course, the question for all forgotten wives. But her case study is an outstanding illustration of how women are often subject to moralising concerns about personal conduct from which men are free. Women who speak their minds and occupy positions of some authority vis-à-vis men are always vulnerable to being typecast as she-devils. That this was Janet's fate during her 18 years serving LSE probably owes a good deal to the irascibility of established academics who can sometimes see no further than the limits of their own disciplines. It was characteristic of Janet, with her strong convictions and keenly felt interests, to make connections in her work at LSE between her province as an administrator and matters of academic policy or academic personnel; herein also lay some of the bitterness with which her work was greeted at LSE. Some of the male academics may simply have resented, in an era before our modern self-consciousness of gender issues, being ordered around by a woman. Janet's status as a lonely woman in a hierarchically masculine environment is neatly portrayed in the photo on page 155, where she sits demurely among the members of LSE's 'Army Class' (an experiment in military education that ran from 1907 to 1932). Academics have always been very good at discriminating against women, and in the 1920s and 1930s it was still unusual to find women in powerful positions of any kind.

Beyond the parochial squabbles of academia, Janet Beveridge's alignment with the scientific social science lobby was of considerable significance both in securing funds and in supporting academic scholarship at LSE. The dream of social biology might have failed, but the rationale for the methodological rigour of natural science impressed itself on LSE scholarship and on British social science more generally. Social science did go on to distance itself somewhat from armchair theorising and it did form a friendlier alliance with empirical research as a sounder base for formulating statements about society and public policy. In this and other ways the School, and British social science, were the net beneficiaries of the Beveridge-Mair regime. A related and (as yet) untold story is Janet Beveridge's high-level negotiation with the Commonwealth Fund in the US for funding from 1927 onward to support a mental health social work course at LSE. This was effectively how the child guidance movement entered Britain.[104] With respect to the fate of the natural bases of the social sciences at LSE, one can speculate that, had the outcome been different, William Beveridge might not have been disposed to take on the forbidding task of reviewing the country's social insurance system. He was, as we know, reluctant to do this anyway, and it was Janet who saw the opportunity the invitation offered to steer social policy in a more rational and progressive direction.

The records of Janet Beveridge's life and work, set alongside the various biographies and histories in which she features, pose really serious questions about the methodology used to tell stories about people's lives. José Harris, William Beveridge's biographer, does admit that Janet's unpopularity at LSE was never as universal as her enemies liked to suggest. Harris also acknowledges that, 'Jessy Mair has had a bad press from historians, including myself. She perhaps deserves a more sympathetic treatment, as a woman trapped in the powerful cross currents of early 20th-century social transformation.'[105] What we see in most existing accounts of Janet Beveridge's life and work is the elision of a wife's private and public contribution by means, almost, of a caricature: a wife who doesn't hide her light under a bushel, as Mary Booth, Charlotte Shaw and Jeannette Tawney all did (the latter somewhat unwillingly), risks becoming a kind of she-devil, a woman who departs from conventional norms, not merely by smoking cigars, but by being an outspoken claimant of her own achievements and of the right to an acknowledged share in his. The unorthodox triangular relationship that developed between Janet and the two Beveridge cousins clearly flaunted the precepts of wifehood, and it is also something for which, strangely, Janet, rather than either or both of the two men, is held responsible.

These methodological questions about interpretation and about repetition (of the same story over and over again) run through all the case studies in this book, but they are most urgent with respect to Janet Beveridge. How does one disentangle what a wife does from what a husband does, and what injuries may occur in the process, if we always assume that she was, and is, the subsidiary one? We may like, or dislike, the people we write about, but to what extent should these personal opinions influence our judgement and our choice of language? The words used to describe Janet Beveridge and her interactions with others are astonishingly emotive and damning. It's actually difficult to believe that anyone could have been quite as awful as she was said to be, and have got anything useful done, as she patently did. Any praise she does get tends to be given rather grudgingly, as here in Dahrendorf's history of LSE: 'Whatever else one may say about Jessy Mair, she kept her man going. Without her he would have been lost and ineffectual.'[106] As Janet's son put it: 'That she caused annoyance is well known; that she won wide allegiance is less commonly recognised. The ill that she was thought to have done has lived after her to the point that those who have written in recent years have emphasised it rather than merely commented on it. The good, for which without question she should be credited, has been given much less notice.'[107]

How, then, should we remember her? Shortly before she died, Janet wrote to her old school friend Agnes Savill: 'I think that you and I are two of the most remarkable octogenarians alive and that we get far too little credit for having lived so long and done so many remarkable things.'[108] Among the appraisals that followed Janet's death, there was one from perhaps a surprising source, the economist Sydney Caine, who took over the Directorship of LSE in 1957. His memorial service oration for Janet acknowledged that there was more to her than a she-devil and a limpet. Caine said: 'whether as Mrs Mair, the name under which I first knew her nearly forty years ago, or as Janet Beveridge, it is of her work with William Beveridge that the world will first think. Her devotion to their joint activities, her loyalty to him, were outstanding and he has paid frequent tribute to the value of her constant support and encouragement whether in the great building up of the School of Economics, in the preparation of the Beveridge Report, in his Mastership of this College, in the building of the new community of Aycliffe or in his many other public services. But it would be entirely wrong to think of her as a mere shadow to him or to anyone else. Of no one was it more true that she was an individual in her own right.'[109]

6

A life of her own

Wives, like everybody else, are individuals with lives of their own. But history and ideology can conspire to strip them of this identity. In the process something essential about the social condition of being a woman is revealed. Of course it isn't a conspiracy; if it were, the story would be simple, with none of the devious tricks and turns that beset the real narratives. It's the complexity of the story – the layers of stories – that gives the story-teller such a headache, and puts the reader in such a position of agnosticism about where the truth lies, or may be hiding, or may actively have been hidden. Was Janet Beveridge a shrew with no academic intelligence of her own, and William Beveridge simply too besotted with her? Did Jeannette Tawney really obstruct Harry Tawney's scholarship with her frivolous and untidy ways? What was Mary Booth really doing in that damp mansion apart from having babies and minding the servants while her husband journeyed abroad? Are we allowed any truthful glimpse of Charlotte Shaw behind the thick veil of her labours helping two men write their own mixtures of fact and fiction?

Digging around in the archives of these four lives was for me a kind of revelatory archaeology. The remains produced didn't always match the catalogue description. I was surprised, for example, to learn about the immense networks Mary Booth orchestrated to facilitate her husband's work, and without which it undoubtedly wouldn't have been what it was. I was amazed to find Charlotte Shaw playing such a key role in the establishment of LSE – whose origins I thought I already knew – and to discover her roles as a translator of radical French literature and as Lawrence of Arabia's muse, editor and friend. Jeannette Tawney's independent life as a writer and pioneering factory inspector was another exposed secret. The architecture of Janet Beveridge's contribution to the budding LSE, to the development of social science, and to William's report on social insurance was much more substantial than I had suspected. In all four cases the stereotypes dominating biographical accounts turned out to hide interesting and authentic stories of wifely life and labour.

This chapter distils some of the central themes from these four narratives of wifehood. It looks at aspects of what the women had in common, and what is communal about the ways in which their lives have been represented by others. In doing this it extends the landscape a little by referencing the treatment of other famous men's wives across the territories of science, social science, literature, music and art. Mrs Einstein, Lady Elgar, Swedish Nobel Prize winner Alva Myrdal, Auguste Rodin's companion Rose Beuret, and two Russian literary wives, Sofia Tolstoy and Anna Dostoevsky, put in brief appearances, and the story of philosopher Harriet Taylor Mill's wifehood, mentioned in Chapter 1, is returned to as a source of methodological insights. The researcher looking for examples of forgotten or misremembered wifehood is absolutely spoilt for choice: these are only a few of many neglected wives who clamoured to be let in. A small deviation into the territory of office wives has also been allowed, on the grounds of the elision that seems perpetually to occur between the services provided by wives and secretaries.

Then we need to confront the methodological problems of writing about wives and wifehood. These problems cover both generic issues about archives and interpretative history, and specific matters relating to how women are seen and written about. Rather strangely, the sociology of work and the family, which might be expected to dwell for a while on the 'vicarious' occupational identity wives acquire, has largely ignored the importance of husbands' work for women's lives.[1] The stories in *Forgotten Wives* point to the forgetting of wives as a systemic phenomenon: far from being an accident, this amnesia is often a matter of actively failing to look, discover and thus remember. There are various strategies at work. Women become invisible by being disregarded; they may be included in the narrative yet be marginalised; wives' experiences may be assimilated but in a distorted fashion. Assumptions, vantage point and sensitivity to bias and silence are all-important. There are lessons to be learnt here about the continuing habit of relegating women who are attached to men as husbands or proto-husbands to some kind of inferior and pre-judged position.

The virgin territory of archives

This book couldn't have been written, or it would have been written very differently, without the plundering of archives. 'Plundering' here is a metaphor: the researcher/biographer/historian storms into those places where life materials are stored and takes from them what s/he wants. This, indeed, may sometimes be what happens. It's entirely consistent with the masculinist 'romantic' fantasy of the archives as secretive places full of stuff that passively awaits the explorer's attention.

The German historian Leopold von Ranke, whose work shaped the profession of history in Europe and the US in the late 19th century, spent much of his life in archives. He described these as 'so many sleeping princesses, possibly beautiful, all under a curse and needing to be saved'.[2] Archives as 'virgin territory' are permanently susceptible to rape. Although archive-explorers aren't always men, the masculinity of the professional historian, ideally objective and detached from everyday life, is an integral part of the archival fantasy. It's key to the kind of history that singles out the nation-state, war, empire, conquest, lineage, and the lives of great men for privileged scrutiny. The two strategies followed by young men wanting to take up history as a profession in the 19th century were training in seminars and working in archives. 'Disciplined by the seminar to become venturesome "citizens," young professionals set out for the archives, where they hoped to break open the gates of the documentary "harem," save the "fairy princesses" residing there, and find truth in the process.'[3]

Archives can be buildings, cardboard boxes, files, cupboards containing letters, postcards, telegrams, diaries, manuscripts, photographs, sound recordings, medical records, certificates of birth, marriage, death and national identity and other multifarious material objects. They are assemblages 'of faded presences and shadowy absences',[4] 'tiny pieces of flotsam, floating on the great dark limitless river of Everything.'[5] Which of these pieces of flotsam should we look at? Who put them there, and why? What might have been there but isn't? And how do we read what *is* there? What do we notice and what passes us by?

Alongside the romance of the archive sits the ordinary reality: the archive-plunderer wanders in one day, wet from the rain, and struggles with the key or the code of the locker in which personal possessions have to be enclosed before anyone is let loose on the precious virgin territory; s/he is uncertain about what will be found here, and confused about the right questions to ask, and then is either submerged in a veritable tsunami of flaky documents or confronted with almost nothing at all. (The absence of evidence isn't evidence of absence, but not everyone remembers this.) It's not romantic working in archives; they're often extremely dusty, cold, lonely, insufficiently signposted places whose guardians give one the impression that it would be better (for the archives) if one wasn't there at all.[6]

My social science degree in the early 1960s contained nothing about method, even though it covered sociology, economics and political history, all subjects which cry out for some consideration as to how knowledge is arrived at. Since matters have advanced in the intervening decades, I turned to the literature on archival and historical methods for an enlightening discussion of the archive plunderer's travails. Astonishingly, archival methods appear to be largely a non-issue. 'I am not aware that we have consciously sought to describe a method,' says the biographer and literary critic Leon Edel.[7] 'The few articles on methods available to new researchers either lament the lack of methods in our field or offer overly simplistic advice – read widely in your field, have a good time, formulate a research question,' says Barbara L'Eplattenier, an American teacher of rhetoric and writing.[8] Yet once you enter the black box of archival territory an avalanche of complications await you. The past isn't a stable matter: it changes all the time, because the present is constantly evolving, and we look back at the past *from* the present with its own particular social and ideological circumstances. This makes pure 'resurrection' of the past an impossible venture.[9]

Archival research is a form of ethnography. As such, it doesn't seem to have caught up with the enormous strides that have been made in recent decades developing criteria for evaluating 'qualitative' research data.[10] There are no accepted guidelines for dealing with the tricky questions: what to do when primary sources conflict? How should gaps and absences be dealt with, and/or how should allowances be made for the uneven treatment different sets of archives have received at the hands of archivists, funders, institutions and families? What do we do when changing values and ideologies alter the lens through which we see history? The sociologist Stina Lyon, writing about the use of biographical material as evidence, puts the case very clearly: such material 'needs to be guided by the same principles as the search for validity and representativeness as in other areas of social research'.[11] Access to the past through people's memories – the use of 'living human mediums' – is also 'a dodgy business', like any form of séance.[12] What people remember is shaped, not only by vantage point, but by the logic of memory itself, which has an unnerving capacity to short-circuit and reinterpret what actually happened. Anyone writing someone else's life, or fitting it in to some particular argument or other, must be perpetually on the lookout for such pitfalls. But, however careful we are about the evidence, an element of judgement is ultimately involved in choosing who to believe about what. Here the notion of 'triangulation' is relevant. Taking data from more than one place and/or using different methods to sample the data is a way of settling on one interpretation over another and avoiding the bias of a preselected viewpoint. How different narratives fit, or fail to fit, together is very important.

The gender of history

Asked why he'd never written a biography of a woman, Michael Holroyd, the biographer of such great men as George Bernard Shaw and Lytton Strachey, said that all such invitations came his way at impossible moments when he'd just started another biography of a bearded man.[13] Biography writing as a genre has, for most of its history, been a tool for the reproduction of dominant values: this is why it has ignored women, people of minority ethnicity, poor people and those who are uncelebrated by, and within, the dominant culture. It's also why biographical dictionaries such as the *Oxford Dictionary of National Biography* specialise unthinkingly in alpha males – a practice encouraged by the absence of female editors.[14]

'By and large gender is not a significant question in mainstream accounts of history-writing as a professional practice.'[15] The lives in *Forgotten Wives* played themselves out against a background of a newly professionalising history writing that focused on public life and 'great men' narratives. It's the residue of this tradition that has so often pushed wives into a limited place. In the early 20th century, university departments of history became 'places where men communed with one another about the histories of other men'.[16] Over time, masculinist history with its core nationalist, elitist and imperialist values predominated, filled school textbooks, became how we all think of history. Scenes and experiences of domestic labour, the life of the body, all those fascinating intersections of the private with the public – these topics took a back seat to the grand masculinist dramas; they became the uninteresting and trivial shadow of what really matters. One consequence of this trajectory is women's absence from the archival record. This record, anyway, privileges the literate, and literacy has traditionally been much more the reserve of men. Where records of women's lives do exist, they must generally be looked for under the names of men: nearly all the archive materials drawn on for *Forgotten Wives* are catalogued using the names of husbands or other male relatives.

Her sympathetic smile

Ideologies and assumptions mist the lens through which wives are seen. For Mary Booth, her very conformity to Victorian ideals of wifehood and motherhood – the many children, the house administration, the entertaining and coordination of the networks, the commitment to supporting her husband's career and guarding his physical and mental health – were her downfall, in the sense that not much else of her life is visible unless you actively look for it, put yourself in the position of being on the alert for traces of agency, autonomy, initiative and significant intellectual labour. As scholarship on the great Booth poverty inquiry has developed in recent years, more of Mary has emerged, because the point of view has shifted to see the inquiry as a collaborative venture involving Mary and many others. But Mary's part in the Booth archives remains minimally catalogued, compared with Charles's, and her diaries, letters and family archive are still a largely untapped resource. One reason is that the astonishing detail they offer about the life and work of a late Victorian/Edwardian upper-middle-class mother is too ordinary to interest many professional historians. Who wants to know how to bottle fowls (her 1922 diary) or make carpet soap (in 1938) or treat bronchitis ('equal parts of spirit of wine & vinegar rubbed into the throat after washing' – the 1896 diary)?[17]

Charlotte Shaw has been more of a puzzle than Mary Booth for the conventionally gendered biographer. First of all, she apparently refused the wifely duty of sexual intercourse (of this more later) and thus she avoided motherhood also. But perhaps she was a kind of mother to the two men in her life – George Bernard Shaw and T.E. Lawrence? This would make her more of a normal woman. Never mind that her collaboration in GBS's ventures was not what a mother would do, or that her allure for T.E. Lawrence was precisely that she bore no resemblance to his mother. At 65 she was old enough to *be* his mother, and this mathematical calculation led to a suitable accompanying image: 'She was a plump, dignified figure, fond of flowered hats, fur collars, and veils. Her eyes sparkled behind rimless glasses and she had a sympathetic smile.'[18] There seems to be a fair preoccupation among biographers with detecting motherhood in implausible places. In the effort to cast her wifehood in a more conventional mould, Janet Beveridge has also been assigned a role as William Beveridge's mother.[19]

Psychological understandings, endemic in modern biography, are easy to misapply, especially when self-consciousness of point of view is lacking. Of the four women in *Forgotten Wives*, the second two have probably suffered most from the application of stereotypes: Jeannette Tawney, for being a bad housewife, a spendthrift, and speaking her mind; and Janet Beveridge for behaving as though she were married to William when she wasn't, for also speaking her mind, and for not being reticent in telling the staff of the Ministry of Food, LSE, and University College, Oxford, what to do. In accounts of her husband's life, Jeannette Tawney has usually been regarded as so hopeless that the assumption of incompetence was extended by association to all departments of her life. Particularly striking in her case is the ascription to her of full responsibility for domestic chaos. In contrast, Jeannette's voice in the Tawney and Beveridge archives can be heard plaintively asking Harry to take standards of cleanliness and tidiness more seriously, and to pay her better attention as a woman. In her work as a factory inspector and would-be novelist Jeannette Tawney was not incompetent, although she was impeded in both these areas by the protective misogyny of her husband.

One of the most startling stories of gender stereotyping's interference with an understanding of wifely behaviour concerns Harriet Taylor Mill, whose marriage to the philosopher and political economist John Stuart Mill was touched on in Chapter 1. Harriet's first marriage in 1826 was to John Taylor, a prosperous wholesale druggist ten years older than she was. The Taylors had three children together, but Harriet became increasingly disenchanted with her husband, both because he wasn't an intellectual like she was, and because he imposed himself on her sexually. While this latter experience probably helped to fuel Harriet's highly radical ideas about marriage, it also gave rise to the idea among biographers that sex disgusted Harriet, and that she was frigid. Biographers decided that this deficit of Harriet's was responsible for the non-consummation of her 23-year-long alliance with John Stuart Mill. Yet another black mark against Harriet was that, for the last 17 years of her life, before dying at the early age of 51, she was ill with multiple symptoms including intermittent difficulty in walking, pain, numbness, headaches, broken blood vessels in the lungs, nose bleeds and fevers. Tuberculosis would have explained some of these maladies, but the rest were considered by biographers to be probably psychological in origin (see next section, on wifely hypochondria). In 2002, Jo Ellen Jacobs, an American philosophy professor, published a book based on many years of research aimed at finding out more about Harriet as a person in her own right – not just her sexuality, but her work as a radical philosopher and economist, and her side in the sustained collaboration with Mill. Jacobs' book, *The Voice of Harriet Taylor Mill*, takes a closer look at Harriet's symptoms, her medical records, and the remedies she used; it concludes that Harriet Taylor Mill was almost certainly a victim of that unmentionable and common scourge of Victorian life – syphilis.

Harriet probably caught syphilis from her first husband, who, marrying relatively late, at almost 30, is likely to have followed the habit of many middle-class Victorian men in visiting prostitutes. Medical advice at the time was that, once the primary genital sore had healed, men couldn't possibly give the disease to their wives. (Correcting such false ideas was one of Charlotte Shaw's projects, see Chapter 3; the unwitting transmission from husbands to wives is the theme of the Brieux play she translated as *Damaged Goods*.) Doctors refused to tell women that their husbands or future husbands had syphilis, regarding it as the husband's 'moral duty to deceive her in this matter'.[20] Syphilis as an explanation of Harriet's invalidism uniquely makes sense of various Taylor-Mill puzzles: in its light we can understand why Harriet may have discovered a dislike of sex with her first husband John Taylor (she found out he'd infected her); Taylor's benevolence in putting up with her relationship with Mill, and continuing to provide for her financially, becomes more reasonable; the non-consummation of her bond with Mill makes perfect sense; and, most sadly, the paralysis, mania and insanity that afflicted Harriet and John Taylor's children and grandchildren also has a plausible cause.

The clues Jacobs excavates as to Harriet Taylor Mill's condition better fit the known facts than other versions. The explanation of syphilis fits *different* bits of evidence, and this is important.

Female maladies

Whether or not he knew what was really ailing Harriet, John Stuart Mill displayed a much more sympathetic attitude than did his biographers to his wife's illness, caring for her and bearing her off to warm climes for the sake of her health. Charlotte Shaw's husband also looked after her well through the long debilitating decades of Paget's disease, and the other man in her life, T.E. Lawrence, expressed much concern for Charlotte's health in his letters to her. Still, Charlotte was accused of hypochondria by GBS's biographer and others: she 'took refuge in a myriad of aches and illnesses, as she did throughout her life',[21] comments one student of the Shaws of the period following Charlotte's encounters with the charismatic Dr Axel Munthe, who himself specialised in a cynical, and financially profitable, outlook on idle women's proneness to imaginary illnesses. Jeannette Tawney, born a generation after Charlotte Shaw, wasn't quite so fortunate in the attentions of her husband, as Harry didn't really know how to be a husband. Jeannette, too, was considered by celebrators of her husband's life to be prone to inventing illness, although the medical records in the Tawney archives say otherwise.[22] The writer Storm Jameson, giving Jeannette advice about the writing of fiction, thought she ought instead to write about being Jeannette Tawney and especially about her 'dreadful illness'.[23]

Mary Booth was much given to mentions of illness in her correspondence and diaries: with all those children, and servants, and Charles's strange afflictions to attend to, her role in caring for other people's health was a critical one. Interspersed with the records of other people's ailments are notes on her own: 'I find it rather a struggle here,' she writes from Gracedieu to Charles in the winter of 1889, when their six children were aged from 3 to 16; she feels sick all the time and has 'head aches even at night ... I keep on being afraid of having to give up'.[24] Charles worried about her, and so did her father, and she was probably quite exhausted a lot of the time. Exhaustion in women can often be mistaken for psychological illness. It was Mary Booth's daughter Imogen who complained to one of Charles's biographers, Margaret Simey, about the phrase the Simeys had used: 'vague ill-health'. Mary, said Imogen, had never been vague about anything in her life, but, on the other hand, she *had* suffered from malaria for many years.[25]

The case of Janet Beveridge is a particularly acute illustration of the critical issues that abound in constructing a person's life story: the reading of personality, the imputation of motives, assumptions about action and inaction. Biographers 'look for facts to suit the character' they have already decided on: 'inconvenient facts can be ignored or minimised, and equivocal facts may be weighted in the direction of a predetermined interpretation.'[26] As noted in Chapter 5, William Beveridge's biographer, José Harris, could find very little of value in Janet Beveridge's contribution to William's life and work, or, indeed, in her own, and this evaluation persisted through both editions of Harris's biography. The epithets applied to Janet – 'paranoid and depressive', 'obsessively anxious', 'suppliant and demanding', the writer of 'streams of hysterical letters' – are disturbingly in line with a long tradition of negative stereotypes of female character.[27]

These two designations of women – of imaginatively creating illness, and of being highly prone to nervous disorders of one kind or another – tie the stories of the four wives in this book to a whole appalling history of medical theories about the pathological vulnerability and 'otherness' of women. In the 19th century, nervousness or 'neurasthenia' and 'hysteria' became technical medical terms justifying women's commitment to mental institutions and their enforced submission to horrible genital and reproductive surgeries. Upper- and middle-class women were subjected to something called the 'rest cure', which meant no physical or mental activity of any kind. The inventor and proselytiser of the rest cure, the American doctor Silas Weir Mitchell, saw it as a useful means of disciplining women who were neglecting their household duties.[28] The most famous record of how the histories of women, nerves and Western medicine interlocked to produce a special form of wifely oppression is a short story called *The Yellow Wallpaper* by the American writer and feminist Charlotte Perkins Gilman who passed some time with the Webbs and the Shaws in 1896 (see Chapter 3). *The Yellow Wallpaper* regales the misadventures of a wife suffering from 'nervous depression' who was locked up by her physician husband and told to do absolutely nothing at all.

Writing women

The rest cure demanded that one thing women had urgently to be prevented from doing was writing. Because, if they wrote, what on earth might they write about? Women's relationship to writing is relevant to the stories of the four wives in this book. Two of them (Mary Booth and Jeannette Tawney) wanted to be writers, and two of them (Jeannette Tawney and Janet Beveridge) had their publishing ambitions obstructed by their husbands. So also, not coincidentally, did Mary Booth's friend the historian Alice Stopford Green.[29] Three of the four wives in *Forgotten Wives* wrote novels: Mary Booth destroyed hers; fragments of Janet Beveridge's remain; and there are various jumbled versions of Jeannette Tawney's in the Tawney archives. None of these novels was published. Their authors joined the huge contingent of women writers who in this period weren't able to usher their fiction into the light of day. We don't know what proportion of women wrote – they needed some sort of education, of course, in order to do so, which many lacked – but, 'For every novel in print there may have been half-a-dozen mute inglorious Brontës', whose works reached the publisher's desk only to be rejected.[30]

What should we make of this frustrated fiction? Novels are the least elitist form of writing: they can be mundane, in the uncorrupted sense of being about ordinary life, and they can – most dangerously – be autobiography in disguise. Virginia Woolf pointed out that fiction is the easiest thing for women to write because it can be picked up or put down at will. 'George Eliot left her work to nurse her father. Charlotte Brontë put down her pen to pick the eyes out of the potatoes.'[31] Another advantage is that women's socialisation, argued Woolf, is an excellent training for novel writing, because in their ordinary social intercourse women learnt to excel at observation and the study of character.

All four wives in *Forgotten Wives* wrote and published other material successfully – essays, academic articles and other pieces. To his credit

Charles Booth encouraged Mary in her writing, and there's no evidence that Charlotte Shaw was held back by any complaints from GBS. But it would be interesting to know just why Jeannette Tawney was so afraid even to tell her husband she was writing a novel: 'Please do realise that it is a complete secret,' she told her brother's secretary, Lucia Turin. 'Harry does not know that I have written it, and does not wish to read it ... I feel his lack of faith in my capacity to do it is a slightly cramping thing so I do not above everything want him to know about it until it is a success.'[32] It would also be informative to find out what it was about the revelations that might ensue from Janet Beveridge's lucrative American publishing deal that convinced William to put a stop to it.

Sofia Tolstoy provides one of the saddest stories of 'great man wifehood' and women's unfulfilled project to be a writer. Buried in the gigantic Tolstoy archives is Sofia's own vanished record as a writer. She wrote poetry, fiction and children's stories, and her husband, Leo Tolstoy, published some of her stories under his own name.[33] Her legacy, that of a 'highly independent, cultured, intelligent and literarily talented professional, who was well in advance of her time,' has been almost totally ignored by contingents of Tolstoy scholars.[34] Sofia, married at 18, endured 16 pregnancies, which added up to more than 23 years spent pregnant or breastfeeding. She ran the Tolstoy households; administered the substantial Tolstoy estate; educated the children (in whom their father showed only a sporadic interest); looked after the man himself, a duty that included giving him enemas; and throughout all this she worked as Leo's amanuensis, making sense of his horrendous handwriting at night when there wasn't time enough in the day, and placing the neat versions on his desk each morning. She is said to have copied out some of his manuscripts as many as 20 times. 'My assistance in this work,' she noted uncomfortably in her autobiography, 'ceased only when I was completely incapacitated by my labour pains, my illnesses or the children's, or when the children died.'[35] For the first 15 years of the marriage the system worked reasonably well, although better for him than for her. 'I don't know if it was such a good thing for me,' she reflected, looking back, and rather mildly given the circumstances, 'constantly assisting my husband with the transcribing, as well as caring for him, to stifle all these talents within myself.'[36] Then Leo had his crisis; he repudiated art, family life and all the trappings of upper-class life, becoming a prophet of a new self-invented religion. Marital antagonism hardened. Sofia found herself defending the rights of their children to an education, and Leo's duty to share the profits of his writings with her and the children.

During the ensuing battles Sofia was deemed hysterical and paranoid and psychiatrists were called in.

Sofia Tolstoy wrote a short autobiography in 1913 to contest her reputation as a nagging unhelpful wife, and then a much longer one, more than a thousand pages, which she was still working on shortly before she died. *My Life: The Memoirs of Sofia Andreevna Tolstaya* eluded publication for a century. It shows Leo Tolstoy to be 'an idol with feet of clay', a man who always put his own needs first, who was terrified of babies, and quite infantile himself in his dependence on his wife. We might call *My Life* her masterpiece, says the Tolstoy scholar Hugh McLean, 'but perhaps it would be better to call it the literary record of her true masterpiece, which was the nurturing and support she gave for over five decades to one of the greatest literary talents the world has produced'.[37]

In the aftermath of Leo Tolstoy's death Sofia consulted another Russian literary wife, Anna Dostoevsky, about self- or rather husband-publishing. Anna Dostoevsky had been hired to take dictation by her husband-to-be when she was 21 and he was locked into an impossible publishing contract, which required him to complete a novel in four weeks or lose the rights to all his work. The novel (*The Gambler*) was duly finished and Fyodor Dostoevsky asked Anna to help him work on the much more famous *Crime and Punishment*. A marriage was established; he called her his collaborator and guardian angel; she nursed him through epileptic fits and a gambling addiction, became his business manager and paid off his debts by setting up a publishing company and getting his work out into the public domain. Both Anna Dostoevsky and Sofia Tolstoy left records of their experiences in diaries, memoirs and correspondence, although Anna was more circumspect than Sofia, using a code that took almost half a century to break. The Dostoevsky marriage lasted for 14 years. Fyodor died when Anna was 35, and she spent the last 37 years of her life publishing his books, organising his archives, donating 4,230 items to the Moscow Historical Museum for a special room dedicated to his memory, and creating a 400-page index of these items – 'a unique achievement in Russian literary bibliography'.[38] The publishing business was very successful. Anna Dostoevsky used the profits from the business to establish a school for peasant children from which by 1917 over a thousand girls had graduated as rural teachers.

Family voices

Trying to tease out the 'true' story of someone's life is especially problematic when the accounts of different people connected to that person diverge. Both Janet Beveridge's son, Philip Mair, and Mary Booth's grand-daughter, Belinda Norman-Butler, wrote book-length accounts intended to remedy what their authors saw as unfair biographical treatment of their mother and grandmother respectively. The Norman-Butler volume rehabilitates Mary Booth as a central figure in Charles Booth's work: 'While Charles Booth's place in social history is well established, very little is known of that working relationship with his wife which puts their marriage into the Curie class, except that the Curies were never apart and the Booths seldom together.'[39] Philip Mair's *Shared Enthusiasm: The Story of Lord and Lady Beveridge* goes a good deal further than rehabilitation in directly contradicting the characterisation of his mother that appears in the Harris biography. Yes, Janet Beveridge spoke her mind, and yes, she could be officious as an administrator, and yes, there were some academics at LSE who disliked her, but these disparagements were counterbalanced by the warmth of the regard in which many other staff and students held her, by her achievements in helping to secure a financially and academically sound future for LSE, and by the strength of her intellectual partnership with William Beveridge. Philip Mair says that Harris's perspective was over-influenced by a reliance on the opinions of Janet Beveridge's critics. He also suggests that one aspect of the calumnies heaped on Janet's head was moralising about the 'irregular' relationships that existed for some years between Janet, William, and Janet's first husband, Philip's father, David Beveridge Mair. Can one really trust and respect a wife who has a close relationship with another man? (The same suspicion isn't usually applied to the 'another man' in these triangles.) The fate of Janet Beveridge in the biographer and historian's hands has been unerringly like that of Harriet Taylor Mill, who similarly loved and worked closely with John Stuart Mill during her first husband's lifetime. The descriptions of Harriet and Janet as tempestuous and domineering shrews, vituperative, paranoid, unpleasant women are also more or less interchangeable.[40] And both John Stuart Mill and William Beveridge were said to have been 'bewitched' by these women, to such an extent that no one should believe the highly complimentary comments the men made about their wives

Lucy Mair, Philip's anthropologist sister, made it clear to Philip that she didn't want to be associated with his book about their mother. She wanted to stay clear of these discussions about family dynamics. In this (under-studied) genre of biographies by sons and daughters, the most arresting example is that of the Swedish social scientist Alva Myrdal, whose three children published five books about her and their family life. Alva Myrdal, born in 1902, was married to the economist Gunnar Myrdal. Both Myrdals were extremely well known in Sweden and internationally in the 1930s, 1940s and 1950s for their contributions to research and policy development, their analysis of contemporary social issues, and their promotion of the need for a family-friendly welfare state. They were both government ministers and members of public commissions in Sweden and elsewhere in Europe. Alva worked in the United Nations Department of Social Welfare and as Director of the newly formed UNESCO Social Science Division. Later she was Swedish Ambassador to India and she led the Swedish delegation to the Geneva Disarmament Conference in the 1960s and early 1970s. For her work on peace and disarmament she was awarded the Albert Einstein Peace Prize in 1980 and the Nobel Peace Prize in 1982. Gunnar Myrdal also received a Nobel Prize for work on the theory of money, jointly with Friedrich Hayek, the very man who first exposed the voice of Harriet Taylor Mill (see Chapter 1).

Despite Alva's distinguished career, Gunnar is altogether more celebrated. He's particularly remembered for the extensive report he wrote on American race relations, *An American Dilemma: The Negro Problem in Modern America*, which was published in 1944. Rather paradoxically, in view of Gunnar's own behaviour as a husband and a father, this incorporated a startling appendix drawing parallels between the cultural treatment of black people and women. Gunnar Myrdal's sensitivity to gender issues was clearly influenced by Alva, who is best known in the UK as the joint author with the sociologist Viola Klein, of one of the first books, *Women's Two Roles* (1956), to put squarely on the table the policy and personal problems consequent on the trend towards the increasing employment of married women outside the home.

The Myrdals' son, Jan, published the first of his three volumes about the Myrdal family's life the year his mother was given the Nobel Peace Prize. His *Childhood* was a literary sensation in Sweden for its portrayal of Alva as a neglectful, cold mother, a wife in a failed marriage who ran a hostile and an unforgiving home, a woman who repeatedly abandoned her children in favour of professional success and social status. This unflattering picture was strengthened in Jan Myrdal's two subsequent volumes, the second of which, in an extraordinary step, Jan Myrdal arranged to have distributed free to 100,000 Swedish schoolchildren. Jan's sister Sissela Bok, a philosopher (and, as Jan was quick to point out, the author of a book called *Lying*) followed this with *Alva Myrdal: A Daughter's Memoir* (1987) showing Alva in an utterly different light as a serious analyst of social and economic issues, and a revolutionary role model for women caught in the snarled space between the old ideas of wifehood and the new tradition of women's two roles. Bok's account details how Alva's relationship with Gunnar, which began when she was 17, triggered 'submissive "self-denial"': Alva burned all her fictional writings and diaries in order to dedicate herself to Gunnar's career.[41] In the early years she did Gunnar's typing, and throughout the marriage she assumed full responsibility for childcare and running the home. Gunnar wasn't interested in his children: on that Sissela and her brother's accounts agree. The Myrdals' younger daughter, Kaj Fölster, extended her sister's perspective in a book subtitled a 'Myrdalian postscript', which fastens on the major dynamic of Alva's domination by both her husband and son: 'Alva's faith in the power of reason, talk, diplomacy and collaboration falls apart in front of their masculine power and control.'[42]

The contents of the 1,600 boxes and 120,000 letters inhabiting the Myrdal archives in Stockholm show that the formula of Gunnar as the brilliant economist, and Alva as the practical-minded policy person, just won't do; they worked on theory and policy together, spanning issues of both family and public policy. Caring for homes, husbands and children doesn't strip women of their intellectual power, although it has created an insidious caricature of wives as too practical and concerned with the everyday to have anything at all significant going on in their minds.

A generic issue in the Myrdal story runs through many narratives on wifehood. Since wifehood is, traditionally and systemically, a condition of subjection to the dominance of husbands, collaboration is difficult for the outsider to perceive and name. If a wife and husband appear to work together, she must be helping him; she will be the midwife, but hardly a progenitor, of his ideas. The archival material can then be adjusted to fit this view. Actually, the bias against collaboration as a working practice is fundamental to our cultural perspective on knowledge. Medieval texts had multiple authors, and if any author was named it was the one who had copied out the text. When printing arrived on the scene it brought a financial incentive to the claim of sole authorship. This, plus the developing ideology of the individual self as the 'knower', helped to eradicate the notion of collaborative knowing and writing.

Individualism, and individualisation, as hallmarks of modern capitalist culture directly oppose what the sociologist Carol Smart has called 'the connectedness thesis', which sets the sociological imagination off on a totally different intellectual path.[43] This path leads away from the geography of modern academic life, which 'is founded in some peculiar assumptions about the relation between doing work and competing with others, competing with others and getting credit for work, getting credit and building a reputation ... minimising family life and leaving it to your wife'. The traditional academic career is wife-unfriendly. Hence those many book prefaces which thank wives for doing everything while never explaining why this doesn't qualify them to be co-authors.[44]

Einstein's wife

The example of Mrs Einstein is an exceptionally commanding case of buried co-creation. Mileva Marić and Albert Einstein were both physicists. They met in 1896 when she was 20 and he was 17, and both were enrolled in a mathematics and physics programme at the Zurich Polytechnic Institute. Marić, born in Serbia, which didn't allow women to enter universities, had come to Switzerland in search of higher education. She was talented and ambitious. She and Einstein studied physics together and got similar grades, Marić doing better at experimental work but suffering from a prejudiced examiner who downgraded her final mark because of her sex. In 1902, the year before they married, Marić gave birth to a baby girl whose fate is unknown: she may have been given up for adoption or died as an infant; two sons were born later. Einstein's family opposed the match: his mother said of Marić to her son, 'Like you, she's a book. And you should have a wife.'[45] Marić believed in the value of Albert's work long before anybody else did, and she supported him while he struggled to get a job and to have his scientific ideas taken seriously. Eventually he found employment as an official in the Bern patent office, and he and Marić worked on physics by the light of a kerosene lamp in the evenings. They discussed science and philosophy with like-minded friends including Marie and Pierre Curie, another scientific husband-wife team.

A Serbian physicist, Desanka Trbuhović-Gjurić, published a full-length biography of Mileva Marić in Serbian in 1969; it was later published in German and French but has not yet been translated into English.[46] A second biography was published in 2015.[47] Like the first, this presents a record of an actively collaborative partnership. It was during the early years of his relationship with Mileva Marić that Albert Einstein's groundbreaking papers, the foundation of modern physics, on motion, photoelectricity and relativity were written and published (in 1905). It seems that Marić's name as well as Einstein's was attached to several of these key papers, afterwards mysteriously disappearing.[48] The year the papers were published, Marić, visiting her family in Serbia, told her father, 'Before our departure, we finished an important scientific work which will make my husband known around the world.'[49] Einstein himself acknowledged the collaborative nature of their work. For example, 'How happy and proud I will be when the two of us will have brought our work on relative motion to a victorious conclusion'; and, 'I am very curious whether our conservative molecular force will hold good for gases as well.'[50]

After their early years of passionate work and life together, Einstein became quite uninterested in his family, and some years into the marriage he began an affair with a cousin. He and Marić separated in 1914 and divorced in 1919. The conditions Einstein laid down for an attempted reconciliation between these two dates make chilling reading: 'You will make sure,' he instructed Marić, 'That my clothes and laundry are kept in good order ... That I will receive my three meals regularly in my room ... That my bedroom and study are kept neat, and especially that my desk is left for my use only ... you will stop talking to me if I request it'.[51]

Albert Einstein isn't the only 'great man' to have treated women badly, nor is Mileva Marić the only great man's wife to have self-effacingly failed to put herself forward as an intellectual equal. But material suggesting that Einstein's theory of relativity might originally have been a collaborative enterprise has been deliberately excluded from the Einstein legacy. When the Einsteins' daughter-in-law tried to publish the letters the Einsteins had written to their sons that discussed their joint lives and work, she was blocked in court by the Einstein Estate Executors who wanted to preserve the 'Einstein myth' as a brilliant and saintly man who made his giant discoveries all on his own.[52]

One question recurs time and again: what might *he* have accomplished without *her*? (The parallel question, what could *she* have done without *him* to cater for, has puzzled many wives.)

Enigma variations: Lady Elgar

Caroline Alice Roberts, who married the composer Edward Elgar in 1889, was herself a person of considerable creative stature, and the musicologist Percy Young was sufficiently fascinated by the enigma of her wifely life to publish a book about her in 1978. Alice, as she was known, 'flitted across the musicological landscape' as the good wife, submissive, tactful, dutifully inspiring, or as a lady whose 'starched opinions and intellectual limitations' inhibited the full development of her husband's work and life. In short, Alice had suffered from the normal wifely stereotypes. She deserved better. As Young put it: 'Either the inspirational force plus wifely companion thesis deserves further scrutiny; or the woman in her own right principle should be applied to one whose own gifts were closely linked to those of a national cultural hero.'[53]

Alice was almost nine years older than Edward, and this was one reason why their families opposed the marriage. Another reason was that Elgar was a struggling musician, virtually unknown, from a Roman Catholic shopkeeper's family, a man given to moods, depression and hypochondria. Alice met Elgar when he gave her music lessons. She was, at the time, as the phrase goes, 'resigned to spinsterhood', but actually she was happy with her writing and painting, her intellectual curiosity and radicalism constantly driving her to explore new territories (she had begun with geology). She wrote short stories, mainly for children; lyric and narrative poems and novels; and she published translations from German and Italian (she was fluent in five languages). Alice's two-volume novel *Marchcroft Manor* – accomplished, entertaining and funny – had been published in 1882, four years before she met Elgar; a 64-page long poem, *Isabel Trevithoe*, some of which Elgar would set to music, appeared in 1879.

Quite why Alice decided to marry such a person as Edward Elgar is unclear, except of course that women were expected to marry. Whatever the reason, in marrying Elgar Alice sealed her own fate as a writer. She did go on writing, but there was little time for that once she had dedicated herself to proving the family opposition wrong by turning Edward Elgar into a great musician. She believed he was a genius. 'The care of a genius is enough of a life work for any woman,' she wrote in her diary, in order to console herself for not being more successful as a writer.[54] Edward Elgar was as much Alice Elgar's life's work as Leo Tolstoy was Sofia Tolstoy's. Early in their marriage Alice brought them to London from Worcestershire, to an abode near the Crystal Palace where Elgar could be taken to hear the best classical music London had to offer. She introduced him to influential social contacts. She was his business and social secretary, the manager of his accounts and households. After their daughter Carice was born in 1890 Alice made sure that the child didn't disturb Edward's composing: Carice was farmed out to relatives and friends during her father's working hours and then sent to boarding school. By 1901 there had been a prolific flow of pieces, including the best-known *Enigma Variations* (1899), *The Dream of Gerontius* (1900) and the *Pomp and Circumstance March Number 1* (*Land of Hope and Glory*, 1901).

Elgar's talent was increasingly being recognised, and he had an assured place as England's leading composer. In 1904, he was knighted, and Alice became Lady Elgar. The biography that tells the hidden story of Caroline Alice Roberts was made possible because Carice, the child banished from the Elgar home in the interests of his music, passed on many of her mother's archives to the biographer, Percy Young. She wanted the record of her mother's role in the creation of Edward Elgar the composer to be written.

Alice died in 1920. Her obituary in *The Times* called her, 'Devoted Helpmeet of Master Musician'.[55] She had laid out all Elgar's scores, copying in all the voice parts, lining the pages and planning the barring for several thousands of pages of 45 scores. But there was collaboration there too. Elgar set many of Alice's poems to music, and there are even some drafts of compositions that (like Albert Einstein's theoretical physics) carried Alice's name. After her death, Elgar, bereft of her 'self-sacrificing organization of his life', wrote only for the wastepaper basket.[56] Not even the magnanimous encouragement of Charlotte and George Bernard Shaw could change this. The Shaws were both huge admirers of Elgar's music. Charlotte Shaw sent records of his music to T.E. Lawrence in India, and Charlotte and he went together to hear Elgar conducting his first symphony in London.

Model wives

In 1904, Charlotte Shaw heard that the sculptor Auguste Rodin was in London and wanted to meet GBS. She invited him to lunch and suggested that he might like to 'do' her husband in marble. She put £1,000 in Rodin's bank account as an inducement, and in 1906 the Shaws were entertained at Rodin's rather bare and unartistic villa in Meudon just outside Paris (it's now a Rodin museum) while the 30 sittings Rodin required tested GBS's patience. The figure in the background at Meudon was Rose Beuret, Rodin's 'model wife', the beautiful, scarcely literate daughter of a peasant family, a seamstress, who met Rodin when she was 18 and doing modelling work to earn money in Paris. Invited into his studio, Rose became Rodin's first full-size nude model figure. She and Rodin were together for 53 years, though Rodin only got round to marrying her two weeks before she died in 1917. For all that time Rose sat for Rodin; she cooked and cleaned and entertained for him; in their early poverty-ridden days she took in sewing to buy food, and looked after their baby son to whom she'd given birth alone in an institution for poor women; she put up with Rodin's numerous affairs; and, very importantly, she learnt how to wrap his clay sculptures in wet rags to stop them from falling to pieces.

Most people in Rodin's lifetime saw Rose as an unimportant marginal figure, and most of Rodin's biographers see her just as a hardly-worth-commenting-on model-mistress/wife. Ruth Butler, one of these biographers, viewed Rose differently. She has argued that Rodin's art would not have been at all the same without Rose, and not just because Rose put food on the table and did the domestic work, but because her life entered into and shaped Rodin's creations. Model wives such as Rose Beuret bring, 'a whole spectrum of feelings with them, giving their husbands' art emotional texture and substance, contributing elements for art as important as the light in which a scene is bathed'.[57] Butler's book *Hidden in the Shadow of the Master* is about three such women: Rose Beuret; Camille Doncieux, Claude Monet's first wife and great model; and Hortense Fiquet, who modelled for Paul Cézanne. All three women steered their men through poverty to artistic recognition, gave birth to a son early in the relationship, and left a deep imprint on the men's art.

Office wives

They used to be called 'office wives'; now they're known as 'work wives'. Secretaries are often confused with wives, but the two are not the same, except sometimes in the eye of the beholder, and in that saddest of all dedicatory acknowledgements: 'lastly my wife, who did the typing'.[58] In such a perception, important men are surrounded by medleys of unimportant women who are scarcely distinguishable from one another. Here is another history that needs to be written.

George Bernard Shaw's secretary, Blanche Patch, provided an invaluable perspective on life with both Shaws in her memoir *Thirty Years with GBS*. She was first recruited by GBS for secretarial services after they met through the Webbs in 1917. Patch had been trained originally as a dispenser and she was working for a rural GP who counted the family of Laurencina Holt née Potter among his patients: this was the very same Laurencina whose house the young Mary Macaulay had been staying in when she first met Charles Booth. (Biographers love stumbling over such coincidences, but they do convey important clues about social networks.) Blanche Patch thought the Shaws quite similar to the Webbs – both men were very single-minded and both depended heavily on the domestic ministrations of their wives: 'Sidney Webb once remarked to me how thankful he was that all his life he had a good woman to put food before him three times a day,' Patch remarked. 'Shaw from the day of his marriage was equally lucky.'[59] Blanche Patch was given a desk in Charlotte's Adelphi Terrace flat for seven years, and then, when the Shaws moved to a flat in Whitehall Court next to the National Liberal Club, she went with them, her desk sharing a room with GBS's. Patch had a room in their house in Ayot St Lawrence too, although she, like Charlotte, disliked its cold and isolation.

Blanche (they called her Blanche) knitted GBS fingerless mittens in all sorts of colours to ward off the cold, and year after year she turned his scribbles into readable text. GBS wrote to his friend Nancy Astor in the middle of the Second World War about Blanche's all-embracing role in his life: 'Patient Patch does my business, types my shorthand for the printer, fills up all chinks in the housekeeping, knits for the soldiers and makes soft dolls for the Red Cross, and knows more about everybody in the village than I learned in thirty five years.'[60] Blanche's contribution to GBS's writing was a source of tension sometimes. Charlotte, said Blanche, 'was a bit possessive … Although she never showed it outwardly, I sometimes felt that she was even jealous of the fact that I had to read and transcribe his shorthand. I knew the text of the latest play before she did.' But the two women also formed an alliance; for example, when it came to the writing of *An Intelligent Woman's Guide to Socialism* (an explanation of socialism for middle-class women commissioned by Charlotte's sister Mary), which took three years, 'Charlotte told me she was tired of hearing about his intelligent women and their socialism. Both of us implored GBS to hurry up and finish the thing.' According to Blanche Patch, she and GBS had just one argument in the 30 years of their work together; it was sparked by her feeling, and saying, that he was treating her as a secretary and not as a person. In response he wrote, 'You are intelligent, sensible, self-reliant, kindly, useful, competent, and almost unbelievably even-tempered and self-controlled … The trouble you have NOT given me, and the help you HAVE given me are immeasurable.'[61]

The Blanche Patch in William Beveridge's life was called Lydia Lucia Turin, known as Lucia. She worked for Beveridge at LSE and she followed him and Janet to Oxford after they retired, where William paid the rent on the flat she lived in: 'I can guarantee whatever rent you require, providing a home for her as a reward for her work for me,' he told the University College Bursar.[62] The official rationale for this arrangement was that Lucia Turin, whom he termed his 'research assistant', would help him finish volume 2 of his mammoth *History of Prices and Wages in England*. Turin's background is mysterious, but the political theorist Harold Laski, who met her when she was a student at the University of Glasgow in 1912, said she was born in what is now Lithuania in 1893 (the Russian Revolution would have destroyed her birth records). Turin, who may have come from a minor aristocratic family, was thought to have originally studied medicine, to have married a British officer who was killed in the First World War, and then to have studied at LSE where she met and married Sergei Turin, a lecturer in economic theory and Russian economic conditions. In the 1920s Lucia was Laski's research assistant and then from 1929 William Beveridge's secretary.

Over the years Lucia Turin performed many duties for the Webbs, the Beveridges, the Tawneys, and other LSE staff, activities that crop up in the margins, acknowledgements and footnotes of public texts but have never been put together as a coherent story. Fortunately, there is a box, uncatalogued, of Turin papers in LSE, which contains correspondence and photographs that fill in the story somewhat. Both Turin and her husband as Russian speakers were invaluable sources of help to the Webbs in the writing of their *Soviet Communism: A New Civilisation?*; Lucia supplied both the Webbs and Harry Tawney with material about Russia. She was an amateur photographer and her many pictures of people in these circles are tucked away in the archives. As we saw in Chapter 4, she played a key and protracted role in counselling Jeannette Tawney about her own efforts to be a fiction writer: Turin had herself written a novel and had successfully published a number of short stories. Jeannette's reliance on her advice is evident in this letter, written in the winter of 1934, about the manuscript of Jeannette's novel: 'I do want you to be an angel and read it all through again,' urged Jeannette. 'Then if you would mark with a pencil any of the parts that jar or seem very bad I will try and reconsider them … If I have the ill-luck to get ill again and not be able to float my little boat, will you please do it for me as a friend's act.'[63]

There were many other miscellaneous 'secretarial' acts: buying a typewriter ribbon for Jeannette Tawney's Underwood Portable typewriter; delivering a copy of Hardy's *Far From the Madding Crowd* to William Beveridge, paying his laundry bill, and choosing a lampshade, all on Jeannette's behalf; helping Jeannette to find a servant to look after Harry when she was recuperating in the country from a severe thrombosis in her leg; negotiating the loan of William's car to take her to a meeting at a school in Hackney Downs where she was a governor. Despite this extensive service, Lucia Turin gets no mention in Lawrence Goldman's biography of Harry Tawney and there are just two in the first edition of Harris's Beveridge biography. In one, Turin is William Beveridge's 'faithful and effusive Russian secretary', and in the other she 'fussed over him like a child' in his post-Janet years.[64] The second edition of the biography adds four more references to Turin as a source of information on Janet Beveridge's 'almost hysterical resentment and jealousy' of other women in William's life.[65]

In the four years after Janet Beveridge died, Lucia Turin did virtually assume Janet's role in his life. She took care of the cleaning in his Oxford flat, and then of the man himself when he became ill. In 1961, she attended as his companion a Beveridge debate at LSE and a dinner at the Waldorf, and she accompanied him when he returned to LSE later in the year to talk about its history: 'It would be absurd,' William said, 'for me to recount the story of L.S.E. without Lucia also there. She was with me and indispensable there for practically all of 18 years'.[66] Beveridge scholars should be intrigued by the letter she wrote William in October 1961, when Janet had been dead for two and a half years, and Sergei for seven: 'My dear William ... I want to set you free, so that you can make a free choice and decide whether you want me, whether I am of any use to you, whether the whole game is worth the candle ... at our age, and between old and devoted friends as we are, complete faith and freedom is all that matters. Choose freely for both of us ... God bless you and keep you, Lucia.'[67]

Lucia Turin's University College, Oxford, obituary said that she 'never talked about herself ... She was one of those insignificant looking people, easy to overlook, who leave behind them a memory of presence, distinction, remarkableness'.[68] Demonstrably much more than a secretary, Turin was a vital part of the network that produced the institutional growth of British social science in the form of LSE. The LSE story runs in parallel to the lives of the four forgotten wives in this book. Without two of them (Charlotte Shaw and Janet Beveridge), LSE is unlikely to have flourished as an institution at all.

Lessons of wifehood

'Easy stories drive out hard ones.'[69] Offered the easy story and simple paradigm of women as dutiful wives devoted to the servicing of husbands and homes, the injudicious biographer need look no further to explain (or judge) women's conduct, or to understand marriage as a context for husbands' work. Forgetting and misremembering are cultural as well as individual acts. In researching and writing this book my own prior assumption (which is of course another kind of bias) has been that wives are women with lives of their own. In her book *Writing of Women*, Phyllis Rose proposed that, 'Often the most radical perspective you can adopt on a person's experience is his or her own.'[70] The perspectives on the lives and work of Mary Booth, Charlotte Shaw, Jeannette Tawney and Janet Beveridge offered in the last four chapters are, I believe, more radical in this sense than those in other available accounts. I have tried to create space for the women's own voices to be heard, however dimly, through the fractured mounds of archival material and the distracting distortions of other biographical texts.

Studying marriage is a notoriously awkward business. There's not only the guilt about prying into secret places, but the problem that, 'It is nearly impossible to see behind the lacquered surface of almost any marriage.'[71] The Beveridges, the Booths, the Shaws and the Tawneys all presented a certain face to the world; for each couple it was the face of an arrangement that had its own internal logic. Yet each was also a model of gender difference. Mostly the wives managed the private sphere, while the husbands featured in the public one. But this separation between the two spheres wasn't complete: it wasn't, in fact, nearly as complete as the biographical and historical accounts have made it out to be.

The problem with which the text of *Forgotten Wives* has tangled all the way through is how to tell the difference between how lives were lived and how they've been portrayed by others. Social class and other such influential factors skew this gap differently. But the more you study how the experiences of wives have been represented, the more overwhelming the sense of deeply gendered narrative becomes. Wives type their husbands' manuscripts, even if they have already written their own and slipped these into a dark drawer because publishers aren't interested in them. Wives feed and educate the children and keep them quiet so husbands can work. Wives look after husbands' bodies and minds, not like mothers, but like wives. Their unassuming modesty, and the way in which biographers have lapped this up and thought, 'well, she didn't really do much, did she?' brings tears to one's eyes.

The starting point of biography is almost never the home, the private place which houses wifely labour, whose conditions shape the work and personal relationships of the people who live there. It all comes back to the tricky, irremediably dirty and neglected topic of housework. Virginia Woolf, who ruminated a good deal on the practice of life writing, decided that much more could be learnt about the famously miserable but impressively intellectual married couple Jane and Thomas Carlyle by entering their Chelsea home than from all the grand biographies. These omitted to mention that the Carlyles lived in a house without indoor sanitation, water, electric light or gas fires, a house full of coal smoke in which Mrs Carlyle and 'one unfortunate maid' laboured incessantly to keep dirt and cold at bay and to ensure the total silence the great man needed to write his grand histories. 'Both husband and wife had genius; they loved each other; but what can genius and love avail against bugs and tin baths and pumps in the basement?'[72]

The story of wifehood is a story about women, but it's also one about marriage as an institution. We would do well to remember one of the analytical insights of 1970s feminism – that marriage is the system whereby gratuitous work is extorted from wives as a particular population group. Wives' 'back up services', amounting sometimes to a great deal more than that, as we have seen in the examples of *Forgotten Wives*, are a form of *productive* labour. What is construed as personal work done *for* a husband actually benefits those who enjoy the fruits of the husband's work. This function of marriage as a social and economic system also helps to explain why accounts of marriage have difficulty accommodating diversity. People, in their private relationships, can negotiate all kinds of arrangements that may be unintelligible to, or hidden from, outsiders. This is what the Beveridges, the Booths, the Shaws and the Tawneys did. But the 'heteronormative paradigm' of marriage has to be disposed of before these arrangements are visible. Then various things become clear. One is that friendship, as something that happens within marriages, is probably hugely under-acknowledged. Instead, biographers obsessively chase the conventional but not always answerable question as to whether a couple had sex or not. Why should sexual intercourse be considered the defining feature of a marriage? Out of the five Victorian marriages studied by Phyllis Rose in her book *Parallel Lives* two or three were sexless: 'it will not do just to say "How bizarre."'[73] Sexless marriages can be examples of flexibility and friendship, as was clearly the case with the Shaws and the Beveridges, and in their later years, the Tawneys – if, indeed, the marriages *were* sexless, which we will never know.

People do leave traces of themselves, whether they want to or not. They don't choose what we find after they've gone, nor what we say about it. The four women who feature in *Forgotten Wives* aren't here, as I said in Chapter 1, because they were especially important or well known: they weren't major figures in the social and political history of the time. Or were they? Who is major and who is minor? Every time you research and write about someone who is thought of as minor and not particularly successful they become much less minor and much more successful. This is only one reason why wifehood should be taken seriously.

Notes and sources

Abbreviations

BevP	Beveridge Papers, BLPES, LSE
BevP/BS	Beveridge Papers, BEVERIDGE/ SUPPLEMENTARY, BLPES, LSE
BLPES	The British Library of Political and Economic Science
BP	Booth Family Papers (MS797), Senate House Library, University of London
LSE	London School of Economics and Political Science
LSE/CFR	LSE/CENTRAL FILING REGISTRY, BLPES, LSE
ODNB	Oxford Dictionary of National Biography, Oxford University Press
PP	Passfield Papers, BLPES, LSE
SP	Shaw Papers, BLPES, LSE
TP	Tawney Papers, BLPES, LSE
TP/TV	Tawney Papers, TAWNEY/VYVYAN, BLPES, LSE
TuP	Turin Papers, BLPES, LSE
UCA	University College Archives, University of Oxford

Chapter 1: The condition of wifehood

1   'Why Be A Wife', campaign leaflet (1975), London: Why Be A Wife Campaign.
2   Jeger, L. (1958) Obituary, Jeannette Tawney, *The Times*, 20 January.
3   Pašeta, S. (2004) 'Green [*née* Stopford], Alice Sophia Amelia [known as Alice Stopford Green] (1897–1929), historian and Irish nationalist', ODNB.
4   Green, A. S. (1913) *Woman's Place in the World of Letters*, London: Macmillan & Co., pp 19–20, 23.
5   Cited in Jefferson, A. (2007) *Biography and the Question of Literature in France*, Oxford: Oxford University Press, p 128.
6   Webb, B. (1942) Diary, 24 March, cited in Gahan, P. (2017) *Bernard Shaw and Beatrice Webb on Poverty and Equality in the Modern World, 1905–1914*, Cham, Switzerland: Springer International Publishing AG, p 189.
7   Shaw, G. B. (1938) 'Foreword' to Webb, B. *My Apprenticeship, Vol. I*, Harmondsworth: Penguin, pp 9–13, 10.
8   Shaw, 'Foreword', p 9.

9   Webb, B. (1975, Drake, B. and Cole, M. I. (eds, first published 1948) *Our Partnership*, Cambridge: Cambridge University Press, pp 294–5.

10 Mill, H. T. and Mill, J. S. (1983, first published 1851 and 1869) *Enfranchisement of Women* and *The Subjection of Women*, London: Virago, pp 23–4.

11 Mill, J. S. in Mill and Mill, p iv.

12 Mill, J. S. in Mill and Mill, p 168.

13 Holcombe, L. (1983) *Wives & Property*, Oxford: Martin Robertson, p 112.

14 Rossi, A.(ed.) (1970) *Essays on Sex Equality by John Stuart Mill and Harriet Taylor Mill*, Chicago, IL: University of Chicago Press, p 36.

15 Martineau, H. (1981, first published 1837) *Society in America*, London/New Brunswick, NJ: Transaction Publishers, p 291.

16 Blackstone, W. (1765) *Commentaries on the Laws of England, Vol. I*, Buffalo, New York: William S. Hein & Co., pp 442–5.

17 Beveridge, J. (1954) *Beveridge and His Plan*, London: Hodder and Stoughton, p 119.

18 Caird, M. (1897) *The Morality of Marriage and Other Essays on the Status and Destiny of Women*, London: George Redway, p 53.

19 Yalom, M. (2001) *A History of the Wife*, New York: HarperCollins, p 268.

20 Gilman, C. P. (1898) *Woman and Economics*, Boston: Small, Maynard & Co., p 7.

21 Schreiner, O. (1911) *Woman and Labour*, Leipsic: T. Fisher Unwin, p 68.

22 Hamilton, C. (1909) *Marriage as a Trade*, London: Chapman & Hall, p 4.

23 Abel-Smith, B. (1992) 'The Beveridge Report: its origins and outcomes', *International Social Security Review*, 45 (1–2): 5–16, 6.

24 Abel-Smith, B. (1983) 'Sex equality and social security', in J. Lewis (ed.) *Women's Welfare, Women's Rights*, London; Croom Helm, 86–102, 90.

25 Spender, D. (1982) *Women of Ideas and What Men Have Done to Them*, London: Routledge & Kegan Paul, p 136.

26 Caird, *The Morality of Marriage*, pp 144–5.

Other sources used

Astell, M. (1694) *A Serious Proposal to the Ladies for the Advancement of Their True and Greatest Interest by a Lover of Their Sex*, England: printed for R. Wilkin.

Astell, M. (1700) *Some Reflections Upon Marriage Occasion'd by the Duke & Duchess of Mazarine's Case, which is Also Considered*, England: printed for John Nutt.

Baldwin, M. P. (2001) 'Subject to empire: married women and the British Nationality and Status of Aliens Act', *Journal of British Studies*, 40: 522–56.

Bernard, J. (1873) *The Future of Marriage*, London: Souvenir Press.

Blodgett, H. (1990) 'Cicely Hamilton, independent feminist', *Frontiers: A Journal of Women's Studies*, 11 (2/3): 99–104.

Buss, H. M. and Kadar, M. (eds) (2001) *Working in Women's Archives: Researching Women's Private Literature and Archival Documents*, Waterloo: Wilfrid Laurier University Press.

Cockin, K. (2017) *Edith Craig and the Theatres of Art,* London/New York: Bloomsbury Methuen Drama.

Comer, L. (1974) *Wedlocked Women*, Leeds: Feminist Books.

Dooley, D. (2004) 'Wheeler [née Doyle], Anna (1785?–1848), philosopher', ODNB.

Finch, J. (1983) *Married to the Job: Wives' Incorporation in Men's Work*, London: George Allen & Unwin.

Gilman, C. P. (1911) *The Man-made World or Our Androcentric Culture*, New York: Charlton Company.

Green, A. S. [Mrs J. R. Green] (1894) *Town Life in the Fifteenth Century, Vol. I.,* London: Macmillan & Co.

Green, A. S. (1908a) *The Making of Ireland & its Undoing, 1200–1600*, London: Macmillan & Co.

Green, A. S. [Mrs J. R. Green] (1908b) *Town Life in the Fifteenth Century, Vol. II.,* London: Macmillan & Co.

Green, J. R. (1874) *A Short History of the English People*, London.

Green, J. R. and Green, A. S. (1879) *A Short Geography of the British Islands*, London: Macmillan & Co.

Hallstein, L. O. and Bromwich, R. J. (eds) (2019) *Critical Perspectives on Wives: Roles, Representations, Identities, and Work*, Bradford, Ontario: Demeter Press.

Hayek, F. A. (1951) *John Stuart Mill and Harriet Taylor: Their Correspondence and Subsequent Marriage*, Chicago, IL: University of Chicago Press.

Heilman, A. (1996) 'Mona Caird (1854–1932): wild woman, new woman, and early radical feminist critic of marriage and motherhood', *Women's History Review*, 5 (1): 67–95.

Hill, M. R. and Hoecker-Drysdale, S. (eds) (2003) *Harriet Martineau: Theoretical & Methodological Perspectives*, New York/London: Routledge.

Hollis, P. (1979) *Women in Public: The Women's Movement 1850–1900*, London: George Allen & Unwin.

Holton, S. (2002) 'Gender difference, national identity and professing history: the case of Alice Stopford Green', *History Workshop Journal*, 53 (1): 118-27.

Joannou, M. (2004) 'Hamilton [née Hammill], (Mary) Cicely (1872–1952), writer and campaigner for women's rights', ODNB.

Jose, J. (2019) 'Feminist political theory without apology: Anna Doyle Wheeler, William Thompson, and the *Appeal of One Half the Human Race, Women*', *Hypatia*, 34 (94): 827–51.

Kingstone, H. (2014) 'Feminism, nationalism, separatism? The case of Alice Stopford Green', *Journal of Victorian Culture*, 19 (4): 442–56.

Lewis, J. (1992) 'Gender and the development of welfare regimes', *Journal of European Social Policy*, 2 (3): 159–73.

Lücker, K. and Daenschel, U. (2019) *A History of the World with the Women Put Back in*, Stroud: The History Press.

McDowell, R. B. (1967) *Alice Stopford Green: A Passionate Historian*, Dublin: Allen Figgis and Company Limited.

McFadden, M. (1989) 'Anna Doyle Wheeler (1785–1848): philosopher, socialist, feminist', *Hypatia*, 4 (1): 91–101.

Mair, L. (1971) *Marriage*, London: The Scolar Press Limited.

Martineau, H. (1837) *Society in America*, London.

Martineau, H. (1838) *How to Observe Morals and Manners*, London: Charles Knight and Co.

Murray, J. (2016) *A History of Britain in 21 Women*, London: Oneworld.

Murray, J. (2018) *A History of the World in 21 Women*, London: Oneworld.

Newman, C. (2018) *Bloody Brilliant Women: The Pioneers, Revolutionaries and Geniuses Your History Teacher Forgot to Mention*, London: William Collins.

Oakley, A. (2018) *Women, Peace and Welfare: A Suppressed History of Social Reform, 1880–1920*, Bristol: Policy Press.

Pankhurst, K. (2018) *Fantastically Great Women Who Made History*, London: Bloomsbury Children's Books.

Pateman, C. (2018) *The Sexual Contract*, Redwood City, CA: Stanford University Press.

Pedersen, S. (1989) 'The failure of feminism in the making of the British welfare state', *Radical History Review*, 43: 86–110.

Pedersen, S. (2004) *Eleanor Rathbone and the Politics of Conscience*, London/New Haven, CT: Yale University Press.

Perry, R. (1990) 'Mary Astell and the feminist critique of possessive individualism', *Eighteenth-Century Studies*, 23 (94): 444–57.

Quinn, S. (1996) *Marie Curie: A Life*, London: Mandarin.

Rathbone, E. (1924) *The Disinherited Family*, London: George Allen & Unwin Ltd.

Reich, N. B. (2001) *Clara Schumann: The Artist and the Woman*, Ithaca, NY: Cornell University Press.

Robson, A. P. (2004) 'Mill [née Hardy; other married name Taylor], Harriet (1807–1858), advocate of sexual equality', ODNB.

Russ, J. (1983) *How to Suppress Women's Writing*, London: The Women's Press.

Schneller, B. (2004) 'Caird [née Alison], (Alice) Mona (1854–1932), writer', ODNB.

Tabili, L. (2005) 'Outsiders in the land of their birth: exogamy, citizenship, and identity in war and peace', *Journal of British Studies*, 44 (4): 796–815.

Taylor, B. (2004) 'Wollstonecraft [married name Godwin], Mary (1759–1797), author and advocate of women's rights', ODNB.

Thompson, W. (1825) *Appeal of One Half the Human Race, Women, against the Pretensions of the Other Half, Men, to Retain Them in Political, and thence in Civil and Domestic, Slavery*, London: Longman, Hurst, Rees, Orme, Brown and Green.

Walby, S. (1990) 'From private to public patriarchy: the periodization of British history', *Women's Studies International Forum*, 13 (1/2): 91–104.

Walby, S. (1994) 'Is citizenship gendered?', *Sociology*, 28 (2): 379–95.

Webb, S. and Webb, B. (1932) *Methods of Social Study*, London: Longmans, Green and Co.

Wollstonecraft, M. (1970, first published 1792) *A Vindication of The Rights of Woman*, London: J. M. Dent & Sons Ltd.

Chapter 2: Mary Booth

1 The 1881 Census lists a parlourmaid, cook, housemaid, nurse, nurserymaid and governess.

2 Simey, T. S. and Simey, M. B. (1960) *Charles Booth, Social Scientist*, Oxford: Oxford University Press, p 54. See Annan, N. G. (1955) 'The intellectual aristocracy', in J. H. Plumb (ed.) *Studies in Social History*, London: Longmans, pp 256–83.

3 M. Booth to C. Booth, 26 June 1878, BP 1/3205–3288.

4 O'Day, R. and Englander, D. (1993) *Mr Charles Booth's Inquiry: Life and Labour of the People in London Reconsidered*, London: The Hambledon Press, pp 11, 62; Bales, K. (1994) 'Early innovations in social research: the poverty survey of Charles Booth', PhD thesis, London School of Economics, p 78.

5 M. Booth 'Childhood Writings', Mary Booth Papers MS 1227/3, no page number.

6 The 1851 Census lists a 'Thomas Maculey [*sic*] born about 1843 in Mauritius' as a pupil at a school in Sussex.

7 Crow, D. (1965) *A Man of Push and Go: The Life of George Macaulay Booth*, London: Rupert Hart-Davis, p 15.

8 BP 11/78, collection of obituaries for Mary Booth.

9 M. Booth 'Childhood writings'.

10 M. Booth 'Childhood writings'.

11 Meinertzhagen, G. (1896) *From Ploughshare to Parliament: A Short Memoir of the Potters of Tadcaster*, London: The Chiswick Press [privately printed], p 55.

12 C. Z Macaulay to M. Booth, 13 February 1879, BP 1/5297.

13 C. Z. Macaulay to M. Booth, 23 January 1884, BP 1/ 5419.

14 M. Booth to C. Booth, 20 June 1878, BP 1/3220; M. Booth to C. Booth, 16 August 1880, BP 1/3273.

15 M. Booth to C. Booth, 9 October 1888, BP 1/3426.

16 Mary says she left at 'nearly fourteen' (M. Booth, 'Childhood Writings') but the ODNB says sixteen (O'Day, R. (2004) 'Booth [née Macaulay], Mary Catherine (1847–1939), social reformer and philanthropist', ODNB.)

17 Redwood, M. (2013) 'How do networks evolve over time?', PhD thesis, University of Bath, p 284.

18 Norman-Butler, B. (1972) *Victorian Aspirations: The Life and Labour of Charles and Mary Booth*, London: George Allen & Unwin Ltd, Preface, no page number; Simey and Simey, *Charles Booth*, p 38; Rothenstein, W. (1933) *Men and Memories: Recollections of William Rothenstein, 1900–1922*, London: Faber & Faber Limited, p 132.

19 Harris, J. (2004) 'Booth, Charles (1840–1916), shipowner and social investigator', ODNB.

20 Ritchie, M. (1968) Preface, no page number, to Booth, M. (1968, first published 1918) *Charles Booth: A Memoir*, London: Macmillan & Co.

21 Webb, B. (1938) *My Apprenticeship, Vol. I*, Harmondsworth: Penguin Books, pp 219–20.

22 Booth, *A Memoir*, p 10.

23 Booth, *A Memoir*, p 11.

24 Anorexia nervosa was officially named in 1874. See www.history.org.uk/secondary/resource/2685/anorexia-nervosa-in-the-nineteenth-century. It was considered mainly an affliction of young women, but cases in young men were also noted.

25 Draft letter from G. M. Booth to M. Simey, n.d., probably May 1959, BP 1/2413.

26 C. Booth to M. Booth, 2–3 August 1880, BP 1/ 1263; 27 September 1879, BP 1/1244; 20 June 1880, BP 1/1248.

27 Here, for example, is Mary writing to Charles on 16 September 1884: 'Thanks for your long and most interesting account of the business past present & to come … It is all being turned over in my mind, questions occurring to me & remarks of all sorts but some worth writing down' (BP 1/3330). Charles's letters to Mary expose the depth of his dependence on her advice, as for example when there was a crisis at Gloversville in the summer of 1878 (2 June 1878, BP 1/1219); when major reorganization was called for in 1880 and Alfred's lack of confidence in the business needed to be handled delicately (12 September 1880, BP 1/1275 and 18 September, BP 1/1277); and when critical decisions had to be made about ordering thousands of goat skins in 1904 (13 November 1904, BP 1/1613).

28 C. Booth to M. Booth, 3 March 1878, BP 1/1189.

29 C. Booth to M. Booth, 12 June 1878, BP 1/1223.

30 Booth, *A Memoir*, p 12.

31 One of Mary's Potter cousins, Kate, worked with the Barnetts and invited them to stay at Standish, where their visits might well have overlapped with Mary's.

32 M. Booth to C. Booth, 18 June 1878, BP 1/3213.

33 Untitled manuscript, MS 797/II/63. For her other writings see BP II/57–62.

34 Norman-Butler, *Victorian Aspirations*, p 58.

35 M. Booth diary entries for 21 and 22 May 1899, BP V/2/13.

36 M. Booth to C. Booth, 13 November 1884, BP 1/3338.

37 C. Booth to M. Booth, 22 August 1880, BP 1/1269.

38 M. Booth to C. Booth, 4 October 1887, BP 1/3408.

39 Simey and Simey, *Charles Booth*, p 54.

40 B. Webb Diary, August 1887, in N. Mackenzie and J. Mackenzie (eds) (2000) *The Diaries of Beatrice Webb* (abridged edn), London: Virago, p 91.

41 B. Webb, Diary, 28 May 1895, in Mackenzie and Mackenzie, p 194.

42 M. Booth to C. Booth, 29 May 1897, BP 1/3652.

43 Norman-Butler, *Victorian Aspirations*, p 148; Straughan, P. 'Tenants at Ightham Mote – Charles and Mary Booth 1896', courtesy of C. B. Stephens.

44 Simey and Simey, *Charles Booth*, p 61; Booth, G. (n.d.) *A Recollection of Gracedieu*, Pamphlet, no publication details, BP 11/80.

45 M. Booth to B. Webb, 1886, cited in Simey and Simey, *Charles Booth*, p 81.

46 Information from articles reported in local newspapers (*Coalville Times*, *Birmingham Daily Gazette*, *Birmingham Daily Post*, *Nottingham Evening Post* and *Leicester Daily Post*), Nita Pearson, personal communication; 'The unveiling ceremony', www.nwleics.gov.uk/files/documents/clock_tower_banner_3/Clock%20tower%20low%20res%203.pdf.

47 'Women's work in Thringstone', report in *Coalville Times*, The Charles Booth Centre Archives.

48 'The Thringstone Women's Trust. 9. Origin and Terms of the Trust Deed', Thringstone School log books, The Charles Booth Centre Archives.

49 Untitled, 28 September 1910, Thringstone School log books, The Charles Booth Centre Archives.

50 The diaries before 1887 are missing.

51 Untitled and undated talk for Economic Club, handwritten by M. Booth, BP II/65.

52 M. Booth to C. Booth, 30 August 1887, BP 1/3406.

53 G. M. Booth, Notes, in BP 11/86.

54 C. Booth to M. Booth, 28 March 1906, BP 1/1659.

55 Fanny Hugill, personal communication, 14 April 2020. Thanks to Victoria Hatch for recording Fanny's account.

56 M. Booth to C. Booth, 21 June 1886, BP 1/3374.

57 M. Booth to C. Booth, April 1878, BP 1/3183.

58 M. Booth to C. Booth, 16 August 1880, BP 1/3273.

59 C. Z. Macaulay to M. Booth, 22 June 1886, BP 1/5462.

60 M. Booth to C. Booth, n.d., probably July 1886, BP 1/3380.

61 M. Booth to C. Booth, 26 March 1888, BP 1/3414.

62 C. Z. Macaulay to M. Booth, 9 July 1884, BP 1/5427.

63 M. Booth to C. Booth, 13 August 1878, BP 1/3226.

64 M. Booth, Diary, 1901, BP V/2/15.

65 Notes by I. Gore-Browne for draft letter to M. Simey, n.d., probably May 1959, BP 1/2413.

66 G. M. Booth, Notes, n.d., probably May 1959, BP 1/2413.

67 M. Booth, *A Memoir*, p 22.

68 C. Booth to M. Booth, 17 May 1878, BP 1/1214.

69 M. Booth, untitled and undated essay, BP 11/64/1–4.

70 F. Hugill, personal communication.

71 The Simeys (*Charles Booth*, p 157) give the figure of £33,000 – some £3,999,204 in 2020 – as the cost of *Life and Labour* when the final volume was published in 1903. This is probably an underestimate. The assumption that Charles Booth launched his investigation in order to rebut the allegations of the socialist Henry Hyndman that a quarter of London's population were poor doesn't match the facts, since Charles was talking to socialists and others before Hyndman voiced his claims, and had already begun his unsystematic personal excursions into poor districts of London and other towns (Bales, 'Early innovations in social research', p 28).

[72] M. Booth, *A Memoir*, p 37.

[73] Thanks to Mark Stephens for this insight. See Hall, C. (2012) *Macaulay and Son: Architects of Imperial Britain*, London/New Haven, CT: Yale University Press.

[74] Booth, C. (1934) *Zachary Macaulay*, Longmans, Green and Co., no page number.

[75] Simey and Simey, *Charles Booth*, cite this letter on p 64; they give the date as just '1878' and provide no further reference. I wasn't able to locate this item in the Senate House Booth Papers.

[76] M. Booth, *A Memoir*, p 13.

[77] M. Ritchie to G. Booth, 3 and 9 January 1961, BP 1/3115, cited in O' Day and Englander, *Mr Charles Booth's Inquiry*, p 144.

[78] See O' Day and Englander, *Mr Charles Booth's Inquiry*; Bales, 'Early innovations in social research'.

[79] B. Webb, Diary, 15 February 1890, Mackenzie and Mackenzie, p 135.

[80] *Pall Mall Gazette*, 8 May 1889.

[81] B. Webb, Diary, Mackenzie and Mackenzie, pp 57, 67.

[82] B. Webb, Diary, Mackenzie and Mackenzie, p 158.

[83] B. Webb, Diary, Mackenzie and Mackenzie, p 195.

[84] M. Booth to C. Booth, 21 September 1886, BP 1/3888.

[85] Wright, E. H., King, R. J. and Jackson, C. (2015) '"She became a ship passing in the night": charting Virginia Woolf's "The Voyage Out"', *The Nautilus*, VI: 55–93.

[86] M. Booth to C. Booth, 6 November 1895, BP 1/3594.

[87] M. Booth Diary, 2 November 1890, BP V/2/4 and 19 July 1904, BP V/2/18.

[88] Ritchie, Preface, no page number.

[89] Norman-Butler, *Victorian Aspirations*, p 48.

[90] On M. Harkness see Oakley, A. (2019) 'Fact, fiction and method in the early history of social research', *Women's History Review*, 28 (3): 360–79.

[91] M. Booth, Diary, 18 December 1891, BP V/2/5.

[92] M. Booth, Diary, 1891, BP V/2/5.

[93] M. Booth to C. Booth, n.d., probably early June 1891, BP 1/3470.

[94] M. Booth to C. Booth, 5 November 1895, BP 1/3593.

[95] See, for example, the methodological advice given by the sociologist Max Weber 13 years later: Eldridge, J. E. T. (ed.) (1971) *Max Weber: The Interpretation of Social Reality*, London: Michael Joseph, pp 103–55. Thanks to Graham Crow for drawing my attention to this.

[96] M. Booth, Diary, 14 June 1892, BP V/2/6.

[97] M. Booth, Diary, 9 November 1897, BP V/2/11; 10 January 1893, BP V/2/7; 17 January 1893, BP V/2/7.

[98] M. Booth to C. Booth, 22 May 1891, BP 1/3466.

[99] C. Booth to M Booth, 20 April 1878, BP 1/1206.

[100] M. Booth to C. Booth, 19 September 1884, BP 1/3327.

[101] M. Booth to C. Booth, 7 March 1900, BP 1/3772.

102 M. Booth to E. Aves, 13 May 1903, BP 1/3926.

103 M. Booth to C. Booth, 13 May 1903, BP 1/3925.

104 M. Booth to C. Booth, 2 March 1903, BP 1/3900.

105 M. Booth to E. Aves, 15 April 1903, BP 1/3914.

106 M. Booth to C. Booth, 4 May 1903, BP 1/3922.

107 M. Booth, Diary 1903, BP V/2/17.

108 M. Booth to C. Booth, 9 April 1903, BP 1/3910.

109 M. Booth to C. Booth, 13 May 1903, BP 1/3925.

110 A. Booth to C. Booth, 11 May 1903, BP 1/636.

111 The jointness of this venture is missing from most accounts. C. B. Stephens, personal communication, 20 June 2020; see Maas, J. (1987) *Holman Hunt & The Light of the World*, Aldershot: Wildwood House Limited; Potter, M. C. (2007) 'British art and empire: Holman Hunt's "The Light of the World" reflected in the mirror of the colonial press', *Media History*, 13 (1): 1–23; Roskill, M. (1963) 'Holman Hunt's differing versions of the "Light of the World"', *Victorian Studies*, 6 (3): 228–44.

112 M. Booth to C. Booth, 3 June 1907, BP 1/1721.

113 C. B. Stephens, personal communication.

114 M. Booth to C. Booth, 19 September 1893, BP 1/3507.

115 M. Booth to C. Booth, 17 May 1894, BP 1/3509.

116 Simey and Simey, *Charles Booth*, p 74.

117 J. Argyle to M. Booth, 20 January 1915, BP 1/12.

118 M. Booth to C. Booth, 17 May 1894, BP 1/3509.

119 M. Booth to C. Booth, 16 February 1910, BP 1/4214.

120 Booth, C. (1902) *Life and Labour of the People in London, Final Volume, Notes on Social Influences and Conclusions*, London: Macmillan & Co., no page number.

121 Sprott, W. J. H. (1961) Review of Simey and Simey, *Charles Booth*, *The Listener*, 23 November.

122 BP 11/78, collection of obituaries for Mary Booth.

123 M. Booth to C. Booth, 13 March 1912, BP 1/4347.

Other sources used

Bales, K. (1996) 'Lives and labours in the emergence of organised social research, 1886–1907', *Journal of Historical Sociology*, 9 (2): 113–38.

Bales, K. (1999) 'Popular reactions to sociological research: the case of Charles Booth', *Sociology*, 33 (1): 153–68.

Bell, A. O. (ed.) (1978) *The Diary of Virginia Woolf, Vol. 2 1920–1924*, London/New York: Harcourt Brace Jovanovich.

Booth, Charles (1891) *Labour and Life of the People, Vol. I: East London* (3rd edn), London: Williams and Norgate.

Booth, C. (1892) *Pauperism, a Picture, and Endowment of Old Age, an Argument*, London: Macmillan & Co.

Caine, B. (1986) *Destined to be Wives: The Sisters of Beatrice Webb*, Oxford: Oxford University Press.

Channon, G. (2019) *Richard Potter, Beatrice Webb's Father and Corporate Capitalist*, Newcastle-upon-Tyne: Cambridge Scholars Publishing.

Collet, C. E. (1927) 'Some recollections of Charles Booth', *Social Service Review*, 1 (3): 384–9.

Collet, C. E. (1945) 'Charles Booth, the Denison Club and H. Llewellyn Smith', *Journal of the Royal Statistical Society*, 108 (3/4): 482–85.

Englander, D. and O'Day, R. (eds) (1995) *Retrieved Riches: Social Investigation in Britain 1840–1914*, Aldershot: Scolar Press.

Farmer, M. E. (1967) 'The positivist movement and the development of English sociology', *The Sociological Review*, 15 (1): 5–20.

John, A. H. (1959) *A Liverpool Merchant House*, London: George Allen & Unwin Ltd.

Kimber, V. F. (1989) 'The Potters and the Webbs at the Argoed' www.penallt.org.uk/documents/kimber/people/argoed-families.

Methuen, Lord (1981) *Descendants of Richard Potter (1817–1892) and Lawrencina Heyworth (1821–1882): Family Trees*, new edn [private printing].

O'Day, R. (1989) 'Interviews and investigations: Charles Booth and the making of the religious influences survey', *History*, 74 (242): 361–77.

O'Day, R. (1995) 'Women and social investigation: Clara Collet and Beatrice Potter', in D. Englander and R. O'Day (eds) *Retrieved Riches: Social Investigation in Britain 1840–1914*, Aldershot: Scolar Press, pp 165–200.

Radice, L. (1984) *Beatrice and Sidney Webb: Fabian Socialists*, London: The Macmillan Press Ltd.

Redwood, M. www.mikeredwood.com/booth-co/, www.boothandco.com/history.php.

Stephens, M. (1986) *Roots of Power*, Stevenage: SPA Books Ltd.

Thringstone websites, www.friends-of-thringstone.org.uk/, www.charlesboothcentre.org.uk/centre-history.

Trevelyan, G. O. (1876) *The Life and Letters of Lord Macaulay by His Nephew, Volume 1*, New York/London: Harper & Brothers Publishers.

Webb, B. (1979, first published 1926) *My Apprenticeship*, Cambridge: Cambridge University Press.

Chapter 3: Charlotte Shaw

[1]   C. Payne-Townshend to A. Henry, n.d., SP 31/3.

[2]   This letter exists in two forms, as one addressed 'to no one in particular' (LSE, 7RGB/5/03), and as a letter to T. E. Lawrence (J. Wilson and N. Wilson (eds) (2003) *T. E. Lawrence: Correspondence with Bernard and Charlotte Shaw, 1927*, Woodgreen Common: Castle Hill Press, pp 81–6). Both are dated 17 May 1927. Charlotte's description of Ireland as lacking a middle class is hard to substantiate.

3 Dunbar, J. (1963) *Mrs G.B.S. – A Biographical Portrait of Charlotte Shaw*, London: George G. Harrap & Co Ltd, p 68.

4 See note 2.

5 See note 2.

6 Dunbar, *Mrs G.B.S.*, p 254.

7 Jangfeldt, B. (2016) *Axel Munthe: The Road to San Michele*, London: I. B. Tauris, p 169.

8 B. Webb, Diary entry 16 September 1896, in N. MacKenzie and J. MacKenzie (eds) (2000) *The Diaries of Beatrice Webb*, London: Virago, p 205.

9 Cited in Caine, S. (1963) *The History of the Foundation of the London School of Economics and Political Science*, London: G. Bell and Sons, pp 11–12.

10 Donnelly, S. (2014) 'An unsung heroine of LSE – Charlotte Shaw', https://blogs.lse.ac.uk/lsehistory/2014/01/24/an-unsung-heroine-of-lse-charlotte-payne-townshend/

11 Cited in Drake, B. and Cole, M. I. (eds) (1975, first published 1948) *Our Partnership* by B. Webb, Cambridge: Cambridge University Press, p 189.

12 B. Webb, Diary entry 24 March 1942, cited in Gahan, P. (2017) *Bernard Shaw and Beatrice Webb on Poverty and Equality in the Modern World, 1905–1914*, Cham, Switzerland: Palgrave Macmillan, p 189.

13 B. Webb, Diary entry 24 May 1927, in MacKenzie and MacKenzie, *The Diaries of Beatrice Webb*, p 460.

14 Holroyd, M. (1998) *Bernard Shaw*, London: Vintage Books, p 250.

15 C. P. Gilman, Diary entry 6 August 1896, in D. D. Knight (ed.) (1994) *The Diaries of Charlotte Perkins Gilman Vol. 2, 1890–1935*, London/Charlottesville, VA: University Press of Virginia, p 633.

16 B. Webb, Diary entry 16 September 1996, in MacKenzie and MacKenzie, *The Diaries of Beatrice Webb*, p 206.

17 Shaw, C. F. (ed.) (1915) *Selected Passages from the Works of Bernard Shaw, Chosen by Charlotte F. Shaw*, London: Jonathan Cape, p 57.

18 Jaworowski, K. (2010) 'The bachelor Shaw woos with his wit', *The New York Times*, 26 April, www.nytimes.com/2010/04/27/theater/reviews/27engaging.html.

19 Holroyd, *Bernard Shaw*, pp 247–8.

20 Holroyd, *Bernard Shaw*, p 263.

21 Weintraub, S. (2004) 'Shaw, George Bernard (1856–1950), playwright and polemicist', ODNB.

22 Shaw, G. B. (1910 'The husband, the supertax and the suffragists', (letter) *The Times*, 10 June.

23 Dunbar, *Mrs G.B.S.*, p 175.

24 Holroyd (*George Bernard Shaw*, p 280) decides that the Shaws engaged in 'careful sexual experience'.

25 Henderson, A. (1956) *George Bernard Shaw: Man of the Century*, New York: Appleton-Century-Crofts, Inc, p 820.

26 See Vicinus, M. (2013) 'Celibate marriages', *Victorian Review*, 39 (2): 24–8.

27 Dunbar, *Mrs G.B.S.*, p 8.

28 Patch, *Thirty Years with G.B.S.*, p 62.

29 Henderson, *George Bernard Shaw*, p 860.

30 G. B. Shaw to N. Astor, 8 May 1944, cited in J. P. Wearing (ed.) (2005) *Bernard Shaw and Nancy Astor*, Toronto, University of Toronto Press, p 154.

31 Britain, I. (1982) *Fabianism and Culture A Study in British Socialism and the Arts c 1884–1918*, Cambridge: Cambridge University Press, p 185.

32 C. Shaw to B. Webb, 6 November 1898, cited in Dunbar, *Mrs G. B. S.*, p 182.

33 Dunbar, *Mrs G.B.S.*, p 220.

34 Hutchins' forenames are frequently misquoted. See for example Cooper, J. (2017) *The British Welfare Revolution* (London: Bloomsbury Academic, p 95), and Pugh, P. (1984) *Educate, Agitate, Organize: 100 Years of Fabian Socialism*, London: Methuen, pp 107, 114, 117, for whom she is 'Beatrice'; and Alexander, S. (ed.) (1988) 'Introduction', *Women's Fabian Tracts*, London: Routledge, pp 1–13, 5, who calls her 'Barbara'.

35 See Oakley, A. (2020) 'Women, the early development of sociological research methods in Britain and the London School of Economics: a (partially) retrieved history', *Sociology*, 54 (2): 292–311.

36 Special Correspondent (1908) 'Woman suffrage. Demonstration in Hyde Park', *The Times*, 22 June.

37 Shaw, C. F. (1911) 'Woman suffrage and the government', (letter) *The Times*, 21 November.

38 See https://womanandhersphere.com/tag/mabel-atkinson/. Information on the window from Sue Donnelly, personal communication, and Donnelly, S. (2017) https://blogs.lse.ac.uk/lsehistory/2017/09/13/hammering-out-a-new-world-the-fabian-window-at-lse/.

39 Shaw studentships file, LSE/CFR 835.

40 Correspondence between C. Mactaggart and C. Shaw, 1915, Shaw studentships file, LSE/CFR 835.

41 C. Shaw to C. Mactaggart, 22 August 1915, Shaw studentships file, LSE/CFR 835.

42 Shaw, C. (1914) 'Foreword', in J. Pollock (trans.) *Damaged Goods. A Play by Brieux. Translated by John Pollock, with a Preface by Bernard Shaw and a Foreword by Mrs Bernard Shaw*, London: A. C. Fifield, pp v–xv, v.

43 Shaw, 'Foreword', p v.

44 Shaw, 'Foreword', p vii.

45 Shaw, 'Foreword', p viii.

46 Titus, E. W. (1914) '"La femme seule". M. Brieux's original, and Mrs Bernard Shaw's version', *Pall Mall Gazette*, 8 January, p 5.

47 Anon., 'The Woman's Theatre', *The Stage*, 11 December 1913.

48 Pharand, M. (1988) 'Iconoclasts of social reform: Eugène Brieux and Bernard Shaw', *Shaw*, 8: 97–109, p 104.

49 MacKenzie, N. and MacKenzie, J. (1977) *The First Fabians*, London: Weidenfeld & Nicolson, p 387.

50 Dent, A. (ed.) (1952) *Bernard Shaw and Mrs. Patrick Campbell: Their Correspondence*, London: Victor Gollancz Ltd, pp 174, 119, 204, 237.

51 Meyers, J. (2005) *Married to Genius*, Harpenden: Southbank Publishing, p 47.

52 Holroyd, *Bernard Shaw*, pp 427–8.

53 C. Shaw to T. E. Lawrence, 31 May 1927, Wilson and Wilson, *T. E. Lawrence: Correspondence with Bernard and Charlotte Shaw, 1927*, p 102.

54 Brown, M. and Cave, J. (1988) *A Touch of Genius: The Life of T. E. Lawrence*, London: J. M. Dent & Sons Ltd, p 174.

55 T. E. Lawrence to C. Shaw, 14 April 1927, Wilson and Wilson, *T. E. Lawrence: Correspondence with Bernard and Charlotte Shaw, 1927*, p 61.

56 Patch, *Thirty Years with G.B.S.*, p 78.

57 C. Shaw to T. E. Lawrence, 31 December 1922, Wilson, J. and Wilson, N. (eds) (2000) *T. E. Lawrence: Correspondence with Bernard and Charlotte Shaw, 1922–1926*, Woodgreen Common: Castle Hill Press, pp 25–6.

58 T. E. Lawrence to C. Shaw, 31 August 1924, Wilson and Wilson, *Correspondence with Bernard and Charlotte Shaw, 1922–1926*, pp 97–8.

59 C. Shaw, 'Notes by Charlotte Shaw on the *Seven Pillars* proof', Wilson and Wilson, *Correspondence with Bernard and Charlotte Shaw, 1922–1926*, p 106.

60 Patch, *Thirty Years with G.B.S.*, p 80.

61 T. E. Lawrence to G. B. Shaw, 30 November 1922, Wilson and Wilson, *Correspondence with Bernard and Charlotte Shaw, 1922–1926*, p 9.

62 T. E. Lawrence to C. Shaw, 26 December 1925, cited in Fernald, M. H. (1962) 'The literary relationship between T. E. Lawrence and Mr. and Mrs. Bernard Shaw', MA thesis, University of Maine, p 36.

63 Pateman, J. (2012) *T. E. Lawrence in Lincolnshire*, Sleaford, Lincolnshire: The Pateran Press, p 80.

64 T. E. Lawrence to C. Shaw, 28 August 1928, Wilson, J. and Wilson, N. (eds) (2008) *T. E. Lawrence: Correspondence with Bernard and Charlotte Shaw, 1928*, Woodgreen Common: Castle Hill Press, p 155.

65 Charlotte Shaw's *Commonplace Book*, MS.Eng.Misc.d.789, Bodleian Library, Oxford.

66 T. E. Lawrence to C. Shaw, 10 June 1927, Wilson and Wilson *T. E. Lawrence: Correspondence with Bernard and Charlotte Shaw, 1927*, p 109; T. E. Lawrence to C. Shaw, 25 February 1928, Wilson and Wilson *T. E. Lawrence: Correspondence with Bernard and Charlotte Shaw, 1928*, p 36; T. E. Lawrence to C. Shaw, 18 August 1927, Wilson and Wilson *T. E. Lawrence: Correspondence with Bernard and Charlotte Shaw, 1927*, p 141; T. E. Lawrence to C. Shaw, 2 May 1928, Wilson and Wilson *T. E. Lawrence: Correspondence with Bernard and Charlotte Shaw, 1928*, p 78.

67   C. Shaw to D. Walker, 6 March 1939, Wilson, J. and Wilson, N. (eds) (2009) *T. E. Lawrence: Correspondence with Bernard and Charlotte Shaw, 1929–1935*, Woodgreen Common: Castle Hill Press, p 254.
68   'Notes by Charlotte Shaw on the *Seven Pillars* proof', Wilson and Wilson, *Correspondence with Bernard and Charlotte Shaw, 1922–1926*, p 107.
69   Knightley, P. (1971) *The Secret Lives of Lawrence of Arabia*, London: Panther, p 286.
70   T. E. Lawrence to C Shaw, 10 July 1928, Wilson and Wilson *T. E. Lawrence: Correspondence with Bernard and Charlotte Shaw, 1928*, p 119.
71   C. Shaw to D. Walker, 6 March 1939, Wilson and Wilson *T. E. Lawrence: Correspondence with Bernard and Charlotte Shaw, 1929–1935*, p 254.
72   Patch, *Thirty Years with G.B.S.*, pp 261, 82.
73   *The Nottingham Journal*, 18 January 1934.
74   *Lancashire Evening Post*, 7 December 1931.
75   C. Shaw to F. Whelan, 16 June 1911, SP 31/1.
76   *Gloucester Citizen*, 19 September 1932.
77   C. Shaw to A. Carr-Saunders, 4 October 1939, LSE/CFR 120/2/A.
78   'Ought women to have the vote?', *Dundee Evening Telegraph*, 19 March 1907.
79   Henderson, *George Bernard Shaw*, pp 860–1.
80   Holroyd, *Bernard Shaw*, p 290.
81   Dunbar, *Mrs G. B. S.*, Appendix 'The Will', pp 314–15.
82   *The Scotsman*, 18 February 1944.

Other sources used

Anon. (1943) Obituary of Charlotte Shaw, 'End of a felicitous partnership', *The Times*, 15 September.
Ashwell, L. (1922) *Modern Troubadours*, London: Gyldendal.
Ashwell, L. (1929) *The Stage*, London: Geoffrey Bles.
Ashwell, L. (1936) *Myself a Player*, London: Michael Joseph.
Atkinson, M. A. (1914) *The Economic Foundations of the Women's Movement*, London: Fabian Society.
Beilharz, P. and Nyland, C. (1998) *The Webbs, Fabianism and Feminism*, Aldershot, Hants: Ashgate.
Berg, M. (1996) *A Woman in History, Eileen Power 1889–1940*, Cambridge: Cambridge University Press.
Blagg, H. and Wilson, C. (1912) *Women and Prisons*, London: Fabian Women's Group Series No. 3.
Clark, A. (1919) *Working Life of Women in the Seventeenth Century*, London: Routledge.
Donnelly, S. (2015) 'Charlotte Shaw's legacy – the Shaw Library', https://blogs.lse.ac.uk/lsehistory/2015/08/13/charlotte-shaws-legacy-the-shaw-library/.

Donnelly, S. (2017) 'LSE Women: women in art – the Shaw Library'. https://blogs.lse.ac.uk/lsehistory/2017/03/22/women-in-art-the-shaw-library/.

Donnelly, S. (2017) 'Hammering out a new world – the Fabian Window at LSE', https://blogs.lse.ac.uk/lsehistory/2017/09/13/hammering-out-a-new-world-the-fabian-window-at-lse/.

Fabian Women's Group (1909) *A Summary of Six Papers and Discussions upon the Disabilities of Women as Workers*, London: Fabian Society.

Fabian Women's Group (1910) *A Summary of Eight Papers and Discussions upon the Disabilities of Women as Workers*, London: Fabian Society.

Fabian Women's Group (1911) *The National Insurance Bill. A Criticism, with a Foreword by Mrs Bernard Shaw*, London: Fabian Society.

Gale, M. B. and Gardner, V. (eds) (2004) *Auto/biography and Identity: Women, Theatre and Performance*, Manchester: Manchester University Press.

Harrison, R. (2000) *The Life and Times of Sidney and Beatrice Webb*, Houndmills, Basingstoke: Macmillan Press Ltd.

Hirschfield, C. (1994) 'The Actresses' Franchise League in peace and war: 1913–1918', *New England Theatre Journal*, 5: 35–49.

Hutchins, B L (1908) *Home Work and Sweating: The Causes and the Remedies*, London: Fabian Society.

Hutchins, B L (1911) *The Working Life of Women*, London: Fabian Society.

Jennings, R. (2010) 'Nancy Astor: letters from T. E. Lawrence and G. B. Shaw', University of Reading, Special Collections Services, www.reading.ac.uk/web/files/special-collections/featurenancyastorletters.pdf.

Jones, C. S. (1993) *Beatrice Webb: Woman of Conflict*, London: Pandora.

Lawrence, A. W. (ed.) (1937) *T. E. Lawrence by His Friends*, London: Jonathan Cape.

Leask, M. (2012) *Lena Ashwell, Actress, Patriot, Pioneer*, Hatfield: University of Hertfordshire Press.

McKernan, J. (n.d.) 'GBS, the Fabian Society, and reconstructionist education policy: the London School of Economics and Political Science', www.jceps.com/wp-content/uploads/PDFs/02-2-08.pdf.

Morley, E. J. (ed.) (1914) *Women Workers in Seven Professions: A Survey of Their Economic Conditions and Prospects*, London: George Routledge & Sons.

Paton, A. (1993) 'The mysterious Dr Munthe', *Journal of Medical Biography*, 1: 31–4.

Paxton, N. (1918) *Stage Rights! The Actresses' Franchise League, Activism and Politics 1908–58*, Manchester: Manchester University Press.

Pease, E. R. (1916) *The History of the Fabian Society*, London: A. C. Fifield.

Power, E. (1924) *Medieval People*, London: Methuen & Co.

Reeves, M. P (1914) *Round About a Pound a Week*, London: Bell.

Shaw, Mrs. Bernard (trans.) (1907) *Maternity. A Play in Three Acts by Brieux*, London: G. Standring.

Shaw, Mrs. Bernard, Hankin, St. J, and Pollock, J. (trans.) (1914) *Three Plays by Brieux. With a Preface by Bernard Shaw*. London: A. C. Fifield.

Shaw, Mrs. Bernard, Fagan, J. F. and Miall, A. B. (trans.) (1916) *Woman on Her Own, False Gods and The Red Robe: Three Plays by Brieux. With a Preface by the Dramatist.* London: Herbert Jenkins Limited.

Shaw, C. F. (1909) *Rent and Value (Adapted from the First Fabian Essay)*, Fabian Tract No. 142, London: Fabian Society.

Shaw, C. F. (1911) 'Woman suffrage and the government', (letter) *The Times*, 21 November.

Shaw, C. F. (1914) *Knowledge is the Door. A Forerunner. Being the Introduction to the Science of Self-Conscious Existence as Presented by Dr. James Porter Mills.* Condensed and adapted from his book by C.F.S. London: A. C. Fifield.

Stang, C. M. (ed.) (2002) *The Waking Dream of T. E. Lawrence: Essays on His Life, Literature and Legacy*, Basingstoke: Palgrave.

Townshend, E. C. (1909) *The Case for School Nurseries*, Fabian Tract No. 145, London: Fabian Society.

Townshend, E. C. (1911) *The Case Against the Charity Organization Society*, Fabian Tract No. 158, London: Fabian Society.

Vietzen, S. (2008) 'Fabian connections: Bernard Shaw in Natal, 1935', *Natalia*, 38: 8–26.

Wearing, J. P. (ed.) (2005) *Bernard Shaw and Nancy Astor*, Toronto: University of Toronto Press.

Weintraub, R. (1977) *Fabian Feminist: Bernard Shaw and Women*, The Pennsylvania State University Press.

Wilson, J. (1989) *Lawrence of Arabia: The Authorised Biography of T. E. Lawrence*, London: Heinemann.

Chapter 4: Jeannette Tawney

[1] Brooks, J. R. (1991) 'Labour and educational reconstruction, 1916–1926: a case study in the evolution of policy', *History of Education*, 20 (3): 245–59.

[2] R. M. Titmuss to J. R. Williams, 9 August 1960, Arthur Creech Jones Papers, MSS. Brit. Emp. s332 Box 6, File 7, Bodleian Library, University of Oxford. Thanks to John Stewart for drawing my attention to this.

[3] Stewart, J. (2020) *Richard Titmuss: Commitment to Welfare*, Bristol: Policy Press, pp 396–7.

[4] Goldman, L. (2004) 'Tawney, Richard Henry (1880–1962), historian and political thinker', ODNB; Rowse, A. L. (1979) 'R. H. Tawney's influence', in *Portraits and Views: Literary and Historical*, London: Macmillan, pp 225–8; Terrill, R. (1974) *R. H. Tawney and His Times: Socialism as Fellowship*, London: André Deutsch, p 108.

[5] J. Tawney, *Restitution*, chapter 1, TP/TV 18B.

[6] Atherton, J. R. (1979) 'R. H. Tawney as a Christian social moralist', PhD thesis, University of Manchester; Armstrong, G. (2007) 'Change, Christianity and confusion in the political thought of R. H. Tawney', PhD thesis, University of Newcastle upon Tyne; Brooks, R. (1974)

'R. H. Tawney and the reform of English education', PhD thesis, Bangor University; Mulligan, M. F. T. (2006) 'R. H. Tawney: the integrated life and the reform of education in England 1905–1944', PhD thesis, Simon Fraser University; Passes, E. M. (1994) 'The Christian socialism of R. H. Tawney', PhD thesis, London School of Economics and Political Science; Robinson, S. J. (1990) 'R. H. Tawney's theory of equality: a theological and ethical analysis', PhD thesis, University of Edinburgh; Slater, S. C. (2011) 'A comparative evaluation of the ethical socialism of Tawney and Crosland', PhD thesis, University of Liverpool; Woolley, R. J. (2004) 'Tawney, Temple and acquisitiveness: the legacy of English ethical socialism', PhD thesis, University of Sheffield.

[7] Cited in Beveridge, Lord (1947) *India Called Them*, London: George Allen & Unwin Ltd, p 92.

[8] J. Tawney, *I Learn to Live*, Chapter 5, TP/TV 21.

[9] J. Tawney, *A Learner's Life*, Chapter 6, TP/TV 22.

[10] J. Tawney, *A Learner's Life*, Chapter 2, TP/TV 22.

[11] Beveridge, *India Called Them*, p 373.

[12] Beveridge, A. J. (1906) 'A holiday in Italy', *Eastbourne Ladies' College School Magazine*, December, pp 15–18 in TP/TV 20.

[13] J. Tawney, *A Learner's Life*, Chapter 13, TP/TV 21

[14] Beveridge, J. (1954) *Beveridge and His Plan*, London: Hodder and Stoughton, p 39.

[15] Chisholm, A. (2009) *Frances Partridge: The Biography*, London: Weidenfeld & Nicolson.

[16] Partridge, F. (1981) *Love in Bloomsbury: Memories*, London: Victor Gollancz, pp 24–5.

[17] Beveridge, *India Called Them*, p 350.

[18] J. Tawney, *A Learner's Life*, Chapter 18, TP/TV 22.

[19] W. H. Beveridge to R. H. Tawney, 31 August 1958, BevP 2A/108.

[20] J. Tawney, *I Learn to Live*, Chapter 15, TP/TV 21.

[21] J. Tawney, *I Learn to Live*, Chapter 18, TP/TV 21.

[22] Harris, J. (1977) *William Beveridge: A Biography*, Oxford: Clarendon Press, p 68.

[23] J. Tawney, *I Learn to Live*, Chapter 18, TP/TV 21.

[24] J. Beveridge to R. H. Tawney, 7 December 1903, TP/TV 36.

[25] J. Tawney, *I Learn to Live*, Chapter 25, TP/TV 21.

[26] J. Beveridge to A. Beveridge, n.d., probably 1899–1902, BevP 2A/86.

[27] J. Tawney, *I Learn to Live*, Chapter 23, TP/TV 21.

[28] J. Tawney, *I Learn to Live*, Chapter 23, TP/TV 21.

[29] J. Tawney, *I Learn to Live*, Chapter 23, TP/TV 21.

[30] Ryan, A. (1980) 'R. H. Tawney: a socialist saint', *New Society*, 27 November; 'R. H. Tawney', *Wikipedia*. However, Tawney's socialism was of the moderate kind: see Blackburn, S. C. (1999) 'A very moderate socialist indeed? R. H. Tawney and minimum wages', *Twentieth Century British History*, 10 (2): 107–36.

[31] Goldman, L. (2013) *The Life of R. H. Tawney: Socialism and History*, London: Bloomsbury, pp 109–10.

[32] See Berg, M. (1996) *A Woman in History: Eileen Power 1889–1940*, Cambridge: Cambridge University Press.

[33] Goldman, *The Life of R. H. Tawney*, p 35; Goldman, 'Tawney, Richard Henry'.

[34] Terrill, *R. H. Tawney and His Times*, p 108.

[35] Dahrendorf, R. (1995) *A History of the London School of Economics and Political Science*, Oxford: Oxford University Press, p 239.

[36] Terrill, *R. H. Tawney and His Times*, pp 108–9.

[37] Goldman, *The Life of R. H. Tawney*, p 50.

[38] Goldman, L. (2019) 'Founding the welfare state: Beveridge, Tawney and Temple', in Goldman, L. (ed.) *Welfare and Social Policy in Britain Since 1870: Essays in Honour of José Harris*, Oxford: Oxford University Press, pp 44–59, p 51.

[39] Herklots, H. G. G. (1958) 'Mrs R. H. Tawney', *The Times*, 29 January.

[40] C. Tawney to R. H. Tawney, 13 July 1908, TP/TV 34.

[41] W. H. Beveridge to A. Beveridge, 23 June 1908, BevP 9A/36.

[42] R. H. Tawney to J. Beveridge, 17 June 1900, TP/TV 1.

[43] R. H. Tawney to J. Beveridge, 30 May 1908, TP/TV 1.

[44] R. H. Tawney to J. Beveridge, Undated, early 1900s, TP/TV 1.

[45] J. Beveridge to R. H. Tawney, 11 September 1908, TP/TV 37.

[46] Goldman, *The Life of R. H. Tawney*, p 51.

[47] Martin, J. (2014) 'Intellectual portraits: politics, professions and identity in twentieth-century England', *History of Education*, 43 (6): 740–67, 756.

[48] J. Beveridge to R. H. Tawney, 13 March 1907, TP/TV 34.

[49] J. Beveridge to R. H. Tawney, n.d., probably 1908, TP/TV 37.

[50] Terrill, *R. H. Tawney and His Times*, p 66.

[51] R. H. Tawney to J. Tawney, undated, probably 1909, TP/TV 1.

[52] J. Tawney to R. H. Tawney, 7 March 1911, TP/TV 38.

[53] R. H. Tawney to J. Beveridge, 29 August 1905, TP/TV 1.

[54] J. Beveridge to R. H. Tawney, 2 September 1908, TP/TV 38.

[55] J. Beveridge to R. H. Tawney, 3 September 1908, TP/TV 38.

[56] R. H. Tawney to J. Tawney, undated, probably 1909, TP/TV 1.

[57] R. H. Tawney to J. Tawney, 6 January 1939, TP/TV 2.

[58] R. H. Tawney to J. Tawney, 5 December 1939, TP/TV 2.

[59] J. Tawney to R. H. Tawney, 22 March 1911, TP/TV 38.

[60] J. Tawney to R. H. Tawney, 23 March 1911, TP/TV 38.

[61] J. Tawney to R. H. Tawney, 11 February 1912, TP/TV 39.

[62] J. Tawney to R. H. Tawney, 2 April 1911, TP/TV 38.

[63] From F. W. Stella Browne, undated, probably 1915, TP 27/6.

[64] Terrill, *R. H. Tawney and His Times*, pp 110–11.

[65] J. Tawney, *Restitution*, Chapter 2, TP/TV 18B.

[66] J. Tawney, *Restitution*, Chapter 13, TP/TV 19.

[67] B. Webb to J. Tawney, 4 August 1933, TP 27/6.

68 Cited in Whittle, J. (ed.) (2013) *Landlords and Tenants in Britain, 1440–1660: Tawney's Agrarian Problem Revisited*, Woodbridge: The Boydell Press, p xxv.

69 Tawney, R. H. (1936) *Religion and the Rise of Capitalism: A Historical Study*, London: John Murray, p xxiv.

70 J. Tawney, *I Learn to Live*, Chapter 25, TP/TV 21.

71 Tawney, J. (1911) 'Women and unemployment', *The Economic Journal*, 21 (81): 131–9.

72 Ashton, T. S. (1958) Obituary of J. Tawney, *LSE Magazine*, July, TP/TV 26.

73 Tawney, A. J. and Tawney, R. H. (1934) 'An occupational census of the seventeenth century', *The Economic History Review*, 5 (1): 25–64, 42.

74 See Oakley, A. (2018) *Women, Peace and Welfare: A Suppressed History of Social Reform, 1880–1920*, Bristol: Policy Press, pp 68–71.

75 J. Tawney, *I Learn to Live*, chapter 25, TP/TV 21.

76 J. Tawney, *I Learn to Live*, chapter 3, TP/TV 21.

77 J. Tawney, *I Learn to Live*, chapter 4, TP/TV 21.

78 Tawney, J. (1920) 'My experience as a factory inspector', *Life and Labour*, November: 276–80.

79 J. Tawney, *Restitution*, chapter 10, TP/TV 18B.

80 R. H. Tawney to J. Tawney, 21 April 1915, TP 27/8.

81 R. H. Tawney to J. Tawney, 6 July 1915, TP 27/8.

82 Goldman doesn't dismiss Jeannette's symptoms, see *The Life of R. H. Tawney*, p 143.

83 Maslen, E. (2014) *Life in the Writings of Storm Jameson: A Biography*, Evanston, Illinois, Northwestern University Press, p 4.

84 Maslen, *Life in the Writings of Storm Jameson*, p 92.

85 Jameson, S. (1936) *In the Second Year*, London: Cassell and Company Limited, pp 87–8.

86 S. Jameson to J. Tawney, 28 September 1935, TP/TV 46.

87 S. Jameson to J. Tawney, 15 March 1937, TP/TV 46.

88 J. Tawney to L. Turin, 16 January 1938, Turin Papers, M1319 Box 1.

89 J. Cape to S. Jameson, 10 May 1938, TP/TV 46.

90 S. Jameson to J. Tawney, 15 March 1937, TP/TV 46.

91 J. Tawney to L. Turin, 20 December 1934, Turin Papers, M1319 Box 1.

92 R. M. Titmuss (1964) 'Introduction' to Tawney, R. H. *Equality* (first published 1931) London: George Allen & Unwin, pp 9–24, 15.

93 J. Tawney, *I Learn to Live*, Chapter 30, TP/TV 21.

Other sources used

Bell, K. N. (1925) Review of *Chapters from Richard Baxter's Christian Directory (1673)*, by J. Tawney, *History New Series*, 10 (39): 263–5.

Beveridge, Lord (1953) *Power and Influence*, London: Hodder and Stoughton.

Birkett, J. (2009) *Margaret Storm Jameson: A Life*, Oxford: Oxford University Press.

Chapman, G. (1975) *A Kind of Survivor: The Autobiography of Guy Chapman*, London: Victor Gollancz Ltd.

Clay, C. (2006) *British Women Writers 1914–1945: Professional Work and Friendship*, Aldershot: Ashgate.

Hall, L. (2016) '"Sentimental follies" or "instruments of tremendous uplift"? Reconsidering women's same-sex relationships in interwar Britain', *Women's History Review*, 25 (1): 124–42.

The Haslemere Society, Shottermill Scrap Book, www.haslemeresociety.org/shottermill-scrap-book.html.

Jameson, S. (1952) *The Green Man*, London: Macmillan & Co Ltd.

Jameson, S. (1957) *A Cup of Tea for Mr Thorgill*, London: Macmillan & Co Ltd.

Jameson, S. (1969) *Journey from the North Vol. 1, Autobiography of Storm Jameson*, London: Virago.

Jameson, S. (1970) *Journey from the North Vol. 2 Autobiography of Storm Jameson*, London: Virago.

Priestman, J. (2004) 'Jameson, Margaret Ethel [Storm] (1891–1986), novelist', ODNB.

Scherer, M. A. (1995) 'Annette Akroyd Beveridge: Victorian reformer, oriental scholar', PhD thesis, Ohio State University.

Stewart, J. (1999) '"This injurious measure": Scotland and the 1906 Education (Provision of Meals) Act', *The Scottish Historical Review*, 78 (205): 76–94.

Szreter, R. (1990) 'A note on R. H. Tawney's early interest in juvenile employment and misemployment', *History of Education*, 19 (4): 375–81.

Tawney, J. (1925) (ed.) *Chapters from Richard Baxter's Christian Directory (1673)*, London: Bell.

Tawney, R. H. (1931) *Equality*, London: G. Allen & Unwin.

Tawney, R. H. (1943, first published 1921) *The Acquisitive Society*, London: G. Bell and Sons Ltd.

Tawney, R. H. (1953) *The Attack and Other Papers*, London: George Allen & Unwin Ltd.

Tawney, R. H. (1964) *The Radical Tradition*, London: George Allen & Unwin Ltd.

Winter, J. M. and Joslin, D. M. (eds) (1972) *R. H. Tawney's Commonplace Book*, Cambridge: Cambridge University Press.

Wright, A. (1984) 'Tawneyism revisited: equality, welfare and socialism', in Pimlott, B. (ed.) *Fabian Essays in Socialist Thought*, London: Heinemann, pp 81–90.

Chapter 5: Janet Beveridge

[1] Beveridge, J. (1954) *Beveridge and His Plan*, London: Hodder and Stoughton, p 58.

[2] BevP/BS 4/15, document headed 'JM, 30/5/39'.

3 BevP/BS 4/17, handwritten document.

4 BevP/BS 4/15, document headed 'JM, 21/11/39'.

5 Mair, P. B. (1982) *Shared Enthusiasm: The Story of Lord and Lady Beveridge by her Son Philip Beveridge Mair*, Windlesham, Surrey: Ascent Books, p 24.

6 BevP/BS 4/17, document headed 'Looking back' by J. Beveridge.

7 Mair, *Shared Enthusiasm*, p 42.

8 Harris, J. (1997, 2nd edn) *William Beveridge: A Biography*, Oxford: Clarendon Press, p 25.

9 M. Cole to W. Beveridge, 29 April 1959, BevP/BS 6/5.

10 Bell, A. O. (ed.) (1978) *The Diary of Virginia Woolf Vol. 2, 1920–1924*, London/New York: Harcourt Brace Jovanovich, entry for 20 May 1941, p 41.

11 According to his great-grand-daughter, Jennifer Ward, David Beveridge Mair had a difficult childhood with an alcoholic father who died when David was seven (J. Ward, personal communication).

12 B. Webb, Diary, 20 August 1925, LSE Digital Library.

13 BevP/BS 4/16, J. Beveridge, parts of autobiography written 1950–54.

14 'Woman larder chief', *Southern Reporter*, 24 January 1918.

15 Cited in Mair, *Shared Enthusiasm*, p 63.

16 BevP/BS 4/16, J. Beveridge, parts of autobiography written 1950–54.

17 See Dahrendorf, R. (1995) *A History of the London School of Economics and Political Science*, Oxford: Oxford University Press, Part 11, 'A Second Foundation'.

18 Dahrendorf, *A History of LSE*, p 114.

19 A. Bowley, 'Materials for the history of the School', LSE/SR1101.

20 S. Webb to C. Mactaggart, 29 May 1919, PP 2/6/A/4.

21 Beveridge, W. (1960) *The London School of Economics and its Problems, 1919–1937*, London: George Allen & Unwin Ltd, p 78.

22 Handwritten note 'as secretary', BevP/BS 4/7.

23 J. Beveridge, 'The near loss of Houghton Street', 5 April 1958, BevP/BS 4/8.

24 Beveridge, *The London School of Economics*, p 22.

25 J. Beveridge, 'The near loss of Houghton Street'.

26 LSE's relationship with the LCC was eased both by Sidney Webb's chairmanship of the LCC's Technical Education Committee, and because Philippa Fawcett, daughter of the famous Millicent, and in charge of higher education at the LCC, was also well known to Janet. St Clement's Press appealed against the LCC decision but lost; William Berry then charitably offered his building to the School and donated £3,000 to the building fund.

27 S. Donnelly, personal communication; and Donnelly, S. (2017) 'Cheerful nonsense with brains behind it' – devising the LSE coat of arms', https://blogs.lse.ac.uk/lsehistory/2017/06/20/cheerful-nonsense-with-brains-behind-it-devising-the-lse-coat-of-arms/; J. Beveridge 'Felix Q Potuit', *Clare Market Review*, Summer 1955, BevP/BS 4/7. On the association of 'Beveridge' with 'beaver' see www.houseofnames.com/beveridge-family-crest.

28 J. Beveridge, (n.d.) 'The jollygoodfellowship porters', BevP/BS 4/7.
29 Beveridge, *The London School of Economics*, p 33.
30 On the correct ownership of Green Street, see J. Beveridge, *Beveridge and His Plan*, pp 91–2; W. Beveridge, *The London School of Economics*, p 40; and Mair, *Shared Enthusiasm*, p 85. Harris, *William Beveridge*, p 283, refers to Green Street as 'his cottage', repeating B. Webb's own attribution of it to William Beveridge (B. Webb, Diary, 1 July 1931, LSE Digital Library). Harris also repeats B. Webb's statement that William handed it over to Janet in 1934 in order to win his freedom (B. Webb, Diary, 20 May 1934, LSE Digital Library). The mistake is repeated in other biographies, e.g. S. Howson (2011) *Lionel Robbins*, Cambridge: Cambridge University Press, p 165.
31 H. Wilson (1982) 'His last words were "I have a thousand things to do"', review of P. Mair *Shared Enthusiasm*, *The Listener*, 9 December. Thanks to David Burn for drawing my attention to this.
32 J. Beveridge, (1957) 'Sic transit gloria', 25 September, BevP/BS 4/7.
33 See Beveridge, W. (1935) 'Origin of social biology in the School of Economics', https://library.lse.ac.uk/archives/beveridge/5_3pdf; Renwick, C. (n.d.) 'Observation and detachment: William Beveridge and "The Natural Bases of Social Science"', https://warwick.ac.uk/fac/cross_fac/esrcdtc/advanced/biological/observation_and_detachment_new_draft_renwick.pdf; Shearmur, J. (2013) 'Beveridge and the brief life of "Social Biology" at the LSE', *Agenda*, 20 (1): 79–94.
34 J. Beveridge (1958) 'The chair of social biology', 17 April, BevP/BS 4/8.
35 J. Beveridge (1930) 'Address of welcome to Lancelot Hogben', BevP/BS 5/2. The LSE Archives catalogue notes that this 'doesn't seem to be by her'.
36 W. Beveridge, 'Origin of social biology'.
37 Cited in Dahrendorf, *A History of LSE*, p 162.
38 Note, 20 October 1931, LSE/CFR 120/1/A.
39 B Webb, Diary, 8 December 1930, LSE Digital Library.
40 Hogben, L. (ed.) (1938) *Political Arithmetic: A Symposium of Population Studies*, London: George Allen & Unwin Ltd, no page number.
41 J. Beveridge, 'The chair of social biology'.
42 W. Beveridge, *The London School of Economics*, p 94.
43 Hogben, L. T. (1938) *Retreat from Reason*, New York: Random House, pp 7, 66.
44 Mair, *Shared Enthusiasm*, p 93.
45 B. Webb, Diary, 20 May 1934, 4 January 1935, 12 July 1936, LSE Digital Library.
46 The reply was that David Rockefeller could attend with John Kennedy, whom he had met at LSE. The Rockefeller correspondence is in BevP/BS 2/2 and 2/3.
47 A. Rockefeller to J. Beveridge, 1938, BevP/BS 2/2.
48 L. Hogben to J. Beveridge, 7 December 1942, BevP/BS 6/2.

49 B. Malinowski to J. Mair, 16 February 1932, BevP/BS 2/1.

50 Harris, *William Beveridge* (1977 edn, pp 73, 278–9), (1997 edn, pp 22, 28).

51 The two staff were Eve Evans, who became School Secretary in 1940, and her friend Kay Lewis. Letters to Janet from Eve Evans in the LSE archives are notably warm in tone (see those in BevP/BS 2/2).

52 Harris, *William Beveridge* (1997 edn), p 28.

53 Harris, *William Beveridge* (1997 edn), p 33.

54 Dahrendorf, *A History of the London School of Economics*, p 156.

55 Berg, M. (1996) *A Woman in History: Eileen Power 1889–1940*, Cambridge: Cambridge University Press, p 147.

56 Shearmur, 'Beveridge and the brief life of "Social Biology"', p 80.

57 Cited in Leeson, R. (ed.) (2015) *Hayek. Part II, Austria, America and the Rise of Hitler, 1899–1933: A Collaborative Biography*, Basingstoke: Palgrave Macmillan, p 183.

58 Hall, J. A. (2010) *Ernest Gellner: An Intellectual Biography*, London: Verso, p 181.

59 Mair, *Shared Enthusiasm*, pp 13–14.

60 Mair, *Shared Enthusiasm*, Appendix E, pp 143–7, gives full details of his relationship to Harris's account. Harris makes considerable use of Janet's diaries (see the second edition of *William Beveridge*, pp 35–7, for example), which she says (pp 7, 500) she read originally in Philip Mair's attic. According to her, most of these, along with the letters that were with them, are now in LSE where they are 'freely available for scholars to read' (p 7). Unfortunately neither I nor the archive staff have been able to track the diaries down.

61 Mair, *Shared Enthusiasm*, p 95.

62 B. Webb, *Diary*, 14 May 1922, LSE Digital Library.

63 B. Webb, *Diary*, 30 April 1928, LSE Digital Library.

64 Cited in Leeson, *Hayek*, p 183.

65 On William Beveridge and Carré, see Harris, *William Beveridge* (1977 edn, p 14; 1997 edn, p 12).

66 *Evening Citizen, Glasgow*, 10 December 1942; *Belfast Telegraph*, 15 December 1942; *The News Chronicle*, 28 November 1942.

67 J. Beveridge, *Beveridge and His Plan*, p 119.

68 Beveridge, W. H. (1960) 'A few words on Janet by Lord Beveridge', in Beveridge, J., *An Epic of Clare Market: Birth and Early Days of the London School of Economics*, London: G. Bell & Sons Ltd, pp x–xiii, xii–xiii.

69 Note by W. Beveridge, BevP/BS 2/7.

70 M. B. Stephens, personal communication.

71 Hennessy, P. (1992) *Never Again: Britain, 1945–51*, London: Jonathan Cape, pp 72–3.

72 J. Beveridge to L. Turin, 13 June 1937, Turin Papers, M1319, Box 1.

73 *The Liverpool Echo*, 27 November 1944.

74 M. Wilson to R. Darwall-Smith, October 2005, UCA/05/314.

75 University College, 'MA46 Papers of Sir William Henry Beveridge (Master 1937–45)', www.univ.ox.ac.uk/wp-content/uploads/2020/01/Papers-of-William-Beveridge.pdf. The University College online archive catalogue describes Janet on the basis of opinions expressed by fellows, students and staff who knew her as being considered 'overbearing and interfering' and not popular.

76 Dr Michael Bull, Univ 1944–47, *University College, Oxford Archives*, Handwritten account of memories of Univ. UC:P214/MS1/16.

77 J. Beveridge to 'Dear Leslie', 26 October 1945, BevP/BS 2/21.

78 D. Burn and J. Ward, personal communication.

79 Speech given at Salford by Lady Beveridge, 19 May 1944, BevP/BS 2/15. William Beveridge shared this concern for 'the problem of peace': see his Australian broadcast in 1948 reproduced as chapter 9 of Beveridge, J. and Beveridge, W. (1949) *Antipodes Notebook*, London: The Pilot Press Ltd.

80 Beveridge, J. (1955) 'Grandmothers: asset or liability?', *The Listener*, 18 August.

81 *The Liverpool Evening News*, 18 May 1944; *Northern Whig*, 6 March 1944.

82 Beveridge, J. (1958) (Letter) *The Times*, 24 October.

83 Beveridge, J. (n.d.) 'Women under The Beveridge Report', BevP/BS 4/1.

84 Beveridge, J. (n.d.) 'A storm in a teacup, or the country totalitarians', BevP/BS 4/21.

85 G. Algase to J. Beveridge, 9 June 1943, BevP/BS 2/9.

86 'Veronica' at Jonathan Cape to J. Beveridge, 15 February, 1944, BevP/BS 2/11.

87 'Contract between Lady Beveridge and D. Appleton-Century Company for the publication of Johanna's family or some similar title, 29 June 1943', BevP/BS 4/20.

88 'Yes, Minister' and 'Yes, Prime Minister' were political satires transmitted by the BBC in the 1980s.

89 J. Beveridge to 'my dear Amy', 7 January 1944; J. Beveridge to 'Veronica' at Jonathan Cape, 3 February 1944; J. Beveridge to 'Miss Chambers', 14 January 1944, BevP/BS 2/11.

90 J. Beveridge to 'Miss Rich' (G. Algase agency), 13 January 1944, BevP/BS 2/11.

91 J. Beveridge to H. Rich (G. Algase agency), n.d., BevP/BS 2/11.

92 Some of these are in BevP/BS 4/6.

93 Beveridge and Beveridge, *Antipodes Notebook*, pp 81–2.

94 Speech given at Salford by Lady Beveridge, 19 May 1944, BevP/BS 2/15.

95 Novy, P. (1945, Foreword by Lady Beveridge) *Housework without Tears*, London: Pilot Press Ltd. *The Times* and *The Daily Telegraph* obituaries of Janet (27 April 1959) both mistakenly attribute the book to J. Beveridge. Priscilla Novy worked for Mass Observation under her maiden name of Priscilla Feare; later, with her husband Henry Novy, she joined the staff of the policy think-tank Political and Economic Planning.

96 Foreword by Lady Beveridge, *Housework without Tears*, pp 7–14, 12.

97 Beveridge, J. (1948) *The Observer*, 7 November.
98 Lady Beveridge (1952) 'About new towns and Newton Aycliffe', typescript for broadcast on 30 January, BevP/BS 4/1.
99 W. Beveridge to J. Beveridge, 27 March 1946, BevP/BS 1/35.
100 J. Beveridge to W. Beveridge, 27 March 1946, BevP/BS 1/35.
101 J. Beveridge to L. Turin, 3 June 1938, Turin Papers M1319, Box 4.
102 J. Beveridge to L. Robbins, 22 April 1949, and L. Robbins to J. Beveridge, 10 May 1949, BevP/BS 2/25.
103 Beveridge, W. (1953) *Power and Influence*, London: Hodder and Stoughton, p 169.
104 Thanks to John Stewart who alerted me to Janet Beveridge's role in securing mental health funding. On the history of child guidance, see Stewart, J. (2006) 'Psychiatric social work in inter-war Britain: child guidance, American ideas, American philanthropy', *Michael*, 3: 78–91.
105 Harris, *William Beveridge* (1997 edn), p 22.
106 Dahrendorf, *A History of the London School of Economics*, p 328.
107 Mair, *Shared Enthusiasm*, p 96.
108 J. Beveridge to A. Savill, 20 March 1959, BevP/BS 2/37.
109 Caine, S. (1960 'Address at the University College Memorial Service for Janet Beveridge', *The LSE Society Magazine*, no. 19, January, pp 6–7. BevP/BS 6/4.

Other sources used

Abel-Smith, B. (1992) 'The Beveridge Report: its origins and outcomes', *International Social Security Review*, 45 (1–2): 5–16.

Ahmad, S. (1991) 'American foundations and the development of the social sciences between the wars: comment on the debate between Martin Bulmer and Donald Fisher', *Sociology*, 25 (3): 511–20.

Ahmad, S. P. (1987) 'Institutions and the growth of knowledge: the Rockefeller Foundation's influence on the social sciences between the wars', PhD thesis, University of Manchester.

Beveridge, W. (1912) *John and Irene: An Anthology of Thoughts on Women*, London: Longmans, Green & Co.

Beveridge, W. (1921) 'Economics as a liberal education', *Economica*, No. 1: 2–19.

Beveridge, W. B. (1931) *Unemployment: A Problem of Industry*, London: Longmans & Co.

Bulmer, M. (1982) 'Support for sociology in the 1920s: the Laura Spelman Rockefeller Memorial and the beginnings of modern large-scale, sociological research in the university', *The American Sociologist*, 17(4): 185–92.

Bulmer, M. (1995) 'Some observations on the history of large philanthropic foundations in Britain and the United States', *Foundations: International Perspectives*, 6 (3): 275–91.

Bulmer, M. and Bulmer, J. (1981) 'Philanthropy and social science in the 1920s: Beardsley Ruml and the Laura Spelman Rockefeller Memorial, 1922–29', *Minerva*, 19 (2): 347–407.

Burn, E. (1965) Antecedents and early life of Jessie Thomson Philip (later Mrs. D. B. Mair/Lady Beveridge) by her daughter Elspeth Burn. Unpublished manuscript.

Campsie, A. (2016) 'Mass-Observation, left intellectuals and the politics of everyday life', *English Historical Review*, 131 (548): 92–121.

Czarniawska, B. (2009) 'Emerging institutions: pyramids or anthills?', *Organization Studies*, 30 (4): 423–41.

Darwall-Smith, R. (2008) *A History of University College, Oxford*, Oxford: Oxford University Press.

Donnelly, S. (2017) 'Cheerful nonsense with brains behind it' – devising the LSE coat of arms', https://blogs.lse.ac.uk/lsehistory/2017/06/20/cheerful-nonsense-with-brains-behind-it-devising-the-lse-coat-of-arms/.

Donnelly, S. (2019) 'A controversial appointment – Jessy Mair, School Secretary, 1920–1939', https://blogs.lse.ac.uk/lsehistory/2019/12/03/a-controversial-appointment-jessy-mair-school-secretary-1920-1939/.

Edwards, K. C. (1964) 'The new towns of Britain', *Geography*, 49 (3): 279–85.

Fleck C A (2011) *A Transatlantic History of the Social Sciences*, London: Bloomsbury Academic.

Galton, F., Geddes, P., Sadler, M. E., Westermarck, E., Höffding, H., Bridges, J. H., Stuart-Glennie, J. S. et al (1906) *Sociological Papers 1905 Vol II*, London: Macmillan & Co.

Garrett, A. C. (1987) 'The quest for autonomy: sociology's advocacy dimension', PhD thesis, University of Durham.

Great Aycliffe Town Council 'The Newton Aycliffe story', www.great-aycliffe.gov.uk/about/newton-aycliffe-story/.

Harris, J. (2004) 'Beveridge, William Henry, Baron Beveridge (1879–1963), social reformer and economist', ODNB.

Hayek, F. A. (1946) 'The London School of Economics, 1895–1945', *Economica* New Series, 13 (49): 1–31.

Hogben, L. and Herman, L. (1933) 'The intellectual resemblance of twins', *Proceedings of the Royal Society of Edinburgh*, 53: 105–29.

Husbands, C. T. (2019) *Sociology at the London School of Economics and Political Science, 1904–2015*, Basingstoke: Palgrave Macmillan.

Lewis, J. (1992) 'Gender and the development of welfare regimes', *Journal of European Social Policy*, 2 (3): 159–73.

Mair, L. (1934) *An African People in the Twentieth Century*, London: G. Routledge & Sons.

Oakley, A. (2014) *Father and Daughter: Patriarchy, Gender and Social Science*, Bristol: Policy Press.

Pedersen, S. (1993) *Family, Dependence and the Origins of the Welfare State: Britain and France 1914–1945*, Cambridge: Cambridge University Press.

Rathbone, E. (n.d.) *The Case for Family Allowances*, Penguin.

Renwick, C. (2012) *British Sociology's Lost Biological Roots*, Houndmills, Basingstoke: Palgrave Macmillan.

Renwick, C. (2014) 'Completing the circle of the social sciences? William Beveridge and social biology at the London School of Economics during the 1930s', *Philosophy of the Social Sciences*, 44 (4): 478–96.

Renwick, C. (2016) 'Eugenics, population research, and social mobility studies in early and mid-twentieth-century Britain', *The Historical Journal*, 845–67 http://eprints.whiterose.ac.uk/94187/.

Renwick, C. (2017) *Bread for All: The Origins of the Welfare State*, Penguin Books.

Robbins L (1932) *An Essay on the Nature & Significance of Economic Science*. London: Macmillan & Co., Ltd.

Robbins, L. (1971) *Autobiography of an Economist*, London: Macmillan.

Shiman, L. L. (1981) 'The Blue Ribbon Army: Gospel temperance in England', *Historical Magazine of the Protestant Episcopal Church*, 50 (4): 391–408.

Tabery, J. and Sarkar, S. (2015) 'R. A. Fisher, Lancelot Hogben, and the "competition" for the chair of social biology at the London School of Economics in 1930: correcting the legend', *Records of the Royal Society London*, 69 (4): 437–46.

Unknown letters from Beveridge www.univ.ox.ac.uk/news/unknown-letters-beveridge/.

Chapter 6: A life of her own

1   Finch, J. (1983) *Married to the Job: Wives' Incorporation in Men's Work*, London: George Allen & Unwin, p 71.

2   Smith, B. S. (1998) *The Gender of History*, Cambridge, MA: Harvard University Press, p 6.

3   Smith, *The Gender of History*, p 105.

4   Moore, N., Salter, A., Stanley, L. and Tamboukou, M. (2017) *The Archive Project: Archival Research in the Social Sciences*, Abingdon: Routledge, p 157.

5   Steedman, C. (2013) 'Archival methods', in Griffin, G. (ed.) *Research Methods for English Studies*, Edinburgh: Edinburgh University Press, pp 17–29, 27.

6   This is not true of any of the archives visited for the present book!

7   Edel, L. (1986) 'The figure under the carpet', in Oates, S. B. (eds) (1986) *Biography as High Adventure*, Amherst: The University of Massachusetts Press, pp 18–31, 25.

8   L'Eplattenier, B. E. (2009) 'An argument for archival research methods: thinking beyond methodology', *College English*, 72 (1): 67–79, 69.

9   Stanley, L. (2017) 'Archival methodology inside the black box: noise in the archive!' in Moore et al, *The Archive Project*, pp 33–67, 59.

10   See Liabo, K., Gough, D. and Harden, A. (2017) 'Developing justifiable evidence claims', in Gough, D., Oliver, S. and Thomas, J. (eds) *An Introduction to Systematic Reviews* (2nd edn), London: Sage Publications, pp 251–77.

[11] Lyon, E. S. (2004) 'The use of biographical material in intellectual history: writing about Alva and Gunnar Myrdal's contribution to sociology', *International Journal of Social Research Methodology*, 7 (4): 323–43, 323.

[12] Spurling, H. (2004) 'Glendower's syndrome', in Bostridge, M. (ed.) *Lives for Sale: Biographers' Tales*, London: Continuum, pp 68–75, 68.

[13] Holroyd, M. (2004) 'Finding a good woman', in Bostridge, *Lives for Sale*, pp 160–4, 162.

[14] Martin, J. (2014) 'Intellectual portraits: politics, professions and identity in twentieth-century England', *History of Education*, 43 (6): 740–67, 742.

[15] Martin, 'Intellectual portraits', p 743.

[16] Bennett, J. M. (2006) *History Matters: Patriarchy and the Challenge of Feminism*, Philadelphia: University of Pennsylvania Press, p 128.

[17] M. Booth diaries, 1922 BP V/2/36, 1938 BP V/2/58, 1896 BP V/2/10.

[18] Knightley, P. (1971) *The Secret Lives of Lawrence of Arabia*, London: Panther, p 286.

[19] Dahrendorf, R. (1995) *A History of the London School of Economics and Political Science*, Oxford: Oxford University Press, p 153.

[20] Jacobs, J. E. (2002) *The Voice of Harriet Taylor Mill*, Bloomington, IN: Indiana University Press; Harsin, J. (1989) 'Syphilis, wives, and physicians: medical ethics and the family in late nineteenth-century France', *French Historical Studies*, 16 (1): 72–95, 85.

[21] Greenburg, R. P. (1987) *Fabian Couples, Feminist Issues*, Abingdon: Routledge, p 115.

[22] Having looked at these records, Lawrence Goldman in his biography of R. H. Tawney revises his opinion of Jeannette (Goldman, L. (2013) *The Life of R. H. Tawney: Socialism and History*, London: Bloomsbury, p 143).

[23] M. S. Jameson to J. Tawney, 5 June 1938, TP 27/6.

[24] M. Booth to C. Booth, 7 November 1889, BP 1/3442.

[25] See Chapter 2.

[26] Jones, H. M. (1932) 'Methods in contemporary biography', *The English Journal*, 21 (2), pp 113–22, pp 117–18.

[27] Harris, J. (1977, 1st edn) *William Beveridge*, Oxford: Oxford University Press, p 27.

[28] Sigurðardóttir, E. R. (2013) 'Women and madness in the 19th century: the effects of oppression on women's mental health', Háskóli Íslands, Hugvísindasvið, Department of English. https://skemman.is/bitstream/1946/16449/1/BA-ElisabetRakelSigurdar.pdf, p 4.

[29] McDowell, R. B. (1967) *Alice Stopford Green: A Passionate Historian*, Dublin: Allen Figgis and Company Limited.

[30] Showalter, E. (1978) *A Literature of Their Own: British Women Novelists from Brontë to Lessing*, London: Virago, p 38.

[31] Woolf, V. (1979) *Women and Writing*, London: The Women's Press, p 46.

[32] J. Tawney to L. Turin, 20 December 1934, Turin Papers, M 1319 Box 1.

[33] Donskov, A. (ed.) (2017) *Tolstoy and Tolstaya: A Portrait of a Life in Letters*, University of Ottawa Press.

34 Donskov, A. A. (2010) 'Sofia Andreevna Tolstaya: a critical look at an insider's perspective', in S. A. Tolstaya, *My Life*, University of Ottawa Press, pp xix–lix, lix.

35 Tolstaya, *My Life*, p 84.

36 Tolstaya, *My Life*, p 113.

37 McLean, H. (2011) 'The Tolstoy marriage revisited – many times', *Canadian Slavonic Papers*, 53 (1): 65–79, 74.

38 Popoff, A. (2012) *The Wives: The Women Behind Russia's Literary Giants*, New York: Pegasus Books, p 55.

39 Norman-Butler, N. (1972) *Victorian Aspirations: The Life and Labour of Charles and Mary Booth*, London: George Allen & Unwin Ltd, Preface, no page number.

40 See pp xxi–xxii of Jacobs, *The Voice of Harriet Taylor Mill*.

41 Bok, S. (1991) *Alva Myrdal: A Daughter's Memoir*, Reading, MA: Addison-Wesley, p 75.

42 Lyon, E. S. (2000) 'Biographical constructions of a working woman: the changing faces of Alva Myrdal', *European Journal of Social Theory*, 3(4): 407–28, 424.

43 Smart, C. (2007) *Personal Life*, Cambridge: Polity, p 189.

44 Hochschild, A. R. (2003) *The Commercialization of Intimate Life: Notes from Home and Work*, Berkeley, University of California Press, pp 224, 243. See also #ThanksforTyping: the women behind famous male writers https://theconversation.com/thanksfortyping-the-women-behind-famous-male-writers-75770.

45 Letter from A. Einstein, July, 1900, in Renn, J. and Schulmann, R. (eds) (1992) *Albert Einstein/Mileva Marić: The Love Letters*, Princeton, NJ: Princeton University Press, cited in Popova, M. 'Albert Einstein's Love letters', www.braimnpickings.org/2015/07/27/albert-einstein-mileva-maric-love-letters/.

46 Trbuhović-Gjurić, D. (1988) *Im Schatten Albert Einsteins. Das tragische Leben der Mileva Einstein-Marić*. Bern: Paul Haupt.

47 Milentijević, R. (2015) *Mileva Marić-Einstein: Life with Albert Einstein*, United World Press. See also Esterson, A. and Cassidy, D. C. (2019) *Einstein's Wife: The Real Story of Mileva Einstein-Marić*. Cambridge, MA: The MIT Press.

48 'Did Einstein espouse his spouse's ideas?', Correspondence, *Physics Today*, February 1989: 10–13, and February 1991: 122–3, 123.

49 Gagnon, P. (2016) 'The forgotten life of Einstein's first wife', *Scientific American*, 19 December.

50 Banovic, R. (2018) 'Does Albert Einstein's first wife Mileva Marić deserve credit for some of his work?', *The Independent*, 13 June.

51 Larvoll, A. 'My little witch – Albert & Mileva Einstein's love letters.' https://vimeo.com/40078358.

52 Gagnon, 'The forgotten life'.

53 Young, P. M. (1978) *Alice Elgar: Enigma of a Victorian Lady*, London: Dennis Dobson, p 12.

54 Kennedy, M. (1987) *Portrait of Elgar*, 3rd edn, Oxford: Clarendon Press, p 115.

55 Lady Elgar, Obituary, *The Times*, 8 April 1920.

56 Kennedy, M. (2004) 'Elgar, Sir Edward William, baronet (1857–1934), composer and conductor', ODNB.

57 Butler, R. (2008) *Hidden in the Shadow of the Master: The Model-Wives of Cézanne, Monet, & Rodin*, London/New Haven, CT: Yale University Press, p xiv.

58 Price, L. and P. Thurschwell (2016) 'Introduction' in Price, L. and P. Thurschwell (eds) *Literary Secretaries/Secretarial Culture*, Abingdon: Routledge, pp 1–11, 1.

59 Patch, B. (1951) *Thirty Years with G.B.S.*, London: Victor Gollancz Ltd, p 16.

60 Wearing, J. P. (2005) *Bernard Shaw and Nancy Astor*, Toronto: University of Toronto Press, p 113.

61 Patch, *Thirty Years with G.B.S.*, pp 32, 235.

62 University College, Oxford 'Unknown letters from Beveridge', www.univ.ox. ac.uk/news/unknown-letters-beveridge/, letter dated 25 October, 1961.

63 J. Tawney to L. Turin, 20 December 1934, Turin Papers, M 1319 Box 1.

64 Harris (1977, 1st edn) *William Beveridge*, pp 283, 468.

65 Harris, J. (1997, 2nd edn) *William Beveridge*, Oxford: Clarendon Press, p 15.

66 W. H. Beveridge to The Warden, Passfield Hall, 12 November 1961, Turin Papers, M 1319 Box 4.

67 L. Turin to W. H. Beveridge, 28 October 1961, Turin Papers, M 1319 Box 4.

68 Bayley, P. C. (1973) Obituary, Lucia Turin, *University College Record*, VI (3): 303–4.

69 Rose, P. (1984) *Parallel Lives: Five Victorian Marriages*, London: Chatto & Windus, Hogarth Press, p 9.

70 Rose, P. (1985) *Writing of Women: Essays in a Renaissance*, Middletown, CT: Wesleyan University Press, p 72.

71 Roiphe, K. (2008) *Uncommon Arrangements: Seven Marriages in Literary London 1910–1939*, London: Virago, p 7.

72 Woolf, V. (2013, first published 1975) *The London Scene*, London: Hogarth Press, p 34.

73 Rose, *Parallel Lives*, p 11.

Other sources used

Astbury. J. (1996) *Crazy for You: The Making of Women's Madness*, Melbourne: Oxford University Press.

Beer, A. (2017) *Sounds and Sweet Airs: The Forgotten Women of Classical Music*, London: Oneworld.

Bok, S. (1990) *Lying: Moral Choice in Public and Private Life*, London: Quartet Books.

Buss, H. M. and Kadar, M. (eds) (2001) *Working in Women's Archives: Researching Women's Private Literature and Archival Documents*, Waterloo, Ontario: Wilfrid Laurier University Press.

Cayleff, S. E. (1988) '"Prisoners of their own feebleness": women, nerves and Western medicine – a historical overview', *Social Science and Medicine*, 26 (12): 1199–1208.

Collini, S. (2009) *Common Reading: Critics, Historians, Publics*, Oxford: Oxford University Press.

Dorney, K. (2010) 'The ordering of things: allure, access, and archives', *Shakespeare Bulletin*, 28 (1): 19–36.

'Einstein's wife: the Mileva question' (2003), Oregon Public Broadcasting, www.pbs.org/opb/einsteinswife/science/mquest/htm.

Ekerwald, H. (2000) 'Alva Myrdal: making the private public', *Acta Sociologica*, 43: 343–52.

Esterson, A. and Cassidy, D. C. (2019) *Einstein's Wife: The Real Story of Mileva Einstein-Marić*, The MIT Press.

Fölster, K. (1992) *De tre löven: en Myrdals efterskrift*, Stockholm: Bonniers Förlag.

Gabor, A. (1995) *Einstein's Wife: Work and Marriage in the Lives of Five Great Twentieth-Century Women*, London: Penguin.

Gilman, C. (1981, first published 1892) 'The Yellow Wallpaper', in *The Charlotte Perkins Gilman Reader: The Yellow Wallpaper and Other Fiction*, London: The Women's Press.

Harvey, J. and Ogilvie, M. B. (eds) (2000) *The Biographical Dictionary of Women in Science*, New York: Routledge.

Heilbrun, C. (1989) *Writing a Woman's Life*, London: The Women's Press.

Holroyd, M. (2003) *Works on Paper: The Craft of Biography & Autobiography*, London: Abacus.

McVeagh, D. (1984) 'Mrs Edward Elgar', *The Musical Times*, 125 (1692): 76–8.

Mair, P. (1982) *Shared Enthusiasm: The Story of Lord and Lady Beveridge by her Son Philip Beveridge Mair*, Windlesham, Surrey: Ascent Books Ltd.

Myrdal, A. (1941) *Nation and Family: The Swedish Experiment in Democratic Family and Population Policy*, New York/London: Harper & Brothers Publishers.

Myrdal, A. and Klein, V. (1956) *Women's Two Roles*, London: Routledge & Kegan Paul Ltd.

Myrdal, G. (1944) *An American Dilemma: The Negro Problem and Modern Democracy*, New York: Harper & Bros.

Myrdal, J. (1984) *Another World*, Chicago: Ravenswood Books.

Myrdal, J. (1991, originally published in 1982) *Childhood*, Chicago: Lake View Press.

Myrdal, J (2010, originally published 1985) *Twelve Going on Thirteen*, University of Minnesota Press.

Pateman, C. and Gross, E. (eds) (2013) *Feminist Challenges: Social and Political Theory*, Abingdon: Routledge.

Robb, P. 'A marriage for the ages: new book reveals the inner lives of Leo and Sofia Tolstoy', https://artsfile.ca/a-marriage-for-the-ages-new-book-reveals-the-inner-lives-of-leo-and-sofia-tolstoy/.

Roberts, C. A. (1879) *Isabel Trevithoe: A Poem*, London: Charing Cross Publishing Company, Limited.

Roberts, C. A. (1882) *Marchcroft Manor* (2 vols), London: Remington and Co.

Showalter, E. (1987) *The Female Malady: Women, Madness and English Culture, 1830–1980*, London: Virago.

Smith, B. G. (1984) 'The contribution of women to modern historiography in Great Britain, France, and the United States, 1750–1940', *The American Historical Review*, 89 (3): 709–32.

Smith, B. G. (1995a) 'Gender and the practices of scientific history: the seminar and archival research in the nineteenth century', *The American Historical Review*, 100 (4): 1150–76.

Smith, B. G. (1995b) 'Whose truth, whose history?', *Journal of the History of Ideas*, 36 (4): 661–8.

Smith, H. L. and Zook, M. S. (eds) (2018) *Generations of Women Historians*, Cham: Palgrave Macmillan.

Steedman, C. (2001) *Dust*, Manchester: Manchester University Press.

Troemel-Ploetz, S. (1990) Mileva Einstein-Marić: the woman who did Einstein's mathematics,, *Women's Studies International Forum*, 13 (5): 415–32.

Troyat, H. (1970) *Tolstoy*, Harmondsworth: Penguin.

Ussher, J. (1991) *Women's Madness: Misogyny or Mental Illness?*, Hemel Hempstead: Harvester Wheatsheaf.

Weintraub, S. (2002) 'Shaw's musician: Edward Elgar', *Shaw*, 22: 1–18.

Index

Note: page locators in *italic* refer to figures, images or tables.

Index

Patch, Blanche 77, 93, 97, 194–5
Payne-Townshend, Charlotte Frances
    see Shaw, Charlotte Frances (née
    Payne-Townshend)
Payne-Townshend, Horace 67–8, 69
Payne-Townshend, Mary Susanna (née
    Kirby) 68, 69, 92
Pearson, Karl 136
Pease, Edward 71, 78, 85
Pember Reeves, Maud 79, 80, *83*, 85
Pember Reeves, William 79, *83*, 141, 142
pensions
    Booths' work on 26, 52–3, 54, 61–2
    at LSE 144
philanthropy 34, 38–40, 65
Philip, Anne Glenday 137
Philip, Jessie Thomson *see* Beveridge,
    Janet (previously Jessy Mair, née
    Jessie Thomson Philip)
Phillips, Marion 80, 85
Pioneer Players 19
Pitfold, Hindhead 107–8
Plant, Arnold 144, 145
positivism 48
Potter, Beatrice *see* Webb, Beatrice (née
    Potter)
Potter, Mary (Mary Booth's grandmother)
    28
Potter, Mary (Mary Booth's mother) *see*
    Macaulay, Mary (née Potter)
Potter, Richard 28
poverty enquiry, Booth's *see* Life and
    Labour of the People in London
Power, Eileen 86, 113, 117, 127, 148,
    152, 157
Prange, Antonia 31
pregnancy test 150
prisons, report on women and 80
public life, underrepresentation of women
    in 80–1

R
Ranke, Leopold von 177
Rathbone, Eleanor 20
'Remembrance' 123
'rest cure' 183–4
Robbins, Lionel 145, 148, 151, 170
Rockefeller, David 153
Rockefeller Foundation funds 146–9
Rodin, Auguste 193–4

Rose Cottage *119*, 120
Rose, Phyllis 197–8, 199
Rossi, Alice 14
Rothenstein, William 60
Round About A Pound A Week 79, 80
Royden, Maude 109
Ruml, Beardsley 147, 148, 149, 150, 151
Russ, Joanna 3
Russell, Bertrand 71

S
Sainte-Beuve, Charles Augustin 9
Sanders, Mary 157
Savill, Dr Agnes (née Blackadder) 137,
    173
scholarships for women 85–7
Schreiner, Olive 18–19, 120
Schumann, Clara 7–8
secretaries 194–7
Sen, Keshub Chandra 104
The Seven Pillars of Wisdom 6, 67, 93, 94
Sex Discrimination (Removal) Act 1919
    17
sex education 87–8
sex in marriage 22, 199
    Beveridges 159
    Harriet Taylor Mill and 181–2
    Shaws 76–7, 90, 96, 180
    Tawneys 123
Shaw, Charlotte Frances (née Payne-
    Townshend) 6, *24*, 65–100
    accused of hypochondria 91, 182
    admiration for Elgar 193
    assists Hepburn with venereal disease
        education 88–9
    Beatrice Webb on 71, 73, 74
    Beveridge connection 107–8
    on Blanch Patch 195
    Commonplace Book 96
    courtship with GBS 74–6
    death 99–100
    diagnosis as frustrated mother 96–7,
        180–1
    domestic labour and married life 77–8
    donations to societies and groups 84
    editing of Lawrence's work 6, 92–4
    endows Shaw Library at LSE 20, 66,
        72, 98
    Fabian Society membership and
        activities 78–9